The Rebellion of Forms in Modern Persian Poetry

The Rebellion of Forms in Modern Persian Poetry

Politics of Poetic Experimentation

Farshad Sonboldel

BLOOMSBURY ACADEMIC
NEW YORK • LONDON • OXFORD • NEW DELHI • SYDNEY

BLOOMSBURY ACADEMIC
Bloomsbury Publishing Inc, 1359 Broadway, New York, NY 10018, USA
Bloomsbury Publishing Plc, 50 Bedford Square, London, WC1B 3DP, UK
Bloomsbury Publishing Ireland, 29 Earlsfort Terrace, Dublin 2, D02 AY28, Ireland

BLOOMSBURY, BLOOMSBURY ACADEMIC and the Diana logo
are trademarks of Bloomsbury Publishing Plc

First published in the United States of America 2024
This paperback edition published 2025

Copyright © Farshad Sonboldel, 2024

For legal purposes the Acknowledgements on p. vii constitute an
extension of this copyright page.

Cover design: Eleanor Rose
Cover image by Bahman Mohassess © Estate of Bahman Mohassess

Whilst every effort has been made to locate copyright holders the publishers
would be grateful to hear from any person(s) not acknowledged here.

All rights reserved. No part of this publication may be: i) reproduced or transmitted in any form, electronic or mechanical, including photocopying, recording or by means of any information storage or retrieval system without prior permission in writing from the publishers; or ii) used or reproduced in any way for the training, development or operation of artificial intelligence (AI) technologies, including generative AI technologies. The rights holders expressly reserve this publication from the text and data mining exception as per Article 4(3) of the Digital Single Market Directive (EU) 2019/790.

Bloomsbury Publishing Inc does not have any control over, or responsibility for, any third-party websites referred to or in this book. All internet addresses given in this book were correct at the time of going to press. The author and publisher regret any inconvenience caused if addresses have changed or sites have ceased to exist, but can accept no responsibility for any such changes.

Library of Congress Cataloging-in-Publication Data
Names: Sonboldel, Farshad, author.
Title: The rebellion of forms in modern Persian poetry : politics of poetic experimentation / Farshad Sonboldel.
Description: New York : Bloomsbury Academic, 2024. | Includes bibliographical references and index. | Summary: "Explores the relationship between aesthetic innovation in poetry and resistance to political and cultural domination in the works of a selected group of pioneer Persian poets from the 1900s through the 1950s"– Provided by publisher.
Identifiers: LCCN 2023030676 (print) | LCCN 2023030677 (ebook) | ISBN 9798765103579 (hardback) | ISBN 9798765103586 (paperback) | ISBN 9798765103593 (epub) | ISBN 9798765103609 (pdf) | ISBN 9798765103616
Subjects: LCSH: Experimental poetry, Persian–History and criticism. | Persian poetry–20th century–History and criticism. | Aesthetics. | Avant-garde (Aesthetics)–Iran–History–20th century. | Politics and literature. | LCGFT: Literary criticism.
Classification: LCC PK6420.E97 S66 2024 (print) | LCC PK6420.E97 (ebook) | DDC 891/.551309–dc23/eng/20231010
LC record available at https://lccn.loc.gov/2023030676
LC ebook record available at https://lccn.loc.gov/2023030677

ISBN:	HB:	979-8-7651-0357-9
	PB:	979-8-7651-0358-6
	ePDF:	979-8-7651-0360-9
	eBook:	979-8-7651-0359-3

Typeset by Integra Software Services Pvt. Ltd.

For product safety related questions contact productsafety@bloomsbury.com.

To find out more about our authors and books visit www.bloomsbury.com
and sign up for our newsletters.

CONTENTS

Acknowledgements vii
A note on transliteration viii

Introduction 1
    Methodology and key theories 3
    Study framework 8
    Research contribution 12
    A note on originality and authenticity of the alternative movements 13

1   The politics of literature and the forms of literary deviation in constitutional poetry 19
    Resistance and transformation in pre-constitutional poetry 22
    Residual forces of the *Bāzgasht-e Adabi* movement 27
    Mohammad Taqi Malek al-Shoʻarā Bahār: Cohabitation of the old and the new 29

2   Constitutional poetry and the performative arts 39
    The politics of singing 41
    Theatrocracy in Mirzādeh Eshqi's dramatic poetry 51

3   The left wing of the poetic revolution and constructive misreading of the literary tradition 63
    The Raʻfat era: From deconstruction to construction 67
    Major Lāhuti: Persian socialist realism and the aesthetic revolution 74
    Remodelling the poetic forms: Prosodic metres and rhyme schemes 88
    Chārpāreh: A collective drive to poetic modernity 98

4 Modernism and high modernism 107
Modernism, experimentalism, and avant-garde 108
Nimā Yushij: Self-revision and conscious misreading of oneself 113

5 Experimentalism in Persian poetry between the 1930s and the 1950s 127
Mohammad Moqaddam, a prose poet: Introducing free verse into Persian poetry 128
Zabih Behruz: A wanderer poet in the city of drama 144
Shin Partow: A bridge between Nimāic and experimental poetry 153

6 Avant-garde poetry between the 1940s and 1950s 159
Tondar Kiā: Poet of cabarets 162
Moods and moments 164
Kiā: Ragpicker in modern Tehran 167
Non-organicity 175
A dialogue with Dadaism 177
Hushang Irāni: Slaughterer of the nightingale 184
Irāni's violet scream 189
A different way of sociopolitical engagement 197

Conclusion 201
Prospects for further research 205

Bibliography 207
Index 215

ACKNOWLEDGEMENTS

This work extends beyond a mere research project; it embodies a personal odyssey as a poet, driven by a fundamental question: Does what I write truly hold significance? To seek an answer, I immersed myself in the works of past poets who courageously challenged the confines of established narratives in modern Persian poetry. In an unconventional quest to recount the stories of my marginalized poetic predecessors from an alternative vantage point, I embarked on a transformative journey.

Concurrently with the creation of this book, my audacious pursuit led me to craft *She'r-e Boland-e Sharāyet* (The Long Poem of Consequences, 2019) – a verse-essay that I envision as the poetic embodiment of the themes explored within these pages.

I am indebted to my beloved wife, Bahar, whose unwavering support has been an indispensable pillar throughout the completion of this research. Her encouragement and steadfast belief in my creative pursuits have served as a perpetual wellspring of inspiration. I also extend profound gratitude to my supervisor, Dr Saeed Talajooy, whose guidance, encouragement, and boundless patience have been instrumental to the realization of this academic endeavour.

A NOTE ON TRANSLITERATION

This book follows the *Iranian Studies* transliteration scheme. All the Persian words and personal names are rendered according to this scheme, except for those words and names established in a certain form in English sources. For more details, see: https://associationforiranianstudies.org/journal/transliteration

All translations are by the author of this book unless otherwise stated in the footnotes.

Introduction

Modern Persian poetry has not followed a linear course of development in terms of its transformation. Since the early 1800s, every period has seen the rise of numerous individuals and movements, representing the various angles of literary change, that have been undermined, ignored, or suppressed by the mainstream. This means that in every period of the history of modern Persian poetry, there have been several parallel or mutually influential poetic movements engaged in polemical dialogues with the bold line representing the mainstream.

Scholars usually portray the process of literary change in Iran as a gradual departure from the fundamentals of traditional aesthetic systems in a rationally moderate process of modernization. These narratives describe modern Persian poetry as a response to, and a reflection of, the sociopolitical changes in, and the consecutive cultural demands of, society in the mid-nineteenth century.[1] Indeed, mainstream narratives often neglect or consciously ignore the role of constant aesthetic experimentations carried out by alternative poets in the initiation and progress of the so-called 'literary revolution'.

In his acclaimed work *Recasting Persian Poetry*, Ahmad Karimi-Hakkak asserts that the mainstream scholars' lack of attention towards the works of alternative poets is a natural phenomenon. He argues that 'all efforts at innovation as they arrive on the cultural scene' are at risk of being considered as 'nonpoetry, nonsense, or both'. The reason behind this judgement might be that the readers have failed to comprehend alternative poems in the way that their creators wished. Karimi-Hakkak then states

---

[1] See Mohammad Shams Langrudi, *Tārikh-e Tahlili-e She'r-e Now*, 4 vols (Tehran: Markaz, 1998), and Yahyā Ārianpur, *Az Sabā tā Nimā*, 2 vols (Tehran: Frānklin, 1976), and Ahmad Karimi-Hakkak, *Recasting Persian Poetry: Scenarios of Poetic Modernity in Iran* (London: Oneworld, 2012), and Mohammad-Rezā Shafi'i Kadkani, *Advār-e She'r-e Fārsi* (Tehran: Tus, 2000).

that the failure of alternative works to connect with their readers is rooted in the absence of aesthetic pleasure in them.[2] This suggests that by deviating from the conventional means of generating aesthetic pleasure in a poem, alternative poets created works which were not compatible with the prevailing public taste of their time. As a result, mainstream literary critics disregarded some of the most forward-thinking Persian poets, dismissing their works as cultural noise, neglecting their experimental efforts, and even excluding them from the literary discourse. In identifying this gap, the aim of this book is to reconsider the role of these poets and their unconventional experiments in different phases of the aesthetic revolution in modern Persian poetry.

This study has been designed to scrutinize various features of this aesthetic revolution and the assumptions dominant in existing studies of modern Persian poetry. In *Recasting Persian Poetry*, Karimi-Hakkak speaks of several paths being concealed in progressing from Qā'āni as a leading figure of classical poetry in the nineteenth century to Nimā Yushij as the founder of modern Persian poetry. However, he builds his arguments on the main narrative of the history of modern poetry and assumes that the mainstream modernist trend has been 'the only, the natural, alternative to classical Persian poetry'. He further states that one should also examine 'the visions enunciated and abandoned, alternatives' [… and] 'efforts undertaken to no avail' as supplements to the main story.[3] However, one may reject the marginalization of alternative poetic movements by challenging the centre-margin model of historiography employed by mainstream narratives. Indeed, my argument posits that these movements, whether collectively or individually, established independent and parallel trajectories alongside mainstream poetry. Furthermore, their aesthetic experiments played a pivotal role in shaping the entire process of literary transformation. In other words, this study deconstructs mainstream literary histories to highlight the journey of overlooked, alternative poems connecting Yaghmā Jandaqi to Tondar Kiā and Hushang Irāni.

Thus, this book reformulates the history of modern Persian poetry by unravelling the intricate relationship between aesthetic changes and resistance to political and cultural domination. In developing this concept, it divides the history of alternative poetry into four periods: Literary Return Movement (1780–1900), Constitutional revolutionary poetry (1900–20), post-constitutional poetry (1920–40), and finally the domination of modernism (1940–60). It also conducts an analysis of the aesthetic, cultural, and political dimensions of the works of a selected group of alternative poets from the aforementioned periods.

---

[2] Karimi-Hakkak, *Recasting Persian Poetry*, p. 283.
[3] Karimi-Hakkak, *Recasting Persian Poetry*, p. 20.

Methodology and key theories

The works analysed in the following chapters have been chosen for their potential to showcase the notable experiments of pioneer movements and individuals in each given period. These experiments hold significance in two distinct ways. First, their impact on the trajectory of poetic modernization differed from that of moderate reformist movements. Second, they proposed alternative paths through which aesthetically innovative poems could actively engage with social reality and effectively resist political and cultural domination.

Through a close examination of the formal properties of the selected poems, each chapter examines their corrective approach towards the immediate literary tradition and the established regimes of poetry. Each chapter then shows how the particular experimentation in the works of the movement or individual poet impacted the Persian poetry of succeeding generations. The pioneer poets of the Constitutional Revolution era used some performative aspects of religious and folklore art forms to highlight the voice of the subordinate. This experience was conducive to the formation of the idea of poetic change through colloquialism and genre integration. Later, debates surrounding the novel concept of poetic change in the subsequent generation of poets during the post-constitutional period propelled the pioneer poets to transcend the mere inclusion of topical subject matter. Instead, they ventured into more radical experiments concerning the formal properties of their poems. Ultimately, the accomplishments of these experiments were further expanded upon in diverse ways by both experimentalist and avant-garde poets during the era of modernism's ascendancy in Persian poetry.

Each section progresses from analysing specific experiments in formal features to presenting critical arguments regarding the notion of literary change and its correlation with various forms of resistance against political and cultural domination. This approach equips this research with the necessary theoretical tools to revive the overlooked practices of alternative Persian poetry over the past two centuries and, ultimately, reconstruct the narrative of poetic change in modern Iran. Brief overviews of selected poets' biographies have also been included in each chapter in order to supplement and extend our perception of the circumstances and intentions behind the particular type of experimentation.

I explore the transformations in literary form as acts of rebellion against the dominance of classical poetic traditions, which, in turn, embodied the undemocratic power dynamics of the real world. To analyse these literary, and in a sense emancipatory, movements I have used the ideas of political philosophers such as Jacques Rancière (1940–) and Walter Benjamin (1892–1940), as well as literary theoreticians such as Harold Bloom (1930–2019), Peter Bürger (1936–2017), and Renato Poggioli

(1907–1963). The book has also benefited from the theories and poetic analyses of Iranian literary scholars and critics, including Yahyā Āriānpur (1907–1985), Ahmad Karimi-Hakkak (1944–), and Rezā Barāhani (1935–2022).

Many of the poets whose bodies of work are analysed in this book have received limited scholarly attention, and their work has yet to be thoroughly theorized by Persian scholars. Current Iranian literary theories are primarily produced to study only mainstream literary trends. Thus, a transcultural approach to creating literary theories is needed to help scholars fill the theoretical gaps in this field. Therefore, I attempted to read and re-evaluate the works at hand within the discourse of world literature as interconnected modernisms, instead of viewing them as isolated, local cultural products. In the absence of Iranian theories on which to build my arguments, I transposed the literary theories developed in the Western critical tradition to the narratives of Iranian scholars from the poetic change in Iran. The following paragraphs present an outline of the theoretical models adopted in this book and brief explanations of key terms.

Through an analysis of some experiential constitutional poems, the first chapter puts forth the argument that the aesthetic transformations of poetry during this era should be regarded as autonomous political acts, rather than as a consequence of the contemporary sociopolitical situation. Merely addressing a sociopolitically engaged topic does not automatically qualify as a political practice of poetry. Jacques Rancière has differentiated between the sociopolitical commitment and 'the politics of literature'. For Rancière, the politics of literature neither deals with the sociopolitical commitment of the author nor addresses 'the modes of representation of political events or the social structure and the social struggles' in the text.[4] Indeed, the politics of literature is concerned with the struggle of the form with the established regimes of aesthetics as well as the power relations between the components of the work. Through this theoretical approach, I argue that most of the sociopolitically engaged poems composed during and after the 1905–11 Iranian Constitutional Revolution were not as 'political' in the true sense of the word as they aspired to be. Therefore, one should investigate the politics of constitutional poetry through determinants such as the emancipation of the work from the solidified regimes of aesthetics as well as its role in the development of the poetic revolution.

Pioneer poets of the constitutional era had various approaches to the idea of reformulating the traditional poetic forms, and, of course, not all of them had the same perspective on the notion of literary change. Some poets were not as radical as others in deviating from the accepted standards and took a moderate, or sometimes conservative, position against literary change.

---

[4] Jacques Rancière, *Politics of Literature*, trans. by Julie Rose (Cambridge: Polity Press, 2011), p. 3.

Harold Bloom, in his introduction to *The Anxiety of Influence: A Theory of Poetry*, articulates conservative and progressive approaches to literary change as weak and strong poetic practices, respectively. He states that weaker poets tend to appropriate accepted traditions, while stronger poets alter the norm by intentionally misreading them. Although Bloom is concerned with the giants of English poetry, he sees the reconfiguration of tradition as the poets' strength. Therefore, some of the poets who have been considered as strong in this book might not have been the greatest poets of their time, but the best among them impacted significantly on the process of poetic change and also inspired ensuing generations of alternative poets. Bloom also conceptualizes a range of revisionary approaches towards the literature of the past, from the most radical, agonistic poetic misinterpretation to mere imitation or conditional acceptance of traditional rules.[5] Reading and re-evaluating the corpus in hand through the Bloomian approach showcases the ways in which a poetic practice accepts or reconfigures its immediate poetic tradition.

Bloom and Rancière provide complementary perspectives as the concept of a revisionary approach towards tradition in order to avoid the anxiety of influence is in line with the determination of the politics of literature as emancipating the literary form from the dominance of the established aesthetic regimes. The new poet rebels against the poetic fathers because she/he sees them as establishments that have predetermined the way a literary work should be created. That is, the poetic father represents the undemocratic, hierarchical, aesthetic regime, the disruption of which is the genuine politics of literature.

In addition, conceptualizing the emancipatory movement of the new poet against the supremacy of the aesthetic tradition leads us to the concept of avant-gardism. Peter Bürger, in his book *Theory of the Avant-Garde*, offers a twofold definition of avant-gardism. He depicted avant-gardism as (1) an attack on institutionalized art, and (2) an attempt at creating non-organic works of art.[6] That is to say, the politics of avant-garde poetry can be seen as its move towards disturbing the dominance of the poetic fathers, as embodied in the established literary rules and organic forms.

Persian avant-gardes struggled with institutionalized literature on two different fronts. First, they had to fight against the traditional aesthetic regime, which confined poets' creativity to the standard principles of classical art. Second, they had to compete with the modernists and high modernists who were rapidly turning into the literary mainstream and were focused on pushing experimentalists and avant-gardes out of their way. On the second

---

[5] Harold Bloom, *The Anxiety of Influence: A Theory of Poetry* (New York: Oxford University Press, 1997), pp. 5–16.
[6] Peter Bürger, *Theory of the Avant-Garde* (Manchester: Manchester University Press, 1984), p. 89.

level, Bürger argues that one should scrutinize an avant-garde work as a non-organic structure. The conception of non-organic composition for Bürger is relational and comparative. In other words, this concept is built upon its contradiction with the idea of organicity of the form in modern poetry. In the organic form, parts are connected cooperatively so as to generate a consolidated body. In contrast, a non-organic work consists of autonomous components. Indeed, the components of a non-organic form are supposed to suggest a more egalitarian form of togetherness – a togetherness which reflects the structure of human identity and society as a body of disparate selves and jumbles of thoughts passing through the mind as a stream of consciousness, without being hammered into shape by the intervention of the tyrannical ego. Yet this has to be done in a way that makes it understood, which in a sense suggests a different kind of organicity.

Bürger delineates two distinct approaches to the sociopolitical engagement of the literary text within avant-garde movements. He argues that avant-garde art suggests a new type of sociopolitical consciousness on the basis of which the old dichotomy between politically committed and uncommitted art may be irrelevant. He argues that the structural principle of the non-organic work of art is emancipatory by nature.[7] Indeed, a non-organic structure liberates itself from the rigid ideology of conventional dominant systems. In other words, the autonomy of parts in a non-organic form democratically allows both political and non-political notions and subjects to exist in a poem concurrently. Producing non-organic forms is a part of the revisionary movement of the alternative poet towards breaking the organicity dictated by tradition. Besides, it is a way to create disruptive equality, which is a significant element in the politics of avant-garde literature in its Rancièrian sense.

Moreover, Renato Poggioli, in *The Theory of the Avant-Garde*, separates the early notion of the avant-garde associated with leftist political activists and writers from its later conception which relates to the aesthetic and figurative sense of this term. Poggioli states that in aesthetically avant-garde poetry, the political notion primarily functions as rhetoric.[8] That is, an avant-garde text engages with politics by revealing what is unacceptable according to the dominant regime of values in society. This attempt to inaugurate a new regime of values, as Poggioli argues, is rooted in an anarchistic attribute of avant-gardism which he terms as 'alienation'.[9]

This sense of social and historical alienation is embodied as the notion of the ragpickers of the modern metropolis in Walter Benjamin's '*Arcades Project*'. The ragpicker occasionally wanders around public places,

---

[7]Bürger, p. 91.
[8]Renato Poggioli, *The Theory of the Avant-Garde* (Cambridge, MA: Belknap Press of Harvard University Press, 1968), p. 12.
[9]Poggioli, p. 110.

while living in the margins and remaining unmarked in history. Indeed, the Benjaminian ragpicker is a historian/artist whose methodology is to reassemble cultural leftovers through literary montage.[10] The last chapter of this book attempts to explain the anti-establishment stance and the non-organicity of Persian avant-garde poetry through the Benjaminian concept of rag picking. It examines several works which employed elements of so-called degenerate art along with both literary and unliterary, verbal and visual pieces in miscellanies.

Other aspects of the anti-establishment stance and the non-organicity of Persian avant-garde poetry in this book are examined through Poggioli's notion of 'the dialectic of avant-garde movements'. Poggioli distinguishes four 'moments' shared among all avant-garde movements. He introduces these moments as a means of analysing avant-garde movements and their approaches to the process of artistic creation, both 'internally and externally'.[11] That is, these shared moments clarify both the ideological and psychological motivation of the artists as well as the practical and sociopolitical significance of their movements. He terms these moments as activism, antagonism, nihilism, and agonism.

Poggioli explains that an avant-garde movement initially emerges as a collective aspiration to achieve recognition and success as a movement, ultimately aiming to disseminate the avant-garde spirit across various cultural domains. The goal of artistic practice for an avant-garde movement is to create a perfect example of a form of art which breaks social and cultural hierarchies. Moreover, avant-garde activism engenders a sense of agitation directed towards mainstream art, traditional norms, public taste, and even the prevailing powers. This state of hostility and opposition in Poggioli's theory is classified as 'the antagonistic moment'. This sense of anarchic antagonism towards established aesthetic regimes may lead the artist to a destructive approach towards tradition and any principle which limits aesthetic experimentations. Poggioli characterizes this disposition as a transcendental antagonism, labelling it as the avant-garde 'nihilism'. He argues that, during this stage, avant-gardes constantly experience a tension between the desire to construct and the impulse to dismantle artistic systems. Finally, at the 'agonistic moment', the artist does not perceive any damage or failure, even when he himself is the subject of the harm. Poggioli describes this phase as a psychological state in which the artist willingly embraces self-destruction and is prepared to sacrifice themselves anonymously for the sake of future artistic movements.[12]

---

[10] Walter Benjamin, *The Arcades Project*, trans. by Howard Eiland (Cambridge, MA: Harvard University Press, 2002), p. 460.
[11] Poggioli, p. 25.
[12] Poggioli, pp. 25–6.

Study framework

The overall structure of this book takes the form of eight chapters, including an introductory chapter and the conclusion. Chapter 1 focuses on the process of poetic change during and slightly after the Constitutional Revolution at the start of the twentieth century. The chapter begins with a concise introduction to the political dimensions as well as unprecedented formal features in the works of three major figures of the *Bāzgasht-e Adabi* (the Literary Return Movement), namely Qāʿem Maqām Farāhāni (1779–1835), Fathollāh Khān Sheybāni (1825–1891), and Yaghmā Jandaqi (1781–1859). The chapter continues by illustrating the impact of the literary revolution on the practices of the followers of pre-revolutionary classical literature or *Bāzgasht-e Adabi* (the Literary Return Movement). The next section is concerned with two different revisionary approaches adopted by Malek al-Shoʿarā Bahār (1886–1951) to the form and function of the poetic templates and literary language used by the classical masters. The chapter then moves on to examine the relationship between colloquialism in the works of the constitutional poets and the popular performing arts of the time. It also discusses why colloquialism, in itself, should be considered as a form of artistic resistance.

Chapter 2 deals with the performing aspect of constitutional poetry, with a specific emphasis on the works of interdisciplinary artists during that era. In so doing, the concepts of collective singing and dramatic poetry are examined in the works of Āref Qazvini (1882–1934) and Mirzādeh Eshqi (1893–1924). Through an analysis of lesser known works by these poet-performers, Chapter 2 delves into the ways in which performance poetry can serve as an emancipatory act in the public space. This chapter attempts to re-evaluate the assumptions made by mainstream narratives of modern Persian poetry about the impact of the mass publication of poetry in the constitutional era on the process of poetic change in Iran. The chapter analyses the works in hand to conceptualize the poetic experimentation in this period as independent politics of literature. Returning to the main thesis, the chapter argues that poetic experimentation and the ways in which poetry was presented in the public space in this era were not merely the result of change in the political sphere. Indeed, the poetic change in this era was a form of self-reliant resistance to sociopolitical and cultural domination, which can be termed as the political act of literary deviation. In other words, the pioneer poets of this period undertook an antithetical movement against the reactionary traditional aesthetic by intentionally misreading it.

Chapter 3 concentrates on the process of literary change in the post-constitutional era. This chapter introduces Taqi Rafʿat (1889–1920), the editor-in-chief of the *Tajaddod* newspaper, as a leading figure of the radical movement in the poetic change of this period. It goes on to examine the theoretical dimensions of critical correspondences between the poets associated with *Tajaddod* and the members of the *Dāneshkadeh* association, particularly correspondence between Rafʿat and Bahār. These disputes are analysed to determine the difference between the radical and the gradualist understandings of the notion of literary revolution. The chapter then reviews Abolqāsem Lāhuti's (1887–1957) life and oeuvre and examines the transformation of Lāhuti's poetry from traditional poetic forms with mystical subject matter to innovative poetic forms with sociopolitically committed, counter-sublime content. This part also analyses the aesthetic changes in Lāhuti's poetry before and after his acquaintance with Soviet socialist realism. Lāhuti's innovative rhythmic systems and unconventional rhyme patterns are discussed as being among the most groundbreaking experiments in poetic forms in this era.

The next section of this chapter analyses attempts by *Tajaddod* poets, particularly Shams Kasmāʾi (1883–1961), at improvising new poetic forms. In so doing, it examines the adaptation of unusual rhyme patterns inspired by French and Russian sonnets in the works of this group. Although *Tajaddod* poets never formulated the results of their experiments with poetic forms as a set of theories, they should be acknowledged as the most significant deviations of Persian poetry from its traditional roots. The last section of this chapter discusses the role of these practices in developing a new conception of the stanza in Persian poetry. It also shows that the new understanding of the stanza resulted in the invention of a novel poetic form called *chārpāreh* (four-liner). The section indicates that *chārpāreh* was inspired by some of the underused classical Persian stanzaic templates and similar European poetic forms. Therefore, *chārpāreh*, with its hybrid spirit, was established as the most popular poetic form among different groups of post-constitutional poets. The final part of this section includes a discussion about the role of *chārpāreh* in challenging the established regime of classical generic classification and bringing about change.

Notwithstanding constitutional poets who understood the politics of literature as a series of thematic changes, post-constitutional poets undertook an antithetical approach to all the aesthetic values of their precursors' works. Responding to the central argument of this book, this chapter attempts to show how the proactive revisionary approach of these poets towards all established literary systems, either traditional or modern, led to a whole new phase of politicizing literature in the post-Constitutional Revolution era. This chapter analyses a selected number of poems to demonstrate how post-constitutional poets revolted against the sublime subject matters and formal properties of their immediate literary tradition as reproductions of the hierarchical political regimes in the aesthetic system.

Chapter 4 begins by presenting a new classification of pioneer poets in this era. The first section reviews some theoretical points on the relationships and distinctions between high-modernism, avant-gardism, and experimentalism in modern Persian poetry. This section is an attempt to offer a framework of categorization for different trends of modernization in Persian poetry that echoes the main argument of this book. That is, it reimages Persian modernist movements in the first half of the twentieth century based on their perspective on poetic experimentation as the main politics of literature. It then examines the career of Nimā Yushij (1887–1957), who is known as the founder of modern Persian poetry, before analysing one of his less studied poems, *Khāneh-ye Sarivoyli* (Sarivoyli's House). This poem, I argue, is a significant turning point in modern Persian poetry. *Khāneh-ye Sarivoyli*, indeed, showcases why Nimā's career should be seen as having had two distinct phases. A close reading of this poem demonstrates that Nimā consciously changed his revisionary approach towards the poetic tradition and the concept of sociopolitical engagement in the course of his career. This transition, in turn, divided Persian poetic modernism into two main branches.

Chapter 5 primarily focuses on the works of three influential experimentalist poets from the 1930s to the 1950s, namely Mohammad Moqaddam (1909–1996), Zabih Behruz (1890–1972), and Shin Partow (1907–1997). The first section in the chapter analyses Mohammad Moqaddam's life and experimental poetic practice. It delves into the analysis of Moqaddam's prose poems and showcases his experimentation with the Persian tradition of versification. It then moves on to an analysis of free verse in Moqaddam's poetry. In doing so, the rhythmic systems employed in his poems are read closely using phrasal, rhythmical, and metrical analysis methods. This section concludes with explicating Moqaddam's rhetorical move to replace dead metaphors and institutional symbols with private ones.

The next poet whose life and works are studied in this chapter is Zabih Behruz. The section briefly reviews Behruz's early practice of creating satirical poems in traditional templates. It moves on to a section examining the application and characteristics of free verse in three of Behruz's poetic dramas. The final section of this chapter analyses the experimental features of Shin Partow's poetry. His prose poetry is studied with a focus on his attempts to extend the conventional literary language of the time, adopting the formal features of modern fiction in his poetry and experimenting with the free verse rhythmic system.

This chapter aims to highlight Persian experimentalists, who perceive political engagement merely as a departure of the literary text towards novelty in aesthetic systems. Indeed, for Persian experimentalists, the politics of literature is an act of disobedience against the sovereignty of their poetic ancestors. Although they did not tend to emancipate their works from the dominance of their immediate tradition in an anarchic way, experimentalist poets paved the way for radical steps by avant-gardes in the process of literary revolution.

Chapter 6 is centred on the poetic practices of Persian avant-garde poets of the 1940s to 1960s, particularly Tondar Kiā (1909–1987) and Hushang Irāni (1925–1973). It begins by identifying Poggioli's avant-garde 'moments' in Kiā's theory and practice. It then investigates disputes between Kiā and his modernist and traditionalist opponents during the first years of his career. The Benjaminian notion of the 'ragpicker' in modern cities is employed to study Kiā's method in creating his works. Kiā gathers various elements of his works from the remnants of art history, purposefully rejecting the hierarchical and archival regime of cultural values. The non-organic nature of his poetic forms and the arbitrary way he arranged his books are also discussed in the same section. The first part of this chapter concludes by drawing a comparison between Kiā's style and the styles associated with historical avant-gardes. This comparison aims to reveal Kiā's dialectical approach to the elements of Western avant-garde movements within the multi-generic spirit of his works.

The subsequent section of Chapter 6 delves into the avant-garde moments of Hushang Irāni's career. This analysis focuses on a manifesto published by Irāni and his associates in the journal *Khorus Jangi* (The Fighting Rooster). The chapter proceeds with a close reading of some of Irāni's most controversial poems. Avant-garde poetic elements, such as non-organic forms and techniques associated with 'automatic writing', are also examined in these poems.

This chapter is an attempt to determine that Persian avant-garde poetry not only plays a significant role in the process of aesthetic revolution but could also actively partake in resistance to the sociopolitical and cultural dominance of the powerholder through suggesting a new kind of sociopolitical consciousness. To articulate this indirect, internal type of political engagement, the chapter investigates both the theory and the practice of Iranian avant-gardes. In alignment with the central thesis, this chapter illustrates that avant-garde work may rebel against hierarchical regimes by implementing non-organic forms and undertaking a confrontational approach to any established system, either sociopolitical or aesthetic.

The conclusion draws upon the entire book, tying up the various strands of the research which set out to determine the relationship between poetic experimentation and resistance to dominant cultural and sociopolitical systems. It gives a synopsis and critique of the findings before summarizing the arguments made in each chapter. It reviews the arguments made in each chapter, attempting to provide the reader with an insight into how each chapter contributes to the main thesis. By discussing the significance of less studied, marginalized poets in the trend of poetic change in Iran, the conclusion restates the contribution this book has made to the field. It then moves on to a brief discussion of the limitations of the current study, such as the difficulties of access to the primary materials and the lack of scholarship about these poets in both Persian and English.

The conclusion ends with some recommendations for developing the findings in future research. It suggests that further research in this field could pursue the historical line drawn in this book and venture to vocalize the avant-garde poetic trend of the 1960s–1970s as well as trends emerging after the Iranian revolution of 1979 to the present. In order to visualize the ways in which this historical narrative could advance, the chapter presents a brief background of these movements.

Research contribution

The present study offers several contributions to the current research approaches in modern Persian literary history by challenging the established narratives of modern poetry. This is the first study to undertake an analysis of some marginalized, radically innovative poets in order to indicate the significance of their experimentations in the process of literary change in modern Iran. This study aims to change the dominant narrative of Persian literary modernization in which the radical frontier is shown as a supplement to, or a deviation from, the mainstream. Offering a new regime of classification, this study breaks the hierarchical dichotomy of central/marginal which has dominated studies on modern Persian poetry. It suggests that the unconventional, formal experiments of the poets discussed in the book have equal weight with the rational and gradual reforms of the moderate modernists.

In contrast to the existing literature, this book posits that the readers and literary community would not have embraced even the slightest reforms in the core elements of Persian poetry if it were not for the groundbreaking works of radical poets who pushed the boundaries of the genre. Paul Mann's theory of 'the anti and its recuperation' provides insight into this dynamic. According to Mann, despite its antagonism towards bourgeois culture, the avant-garde inadvertently reinforces the social mainstream by implicitly acknowledging its authority. Furthermore, the avant-garde rejuvenates the core of this resilient mainstream by introducing novel and vibrant cultural expressions. In essence, the rebellion of the avant-garde indirectly sustains and enlivens the very system it seeks to challenge.[13]

In addition, by examining aesthetic experimentation as a form of literary politics, this analysis contributes to a deeper understanding of different modes of resistance within Persian literature. It is worth noting that this research represents the first application of certain theoretical sources to explore the process of literary change in Iran. These theories have enabled

---

[13] Paul Mann, *The Theory-Death of the Avant-Garde* (Bloomington: Indiana University Press, 1991), p. 81.

a clearer understanding of the contributions of alternative Persian poets to the transformation of the form and function of Persian poetry over the past two centuries.

This book offers a comprehensive analysis of the works of fifteen poets, both marginalized and mainstream, including some who have received limited scholarly attention. Notably, there is a lack of independent academic research on the poetry of Moqaddam, Behruz, Shin Partow, and Kiā, both in English and Persian. Furthermore, there is a scarcity of English academic writings on Sheybāni, Yaghmā, Raf'at, and Kasmā'i.

Another significant contribution of this work to the study of modern Persian poetry is its transcultural approach to the analysis of alternative Persian poetry and its position as a cultural product of a developing society. This book engages with the question of originality and authenticity in poetic experimentation raised by the mainstream narratives of modern Persian poetry in all its substantial aspects. One may argue that the alternative movements of literary change in post-1920s Iran are compelling examples of the rise of avant-garde movements in a non-Western atmosphere. Although in dialogue with non-Iranian avant-garde movements, most alternative poets had particular elements that made them distinct from their non-Iranian counterparts.[14] Indeed, while acknowledging the undeniable influence of Western artistic movements on the process of literary modernization in Iran, it is important to avoid exclusively centralizing theories of European influence in the scholarship of modern Persian poetry. Such an approach can lead to challenges in comprehending the process of literary modernism and, particularly, the emergence of alternative and avant-garde art in a holistic manner.

A note on originality and authenticity of the alternative movements

Most scholars of modern Persian poetry read the oeuvres of the alternative poets as mere borrowings from Western culture. Indeed, these scholars devalue alternative Persian poetry by degrading it to a form of appropriation, thereby suggesting the superiority of Western culture. They assume that the quality and practices of these movements in Iran should be investigated

---

[14] It should be noted that while the dominant scholarship on Persian literary modernization has focused on theories of adaptation and appropriation, there are two noteworthy books that have explored literary exchanges beyond the scope of European influence on Persian and Arabic literary modernisms. These books, *Literary Modernity between the Middle East and Europe* by Kamran Rastegar and *Reorienting Modernism in Arabic and Persian Poetry* by Levi Thompson, offer valuable insights into this subject.

according to their level of compatibility with Western movements, rather than based on their own intrinsic worth. This perspective is based on the 'Eurocentric truism' that Western artists held a privileged understanding of artistic concepts, while non-Western artists were deemed incapable of comprehending them.

According to Partha Mitter, colonial historians of Asian avant-garde movements have rated these (mostly isolated) movements as 'bit players in the master narrative' of Western avant-garde art. They argue that non-Western artists failed to enlarge the canon of avant-garde art and that these artists 'are brought in primarily on account of their compatibility with the avant-garde discourse in the West'.[15] This claim has created, in turn, a mentality in non-Euro-American critics that cultural transmission is a 'one-way process flowing from the occident'.[16]

Although there was a prevailing notion in twentieth-century Iran that the East was the origin of numerous universal cultural developments, Iranian scholars have predominantly adhered to a West-centric perspective when studying the constitutional, post-constitutional, experimentalist, and avant-garde movements from the 1900s to the 1960s. Despite the increasing challenge to the notion of relying exclusively on the West as a primary source of inspiration from the late 1930s, art critics of the time often asserted that Iranian alternative poets were, at best, derivative of early twentieth-century Western movements. For instance, Parviz Nātel Khānlari draws a parallel between Persian sound poems and French Letterism, suggesting that Iranian poets who prioritized the musicality of words over their meaning were influenced by this movement. Similarly, he considers Persian concrete poems of the period as imitations of Apollinaire's collection of poetry, *Calligrammes*.[17] Khānlari, however, does not seem to be aware that by trying to find a Western equivalent for every unconventional experience in Persian poetry, he is implying that all poetic changes are the 'intellectual property rights' of the West. This tendency has been so dominant that the existence of potential sources of inspiration within the long tradition of Persian poetry has been completely ignored.

In other words, scholars like Khānlari, by emphasizing the chronological precedence of Western historical avant-gardes, adopt a 'centre-to-edge/ edge-to-centre framing of the avant-garde' in the context of modern Persian literary scholarship. This approach, as described by James M. Harding, constructs a model that is ideologically biased and laden with assumptions, as it characterizes the leading and most advanced positions of artistic expression in all regions and cultures solely based on the history of

---

[15] Partha Mitter, 'Decentering Modernism: Art History and Avant-Garde Art from the Periphery', *The Art Bulletin*, 4 (2008), 531–48 (p. 531).
[16] Mitter, p. 538.
[17] Iraj Pārsinezhād, *Khānlari va Naqd-e Adabi* (Tehran: Sokhan, 2008), pp. 37–42.

European artistic influence.[18] Consequently, most critical writings about the alternative Persian poets have focused on whether these poets succeeded in their appropriation of Western pioneer poetry for Persian literature.

Mitter states that this type of a question is merely based on the reception of Western avant-garde in peripheral societies. Therefore, any answer to this question is to evaluate a non-Western work through inappropriate criteria. She states that while successful imitation could be seen as mimicking, imperfect imitation signifies a lack of mastery or failure in the learning process.[19] As a result of applying this approach to the history of the avant-garde in Iran, most critics refer to Mohammad Moqaddam and Tondar Kiā's oeuvre as nothing but 'unsuccessful imitation' and a miscomprehension of the doctrine of American free verse and Dadaism, respectively. They also regard Abolqāsem Lāhuti and Hushang Irāni's works as 'successful imitations', which nevertheless should be dismissed as they are absurd copies of Soviet socialist realism and surrealism.[20]

Some argue that the works of alternative Persian poets cannot be genuine as the whole idea of avant-gardism does not work in societies in which modernity has not been fully experienced. Emphasizing the sequence of literary movements in the West as a critical factor, Esmā'il Kho'i states that Persian literature is not in a position to criticize modernism since it has not yet experienced modernism thoroughly.[21] This reasoning on the one hand overlooks the fact that Iran has been through different levels of modernization since the late 1890s. It is also based on the Western-centric ideology of linear progress which defines the development of a nation's art as the ability to follow the exact route paved by so-called Western culture. However, they also argue that it is impossible to understand the history of Western thought without absorbing the critical features of Western culture. Thus, if Iranian artists desire to be recognized as pioneer or alternative, they must compromise their integrity and probably lose their cultural roots as well.

In response, some post-colonial scholars have tied the matter of originality and authenticity in art to the very concepts of avant-gardism. Prita Meier

---

[18] James M. Harding, 'From Cutting Edge to Rough Edges: On the Transnational Foundations of Avant-Garde Performance', in *Not the Other Avant-Garde: The Transnational Foundations of Avant-Garde Performance*, ed. by James M. Harding and John Rouse (Ann Arbor, Michigan: University of Michigan Press, 2006), pp. 18–40 (p. 22).

[19] Mitter, p. 538.

[20] For a thorough discussion of this, see Mohammad-Rezā Shafi'i Kadkani, *Bā Cherāq va Āyeneh* (Tehran: Sokhan, 2011), pp. 588–92, and Sirus Tāhbāz, *Khorus Jangi-e Bi-Mānand* (Tehran: Farzān-e Ruz, 2001), pp. 19–21, and Abdol'ali Dastgheyb, *Sāyeh Rowshan-e She'r-e Now-e Pārsi* (Tehran: Farhang, 1969), pp. 165–243, and Mashi'at Alā'i, 'Hushang Irāni va Sureālism-e Irāni', *Goharān*, 7–8 (2005), 94–9.

[21] Mehdi Jāmi, and Esmā'il Kho'i, 'Esmā'il Kho'i az She'r Miguyad', *Radio Zamaneh*, http://zamaaneh.com/idea/2008/07/post_350.html [accessed 17 February 2020].

roots this idea to the mid-nineteenth century when a group of pioneer artists refused to work within the established styles. They declared that to create an original piece, one must be free to utilize various features of art from any place or period. Meier states that the essence of rebellion against the institutionalized arts was the hinging of avant-garde art onto the reality of the society in which the work had been created. She writes:

> The avant-garde, therefore, propagated what Rosalind Krauss has called a 'discourse of originality,' where work must be vanguardist and new to be authentic. ... in art historical studies, the 'historical avant-garde' designates European artists who practised around World War I; the appropriation of the term for earlier, later or non-European practitioners seeks to claim these now valorised strategies for politicising aesthetic practice for artists in different periods or locations.[22]

Another criticism raised by critics of Persian alternative poetry is that, due to their anti-traditional nature and perceived aesthetic immaturity, these works could pose a potential danger to the public. The argument is that as alternative poets challenge the established and accepted literary values upheld by scholars and intellectuals, they may have a negative impact on the 'literary taste' of regular Persian readers. In a very typical commentary on these poets' careers, Alireza Anushirvani and Kavoos Hasanli state that alternative poets were those who neither comprehended the aesthetic suggestions modernist movements which were still loyal to traditions nor understood 'the nuances and decorum of classical Persian poetry'. They describe these poets' ideas as 'crude and immature' with no 'creativity and poetic imagination' and, at best, as 'a game of words'.[23] One might argue that inculcating so-called 'good taste' is a way of promoting a dominant taste as a solidified and sacred cultural heritage and of emphasizing the necessity for protecting traditional literary standards.

In the case of Iran, the state and other institutionalized cultural bodies, including universities and traditional literary forums, assumed the role of safeguarding traditional standards. The revolt of alternative art against totalitarian regimes, including these cultural bodies, was a means of resisting the old and new hierarchies that threatened and limited the originality of artistic activities. According to Mitter, the avant-garde art is most inspiring for artists raised in traditional societies due to its experimental attitude that

---

[22] Jāmi, and Kho'i, p. 22.
[23] Alireza Anushiravani and Kavoos Hassanli, 'Trends in Contemporary Persian Poetry', in *Media, Culture and Society in Iran: Living with Globalization and the Islamic State*, ed. by Mehdi Semati (London: Routledge Taylor & Francis Group, 2010), pp. 152–66 (p. 155).

constantly seeks to push intellectual frontiers, its ideology of emancipatory innovation, and its agonistic relation to tradition and authority.[24]

I therefore argue that the Iranian alternative poetry cannot be adequately studied unless the critics and scholars of the field make two significant changes to the basis of their analysis. First and foremost, it is necessary to challenge the assumption that modern Western art holds a central position while non-Western art forms are relegated to the margins. They can then examine the quality of cultural dialogue in these works, instead of tracing for signs of external influence in them. Second, to analyse pioneering art in 'developing countries', one should understand that the process of development does not necessarily follow that of Western art history. Modern art in these societies, especially avant-garde art, not only defies the hierarchical regime of values within the local culture but also challenges any institutionalization imposed by other dominant cultures. As a result, artists from various art schools can emerge simultaneously in such societies, irrespective of the region's sociopolitical or economic status of development.

In a similar vein, using Western theoretical frameworks in studies of non-Western art should not be seen as applying central ideas to marginal case studies. Indeed, by acknowledging alternative Persian poetry as an equal party in the process of poetic change in world literature, reading and re-evaluating non-Western alternative literature could feed back into literary theory and expand its perspective. It is, of course, only possible through the reimaging of those dimensions of alternative movements which are exclusive to non-Western literature.

---

[24] Mitter, p. 533.

1

The politics of literature and the forms of literary deviation in constitutional poetry

There is a consensus among modern Persian literary scholars that the era of the Constitutional Revolution is characterized by the number of literary works published in journals and newspapers promoting the emancipatory discourses of the 1890s to the early 1910s. During these two decades, Iranians experienced several periods of economic crisis, initiated a democratic movement with demonstrations, sit-ins, street performances, and lectures, suffered heavy-handed state suppression, and succeeded in changing the structure of the state to that of a constitutional monarchy and establishing the first parliament. Following Mozaffar al-Din Shāh's death in January 1907, they also suffered Mohammad-Ali Shāh's counter-revolutionary coup which, after the bombardment of parliament in June 1908, resulted in a state bordering on civil war, before finally concluding with the conquest of Tehran by the revolutionary forces in 1909.

This was an era of such upheaval that the revolutionary ideas of the public sphere were reflected in the topical literary works of the time. One can argue that the majority of poems published in this period were openly political. Yahyā Āriānpur states that since almost all the publishers and printing presses were controlled by the state, no book was published by liberal writers and poets. Inevitably, the talents and energies of the latter were redirected towards publishing their works in newspapers.[1]

As the number of sociopolitically engaged poems being published in newspapers increased radically, poetry became a medium for the political intelligentsia to convey their message to the masses. A number of poets who

---

[1] Yahyā Āriānpur, *Az Sabā tā Nimā*, 2 vols (Tehran: Frānklin, 1976), 2, p. 26.

were not concerned with upholding the structural rules of traditional poetry attempted to increase the influence of their revolutionary ideas through the innovative forms of their texts.[2] In these works, effectiveness, relevance, and comprehensibility were the top priorities, which in turn led poets towards changes in the formal or generic aspects of their poems. These new priorities, as Ahmad Karimi-Hakkak states, enabled new poets 'to disseminate their ideas in ways that the culture perceived as new and relevant, at least in some aspects'.[3]

The expansion of periodicals in this era and the political aspirations of creative intellectuals resulted in significant changes in the way works of literature, especially poems, were disseminated. Indeed, newspapers spread poems among diverse social classes and throughout many regions of the country. Earlier research on constitutional poetry has suggested that the primary outcome of transferring poetry from conventional establishments to newspapers, thus, enhancing its availability to the general public was the simplification of language and other formal elements in Persian poetry. Nevertheless, it could be contended that the formal alterations in the poetry of that period could be regarded as distinct political expressions rather than solely arising from the contemporaneous sociopolitical circumstances. In essence, the presence of sociopolitically engaged themes in poetry does not automatically imply that every poem serves as a deliberate political act. By drawing on the concept of the politics of literature, Jacques Rancière has been able to differentiate between the sociopolitical commitment and the politics of literature:

> The politics of literature is not the politics of its writers. It does not deal with their personal commitment to the social and political issues and struggles of their times. Nor does it deal with the modes of representation of political events or the social structure and the social struggles in their books. The syntagma 'politics of literature' means that literature 'does' politics as literature – that there is a specific link between politics as a definite way of doing and literature as a definite practice of writing.[4]

---

[2] The first newspaper after the establishment of parliament was *Majles* (Parliament, 1906). This newspaper published several poems by Adib al-Mamālek Farāhāni, along with sociopolitical essays and parliamentary news. Ārianpur lists a considerable number of journals released after the Revolution and mentions their editors and managers. Most of these newspapers, such as *Nedā-ye Vatan* (Call of the Homeland), *Tamaddon* (Civilisation), *Mosāvāt* (Equality), and *Al-Jamāl* (Beauty), published poems with the same political inclination as that of their manager. Some others, such as *Te'ātr* (Theatre), *Sur-e Esrāfil* (Trumpet of Esrafil), and *Nasim-e Shomāl* (Northern Breeze), only published their editor's literary works. See Ārianpur, 2, p. 22.
[3] Ahmad Karimi-Hakkak, *Recasting Persian Poetry: Scenarios of Poetic Modernity in Iran* (London: Oneworld, 2012), p. 15.
[4] Jacques Rancière, *Politics of Literature*, trans. by Julie Rose (Cambridge: Polity Press, 2011), p. 3.

This theory posits that a significant portion of the politically committed poetic works produced during this era may not have fully embodied the true essence of political expression they aimed to convey. To understand the political nature of constitutional poetry, it becomes crucial to delve into factors such as the transformation of the poetic medium and the extent to which the works contributed to the trend of modernizing and reformulating the poetic forms.

One might argue that the politics of literature could differ between poets based on their approach to the notion of literary change and the means of poetic reformulation. Although most poets of the constitutional era experimented with semantic and verbal aspects of Persian poetry, not all of them had the same perspective on the actual concept of literary modernization. One can see a variety of degrees and means of deviation from literary norms in this era. Certain poets exhibited a less radical inclination compared to their counterparts, refraining from significant deviations from established standards and instead adopting a moderate or occasionally conservative stance regarding literary transformation.

New poets are not able to avoid the imperatives of the influence of their precursors. That is, both radical and conservative approaches towards literary change are somehow associated with the position of the new poet concerning the influence of his precursors on his works. The strategy of the poet of pastiches is to imitate his ancestors' works, while the pioneer poet seeks to create a new, divergent style. This corrective approach of the pioneer poet occurs through a process of intentionally misreading the central works of his precursors. In other words, the antithetical stance of pioneer poets leads them to be the exact opposite of their precursors.

Harold Bloom, in his introduction to *The Anxiety of Influence: A Theory of Poetry*, articulates radical and conservative approaches to literary change as weak and strong poetic practices. He states that weaker poets tend to appropriate accepted traditions, while stronger poets alter the norm by intentionally misreading them. He also conceptualizes a range of revisionary approaches towards the literature of the past, from the most radical poetic 'misprision' to the conditional acceptance of traditional rules.[5]

The ensuing chapters aim to demonstrate the specific correlation between these forms of literary deviations and the politics of literature in constitutional poetry. Although the political subject matter of constitutional poetry overshadowed its formal experiential aspects, these chapters aims to demonstrate how different approaches to literary deviation and underlying changes in the structures of classical poetics should be seen as a genuine political act of poetry. The political act of literary deviation will be discussed

---

[5]Harold Bloom, *The Anxiety of Influence: A Theory of Poetry* (New York: Oxford University Press, 1997), pp. 5–16.

through analysing the modification of verbal and semantic systems, as well as the rise of performativity and theatricality in the poetry of this era.

This chapter commences with a concise overview of the origins of resistance and transformation evident in the works of select pre-revolutionary poets. Subsequently, it aims to illustrate the impact of new trends in literary modernization on the works of those who emulated the classical literature of the pre-revolutionary era. The latter part of the chapter delves into the examination of two distinct revisionary approaches undertaken by Malek al-Shoʿarā Bahār, concerning the form and function of the poetic templates and literary language used by his traditional precursors. The chapter then moves on to an analysis of colloquialism in constitutional poetry and its relationship with folk performative arts as a form of artistic resistance.

Resistance and transformation in pre-constitutional poetry

Unexpected changes in the poetic forms and themes of the eighteenth and nineteenth centuries suggest that, in contrast with what Bāzgasht-e Adabi (the Literary Return Movement) promoted in this era, a faction of poets demonstrated a strong inclination towards crafting poems of contemporary relevance and significance.[6] Some of these poets attempted to depict the sociopolitical crises of the Qajar period in works which can be considered as early examples of sociopolitically 'committed poetry'. Although these poems do not represent the modern sense of 'society' and 'liberty', one may identify them as the origin of the innovative, revolutionary poems composed during the 1905–11 Iranian Constitutional Revolution. Indeed, the sociopolitical poetry of the pre-revolutionary era, regardless of the perspective it takes on the crisis, can be seen as a first attempt, paving the way for social commitment in the works of the next generation of poets. In addition, these committed poems contributed to a trend of modernization and reformulation of poetic forms in Persian poetry of the constitutional era.

---

[6]'Bāzgasht-e Adabi' is a classification term used to categorize Persian literature into four main stylistic periods: Khorāsāni, ʿErāqi, Hendi, and Bāzgasht. The Bāzgasht-e Adabi movement emerged in the mid-eighteenth century and persisted until the time of the Constitutional Revolution and beyond. Its objective was to revive the composition of poetry in the Khorāsāni and ʿErāqi styles, which were predominantly practiced between the tenth and fourteenth centuries. In modern literary studies, this movement is often portrayed as a response to the prevalent dominance of the sabk-e Hendi (Hindi style) of poetry in Persian poetry from the fifteenth to eighteenth centuries. Sabk-e Hendi is characterized by its intricate poetic language and imagery, in contrast to the formal aspects emphasized in the earlier stylistic periods.

Among the poets of early and mid-nineteenth-century Iran, three poets are particularly renowned for political poems in which they criticize, or maintain an advisory position in relation to, the corruption of the clergy, lower state officials and the government itself. They are: Mirzā Abolqāsem Qā'em Maqām Farāhāni (1779–1835), Mirzā Fathollāh Khān Sheybāni Kāshāni (1825–1891), and Mirzā Abolhasan Yaghmā Jandaqi (1781–1859).

In my previously published article titled 'Margins, Resistance, and Transformation in Classical Persian Poetry: Yaghmā Jandaqi as the Precursor of Constitutional Revolution Poetry', I explored the works of these poets.[7] The article delved into the political dimensions present in the works of Qā'em Maqām and Sheybāni, as well as unprecedented content and formal features in Yaghmā's poetry. I argued that Yaghmā's poetry introduced new poetic forms that had a profound influence on the subsequent generation of poets.

Qā'em Maqām, as an advocate of Bāzgasht-e Adabi, which approved of adopting the diction and poetic qualities of the ninth- to twelfth-century Khorāsāni or 'Erāqi styles of poetry, made a conscious attempt to imitate classical poetry in his critical poems. However, due to the turbulent societal conditions of the time, his tendency to employ a relatively straightforward language, in contrast to the intricacies of earlier poetry, resulted in a more realistic and politically charged tone. This difference, however, does not extend to other formal aspects of these poems, as their structure remains unchanged and unaltered.

While the context and, to a lesser extent, the language of Qā'em Maqām's poems have embraced elements of modernity, the poetic form he employs continues to adhere to classical conventions. He composed a *masnavi* (poem in rhymed couplet form), *Jalāyer-Nāmeh* (Letter of Jalāyer), which was taken as a model for satirical, classical-like *masnavis* by poets of the next generation, such as Iraj Mirzā (1874–1926) and his *Āref-Nāmeh* (Letter of Āref).[8] Qā'em Maqām endeavours to liberate his work from the language, and occasionally the established norms, of classical poetry, which

---

[7] Sonboldel, Farshad, 'Margins, Resistance and Transformation in Classical Persian Poetry: Yaghmā Jandaqi as Precursive Kernel of the Constitutional Revolution Poetry', in *Poetry and Revolution: The Poets and Poetry of the Constitutional Era of Iran*, ed. by Katouzian Homa and Alireza Korangy (Abingdon Oxon: Routledge, 2022) https://doi.org/10.4324/9781003243335.

[8] *Āref-nāmeh* is a long satirical poem in the *masnavi* template. This work is famous for its homoeroticism addressed to Abo'l-Qasem Āref Qazvini, a poet and musician contemporary to Iraj Mirzā. According to Ārianpur, Iraj Mirzā composed this 515-verse couplet through irritation caused by Āref's discourteous behaviour during his stay in Mashhad in 1920. Ārianpur mentions various historical accounts of the reasons behind the creation of *Āref-nāmeh*, most of which blame Āref for affronting his old friend, Iraj, on purpose. Apparently, Āref, who went to Mashhad in support of the semi-independent government of Colonel Mohammad-Taqi Khān Pesyān, not only insulted the Qajar family in his concert but also behaved disrespectfully when he met Iraj in public. Ārianpur, 1, pp. 391–9.

had become excessively pompous and affected by that time. The poem is composed from the perspective of Jalāyer, the poet's servant, and seeks to demonstrate Qā'em Maqām's critical view of the governors through quips in a relatively simple language and style.

In the majority of his critical poems, Qā'em Maqām directs his criticism towards individuals occupying lower positions of power. His tone towards the Shāh, the crown prince, and other high-ranking members of royalty is soft and gentle, resembling that of a humble supplicant who quietly expresses his grievances. However, when it comes to addressing the shortcomings of lower-level governors, his voice becomes bolder and more assertive.

In a similar vein, Sheybāni's poetry speaks of two different societal demands. On the one hand, he wants to reform Persian poetry so that it is able to expose the tyranny of the age, and on the other hand, he wants to preserve inherited poetical conventions. This ambivalent approach towards literary change is also perceptible in the works of both the traditionalists and the gradualist modernists of the next generation; the poet submits to tradition in his work, while struggling with traditional and hierarchical regimes in social reality. Hence, adopting a moderate and corrective approach towards the past, the poet endeavours to reform and enhance certain aspects of the traditional aesthetic instead of dismantling it completely.

While the innovations of Qā'em Maqām and Sheybāni primarily revolved around content, Yaghmā's contributions extended to the realm of form as well. In his poetic protestations, he espouses elements from *ta'ziyeh* (passion plays) and the *nowheh* (lament) tradition of religious dirges. He also experiments with a more generally spoken idiom in an attempt to broaden the range of his readers from the educated elite and courtiers to ordinary people. Thus, although Qā'em Maqām, Sheybāni, and Yaghmā often address the same issues, in Yaghmā's poetry the language and the tone are not conciliatory, and there is little space for advisory gestures. Yaghmā was not a court poet, and his political criticism is mostly addressed to the people of his class rather than the court. He therefore composed some of his poems in forms more familiar to ordinary people.

Kholāsat al-Eftezāh (The Abridged Account of the Scandal) represents a clear endeavour towards structural innovation, in which Yaghmā has tried to use some *nowheh*-like (lament) monologues to direct the narrative's language towards ordinary people, yoking a built-up colloquial language to a *nowheh*-like discourse. *Nowhehs* with colloquial idiom and different arrangements of rhyme and prosodic patterns point to his rigour in breaking the monotony of classical Persian poetry. *Nowhehs* are used as a sort of poetic respite during the course of the narration and add a theatrical nuance. The story is set in Kashan and describes a big party at which an attack is carried out by a group of bondwomen. In this poem, Yaghmā attempts to illustrate the violence committed by the 'lower class', the bondwomen, against a group of men considered to be of higher rank. The bondwomen assault these drunk and affluent men. They beat them as punishment, saying that they have suffered at the hands of such men of leisure. Yaghmā does not evaluate any of these groups and does not try to depict these bondwomen as revolutionaries. Instead, he affords a theatre of retribution, uncensored and unabashed.

Two other works of Yaghmā, *Āsār-e Morādieh* (Moradi's Works) and *Sayyed Abud*, are ideal for illustrating how he tried to change poetry. *Āsār-e Morādieh* is a satirical poem about Ali Morād Khān Tuni, one of the rulers of Khorasan in the Qajar era. Personally affected by the cruelty of Ali Morād Khān and depicting himself and those in the working class as underdogs, Yaghmā composed a poem that echoed the pangs of a *ta'zieh* passion play, knowing full well the societal impressions this type of performative art would yield. By adopting the theme of banditry and loss, he is, in fact, addressing societal ills to the people, revealing corruption at governmental level.

By token of its idiomatic appeal, a poem like this sets itself apart from a typical satirical poem such as Obeyd Zakāni's fourteenth-century poem *Mush-o-Gorbeh* (Mouse and Cat). Obeyd also created enigmatic dialogues and transgressed the standard diction of Persian poetry to make it colloquial. However, the language of Obeyd's work finds proximity to the idiom of the common folk by following the traditional mode of *monāzereh* (argumentation). Therefore, the purpose of colloquial language or dialogue is not to communicate with common people but to adhere to the conventions/forms of the traditional form of *monāzereh*. *Āsār-e Morādieh*, however, is an experiment geared to finding a new way of using colloquial language by innovating a new form – a new genre in itself. While a narrative poem like *Mush-o-Gorbeh* is imbued with symbolic and veiled depictions, *Āsār-e Morādieh* yawps on behalf of the common folk and speaks of the actual governors of the era.[9]

Another little-studied work by Yaghmā which illustrates his approach towards changes in the formal aspects of Persian poetry is *Sayyed Abud*. This poem is a satire written on behalf of Hoseyn Jandaqi, who was a friend of Yaghmā and a clerk in the court of the governor of Kashan. The target of the satire is Sayyed Abud, who apparently plotted to confiscate Hoseyn's wealth after a dispute in the court of Khorasan's governor. This poem has never been included in Yaghmā's *Divān*, and it has only been published once, in the journal *Yaghmā* in 1954. According to the short preface to this poem, Hoseyn was himself a poet, but his poems were of low quality. Thus

---

[9] The closest work by Yaghmā to a traditional satirical poem is *Shabih-e Hojāj-e Kāshi* (a *ta'ziyeh* about pilgrims to Mecca), which consists of a number of satirical *nowhehs* and *monāzerehs* that could be interpreted symbolically. Unfortunately, this work remains unpublished at present. See Āl-e Dāvud, Sayyed Ali, ed., *Majmu'eh-ye Āsār-e Yaghmā-ye Jandaqi*, 2 vols (Tehran: Tus, 1988), p. 57.

Yaghmā, who adopts Hoseyn as his persona, reflects his predicament, but in a poetic style that reflects his flaws as a poet.[10]

Since the poem was intended to support Hoseyn and deride Sayyed Abud, it seems odd that the poet mocks his friend while lampooning his enemy, but he successfully strikes a balance between a friendly metapoetic commentary on his friend's poetic skills and a heavy-handed satire against Sayyed Abud. In addition, his use of uneven verses, adoption of common idiom, and employment of irregular prosodic rhythm make this more than a simple lampooning satire. Although the subject matter of the poem does not differ greatly from that of his other satire, his innovative poetic form makes this poem unique to the extent that none of Yaghmā's editors have included it in their books of his compiled poetry.

The first two poets seem to have been interested in advising only the ruler and could not find a common tenor with ordinary folk, the masses. However, Yaghmā's poetry has the ironic distinction of being a poetics that both garners common societal elements in its expression and weds elitist learnedness with centuries-old embedded traditional folk cognisance. His form seems to engage an idiom of earthy nagging among common folk. Conscious of the function of religious rituals as theatrical spaces well-equipped for expressing frustration, Yaghmā embarked on writing poetry that combines poetic religious dogma with social protest.

A novel literary form emerges when the crisis of the real world becomes internalized. In order to effectively depict a concept, authors undergo a transformative process of internalization. Only after this process does the internalized concept resurface and shape the form of the literary work in accordance with its specific content. The concept of resistance against corrupt power in Qā'em Maqām and Sheybānī is not internalized, as the infrastructure of their poetry shows that they still defend the hierarchical and autocratic order of traditional poetics. Thus, although they attempted to reflect the crisis of the era, they did not move away from their regular readers of classical poetry, the higher-class groups, towards the subordinates.

In contrast, Yaghmā started a corrective movement towards the classical poetic conventions seeking to render his poetry more appealing and accessible to a broader audience beyond the elite. He fearlessly addressed contemporary societal issues and steered the language of his poetry towards colloquialism. Moreover, he ventured to dismantle the entrenched regime of standard poetic forms by experimenting with metrical patterns and incorporating folk templates. Yaghmā's bold endeavour to reshape the autocratic realm of aesthetic poetics sparked a trend of politicizing Persian poetry, ultimately bearing fruit for the poets of the Constitutional Revolution.

---

[10] Yaghmā Jandaqi, 'Sayyed Abud', *Yaghmā*, 2 (1954), 76–7.

Residual forces of the *Bāzgasht-e Adabi* movement

To date, most researchers of this period in Persian literary history have tended to focus on the pioneering, politically committed poets and have overlooked the impact of the so-called literary revolution and the works of the less politically engaged traditionalists. Āriānpur mentions Fathollāh Khān Sheybāni and Mahmud Khān-e Malek al-Sho'arā (1813–1894), both affiliated with the *Bāzgasht-e Adabi* movement, as the last professional court poets. He contends that after these two poets there was a notable absence of prominent literary figures willing to remain within the courts of the Qajar Shahs. Instead, many poets swiftly aligned themselves with the liberal factions as soon as the Revolution commenced.[11] However, not all of these poets were able to alter their poetry according to the demands of society. He mentions Mohammad Hoseyn Safā'i Esfahāni (1853–1904), Mirzā Na'im Sedehi (1856–1916), Hāji Mohammad Taqi Shurideh (1860–1926), and Sheykh Abdol-Javād Adib Neyshāburi (1864–1926) as technically superior traditional poets who wrote poetry during these two decades, but who nonetheless failed to free their poetry from the verbal and semantic rules of traditional poetry.[12]

However, one can argue that although these poets' oeuvres consist mostly of poems about love and mystical subjects, and panegyric pieces, almost all of them have at least one poem which displays an inclination towards the new trend of literature responding to public demand. For example, Mehdi Hamidi Shirāzi mentions a pre-revolutionary poet named Mohammad Dāvari (1823–1867), who moderately reformed some aspects of traditional poetry by addressing less conventional subjects, with a new tone and infrequently used metres.[13] Hamidi states that even Mahmud Khān-e Malek al-Sho'arā, a well-known court poet, attempted to transform the focus of *qasideh* by writing about nature in poems such as *Bahārieh* and *Khazāniyeh* (Spring letters and Autumn letters) and providing detailed historical narratives.[14] Similarly Jalāl al-Din Homā'i introduces Tarab ebn-e Homā-ye Shirāzi (1860–1912), who, although a prototype of the provincial traditional poet, composed a poem praising the establishment of the first parliament after the Revolution.[15]

Mohammad-Rezā Shafi'i Kadkani categorizes these poets as those whose poetry shows that while they did absorb the constitutional epoch, they

---

[11] Āriānpur, 2, p. 12.
[12] Āriānpur, 2, pp. 12–25.
[13] Mehdi Hamidi Shirāzi, *She'r dar Asr-e Qājar* (Tehran: Ganj-e Ketāb, 1985), pp. 177–8.
[14] Hamidi Shirāzi, pp. 286–7.
[15] Jalāl al-Din Homā'i, *Maqālat-e Adabi* (Tehran: Homā, 1990), p. 474.

only sporadically reflected the literary features of the period in their works. He writes that they are engrossed with the verbal and semantic aspects of traditional literature to such an extent that they avoid the strong tendency of constitutional literature to address itself to the people in the public sphere and to concern itself with social dilemmas. Shafi'i Kadkani characterizes this group by saying: 'If they want to address such topical issues, they do so like a person who in fear of befouling his hands wears gloves when touching everyday objects.'[16] While intentionally engaging with the pressing issues of their society, these poets consciously steer clear of the contemporary literary language that deviates from the sacred and well-established rules of classical literature. Nevertheless, one can argue that even the minimal attempts of these traditionalists to include contemporary issues in their works paved the way for some of their successors to engage classical poetry with modern life.

Bloom considers the corrective strategy of these latecomer poets towards classical literary rules as a revisionary approach termed *apophrades* or 'the return of the dead'. *Apophrades* is the last of Bloom's revisionary terms, in which the poet places his work in the context of classical literature. In this state, the work is not merely a continuation of the precursor's work, but instead introduces new standards by which the works of the classical masters and previous traditionalists can now be read.[17] The strong 'dead' poets keep returning to the works of other significant poets of previous ages. However, this return, as Bloom says, is a 'decisive matter' and, if the return remains 'intact', may result in unnatural and sometimes aesthetically weak poems. On the contrary, it is also conceivable that the poet attains a style that not only captures but remarkably surpasses their predecessors in significance.[18]

This return of the 'mighty dead', as Bloom states, might be visible in the latecomer poet's individualized identity and voice. In that case, the latecomer poet has realized a moment which testifies to his own existence as the central poet, rather than his precursors.[19] The fact that moderate poets such as Sayyed Ashraf Gilāni (1870–1934), Ali Akbar Khān-e Dehkhodā (1879–1956), and Mohammad Taqi Malek al-Sho'arā Bahār succeeded in creating such moments in their works is agreed by most scholars. By analysing the oeuvre of these poets, one can see strong links with the formal aspects of traditional poetry, while the content and the semantic aspects of the work are coloured by contemporary elements.

---

[16] Mohammad-Rezā Shafi'i Kadkani, 'Adib-e Neyshāburi dar Hāshiyeh-ye She'r-e Mashrutiyat', in The *Great Islamic Encyclopaedia* http://cgie.org.ir/fa/news/130399 [accessed 2 August 2016] (para. 7 of 19).
[17] Bloom, pp. 139–44.
[18] Bloom, p. 141.
[19] Bloom, p. 141.

For example, the iconic constitutional poem *Yād Ār* (Remember), composed by Dehkhodā as a tribute to his comrade Mirzā Jahāngir Khān Sur-e Esrāfil, stands out as one of the remarkable achievements of this era. It effectively infuses the literary tradition with contemporary elements, both in its form and in its content, making it a resounding success. The poem satisfies the traditionalists' point of view, because it demonstrates the technical skill of the poet in converting the old template of *mosammat* into a novel form. It also shows the mastery of the poet in classical literary principles while juxtaposing traditional motifs with modern, topical ones. Finally, the historical and contextual specificity of the poem generates a genuine connection between the poet and his readers.

Poets with a gradualist approach to the concept of literary revolution, such as Ali Akbar Dehkhodā, Iraj Mirzā, and Sayyed Ashraf Gilāni, illustrated the most pressing societal issues in the majority of their works. However, the conservative figurative aspect of their works recreates the retrogressive relations between society, the artist, and the state. In other words, the politics in these poems is defined as the implementation of power, or the struggle for power. However, it can be contended that the mere portrayal of this practice and struggle within a poem does not automatically qualify as a political act of poetry. This is because the power relations among the components of a classical poetic form might not be ordered in a way that configures a democratic structure.

Mohammad Taqi Malek al-Sho'arā Bahār, whose life and work I will be examining in the following paragraphs, is one of the poets who, in a number of his classical works, admires freedom and democracy, ironically, in a form which reinforces the elitist aspects of autocracy and maintains the distance between itself and the masses. On the other hand, breaking the existing poetic boundaries in some of his other works, he shows a great deal of enthusiasm for participating in the aesthetic revolution of his age and overthrowing the hierarchical regime of classical poetry.

Mohammad Taqi Malek al-Sho'arā Bahār: Cohabitation of the old and the new

Mohammad Taqi Bahāar was born on 6 November 1884. His father was Mohammad Kāzem Saburi, Poet Laureate of *Āstān-e Qods-e Razavi* (an organization founded on the Holy Shrine of the eighth Shia Imam). Mohammad Taqi studied the Quran and primary Persian literature with his uncle and read Ferdowsi's *Shāhnāmeh* and the principles of Persian rhetoric and poetics under his father's supervision. After he succeeded his father as Poet Laureate of *Āstān-e Qods*, he completed his literary education with some of the well-known, traditionalist men of letters of his time, such as

Adib Neyshāburi and Sayyed-Ali Khān Dargazi (killed in 1913).[20] He joined revolutionaries in the Mashhad branch of *Anjoman-e Saʿādat* (the Society for Prosperity) in his early twenties and became involved in publishing anti-establishment newspapers, namely *Khorāsān*[21] and *Habl al-Matin*. After a while, Bahār, who was recognized as a social democrat activist,[22] established his own newspapers, namely *Now-Bahār* (New Spring) and later *Tāzeh-Bahār* (Fresh Spring), in the cities of Mashhad and Tehran. After 1918, with the contribution of some young critics and poets, he founded *Anjoman-e Adabi-ye Dāneshkadeh* (the Dāneshkadeh Literary Association) and published a journal with the same name between April 1918 and April 1919. According to Loraine and Matini, Bahār's association with Dāneshkadeh and its group of young writers, who possessed knowledge of European languages, played a crucial role in enhancing and modernizing his literary education.[23] However, in contrast with his younger contemporaries and even some of his colleagues in the *Dāneshkadeh* association and journal, he adhered to the gradually developing process of literary modernization.

Loraine and Matini argue that Bahār's position as Poet Laureate of *Āstān-e Qods* required him to compose official religious and personal panegyrics. Most of these panegyric poems had to be modelled after the classical masters of the Khorāsāni style. Because of his religious position in the very early years of his career, they believe 'he had to consider the different elements of local society in his public poems', while years later in Tehran he found enough independence to compose poems more in line with his personal preferences.[24] However, one could argue that, if this religious element of his writing existed only to retain his job as Poet Laureate, he was presumably not so fanatical about the fundamentals of Persian classical poetics at every stage of his career.

Ahmad Niku-Hemmat states that although Bahār was akin to moderate and gradual reforms in the system of signification and communication in poetry, he showed his strong opposition several times to the experiments of the younger generation with formal aspects.[25] One might argue that Bahār's stand against radical changes in Persian poetry was related to his position as the most notable classical poet of his time. While he was not the only pioneer

---

[20] Mohammad-Ali Sepānlu, *Bahār Mohammad Taqi Malek al-Shoʿarā* (Tehran: Tarh-e Now, 2003), pp. 9–12.

[21] Sepānlu states that the young poet radically criticized the Shāh in several poems under the pen name 'Raʾis al-tollāb'. Sepānlu, *Bahār Mohammad Taqi Malek al-Shoʿarā*, p. 16.

[22] Lotfollāh Ajudāni, *Rowshanfekrān-e Irān dar Asr-e Mashruteh* (Tehran: Akhtarān, 2008), p. 143.

[23] M. B. Loraine, and Jalāl Matini, 'Bahār, Mohammad-Taqi', in *Encyclopaedia Iranica* http://www.iranicaonline.org/articles/Bahar-mohammad-taqi [accessed 17 August 2016] (para. 12 of 14).

[24] Loraine, and Matini (para. 11 of 14).

[25] Ahmad Niku-Hemmat, *Zendegāni va Āsār-e Bahār* (Tehran: Ābād, 1982), p. 67.

to change the form and function of poetry in that era, he was considered the last master of classical Persian poetry by many of his contemporaries and also by the next generation of scholars. Ali Akbar Dehkhodā describes him as 'the best Khorāsāni-style poet of the last four centuries'.[26] Similarly, Yahyā Āriānpur exalts Bahār as 'the best of all the poets of the Revolution' because of his mastery in classical poetry.[27]

However, the poet did not remain in this position for long; instead of embarking upon self-appropriation, he attempted to update and complete his precursors' style. Niku-Hemmat differentiates Bahār's poetry from that of other *Bāzgasht-e Adabi* poets by the novelty of his imagery and his relatively modernized language.[28] In terms of novel imagery, Bahār uses well-established metaphors and similes, but attempts to reconsider the relationships between the components of the image. In similes, he chooses conventional *moshabah* and *moshabah-beh* (tenor and vehicle; likened and that whereunto a thing is likened), yet he generates a new *vajh-e shabah* (reason of resemblance) for them. For example, in the following verse the poet analogizes the beloved's eyes, eyebrow and eyelashes to a commander, his sword to the enemies' troops:

فرماندهای است چشم تو ز ابرو کشیده تیغ / پیشش سپاه مژه به حال درازکش

Your eye is a commander and your eyebrow a sword in his hand /
Right in front of him the troop of eyelashes are laid down

He uses a rather common analogy for the beloved's eye and eyebrow, yet he differentiates it from traditional similes through creating a new setting for the image, as well as a new reason for the resemblance between the defeated troops and the eyelashes of the beloved. In so doing, Bahār revives overused analogies and dead metaphors by claiming new similarities between tenor and vehicle. He also experiments with new vehicles to colour old forms of imagery with his own imagination. For instance, in his famous *chārpāreh* called *Kabutarhā* (Pigeons), he says:

بیایید ای کبوترهای دلخواه / بدن کافورگون پاها چو شنگرف
بپرید از فراز بام و ناگاه / به گرد من فرود آیید چون برف

O lovely pigeons come to me / Your bodies are white as camphor, and your legs are red as cinnabar
Fly from the top of the roof and at once / Land around me like snowflakes.

---

[26] Hasan-Ali Mohammadi, *Az Bahār tā Shahriyār* (Arak: [n. pub.], 1993), p. 123.
[27] Āriānpur, 2, p. 126.
[28] Niku-Hemmat, p. 70.

The first verse contains two conventional and overused analogies in traditional poetry, comparing the white feathers and the red feet of the birds to camphor and cinnabar, respectively. However, in the second verse, Bahār creates an innovative image by likening the landing birds to snowflakes. He thereby uses some of the overused motifs of traditional imagery and reassembles them to generate a unique image.

In terms of a refashioned literary language, Bahār initially attempted to consolidate the literary lexical resource with that of everyday life. However, this effort was limited to the insertion of some non-literary or 'alien' words in the same verbal and semantic arrangement as traditional poetry. These words could be colloquial, technological, political, and so on, placed by the poet into the subtle context of classical verse. For instance, in the following verses, the poet draws a comparison between his initial encounter with air travel and Prophet Mohammad's ascension on his beloved horse named Borāq.[29]

چون به پشت آسمان پیما برآمد پای من / آسمانی گشت طبع آسمان پیمای من ...
من پیمبروار کردم نیت معراج و گشت / جنب جنبان زیر پا خنگ برق آسای من

Once I stepped into the aeroplane / My heavenly spirit became a skywalker ...
I intended to ascend like the prophet / my fiery red steed, akin to tinder, galloped onward.

The use of the word 'āsemān-peymā', besides sounding more literary than 'havā-peymā' or 'Tayyāreh' (regular words for an aeroplane in Persian), allows the poet to vividly depict a contemporary experience within the framework of a classical-style poem. However, some scholars, while acknowledging Bahār's efforts at scrutinizing new ways of poetic expression in classical contexts as a response to the demands of modern society, do not endorse these works as 'novel practices'. Āriānpur states that these types of poems were, at most, signs of a vital change in Persian poetry and not a remedy for its underlying problems.[30]

On the other hand, even with minimal alterations to the lexical resources of classical poetry, the poet's increasing consciousness of the politics of literature becomes evident. By inserting some non-literary words, Bahār disturbs the conventional lexical system of classical poetry. He permits the poem to, as Rancière suggests, intervene in the relationship between the practice of poetry and forms of visibility. In other words, he takes a word from a part of the language which was invisible to the literary elite

---

[29] The poet has also formed a pun playing with the vocal similarity between the words 'Borāgh' and 'bargh-āsā'.
[30] Āriānpur, 2, p. 123.

and makes it visible in his poetry, thus attacking the hierarchical regime of classical literary language.[31] Indeed, the incorporation of literary and non-literary names for objects obliterates the hierarchy of lexical values in which elite words have more value than common ones. Considering words such as '*āsemān-peymā*' (aeroplane) as the same rank and value as '*me'rāj*' (ascension) and '*payāmbar*' (prophet) is a configuration of democratic politics in Bahār's poetry in this stage.

Minimal changes such as these in the lexical regime of Persian poetry were at the core of the new regime of signification and of the new politics of literature in this era. Experimenting with the lexical resources of Persian poetry was a point of departure for Bahār, enabling him to shift his poetry from the imitation of past masters to the use of the innovative poetic forms of his own time. One can argue that the essence of the aesthetic revolution of constitutional poetry was realized in the notion of colloquialism. Colloquialism, which should be defined as the use of colloquial language in the freer poetic templates taken from popular folklore and rituals, allowed the poet to share his particular reflections of the world with a broader range of audiences.

As Loraine and Matini have illustrated, the poet's earliest experimentation with a form that he exploited later in his politically engaged works is a *mosammat*, imitated from Manuchehri Dāmqāni's (eleventh century) celebrated works in this template.[32] Āriānpur also cites a number of Bahār's early critical poems which are mostly modelled on masterpieces of classical poetry, such as his outstanding *mosammat-e tazmini* (adaptive *mosammat*) entitled *Pand-e Sa'di* (Sa'di's Advice). However, it is through a *mostazād* entitled *Kār-e Irān bā khodāst* (Just God Can Save Iran) that Bahār is recognized as a poet politically committed to the literary community of his time. *Mostazād* is a popular template for folklore songs and religious laments (*nowheh*), its unequal hemistichs making it a less restricted template for practising colloquial poems.

Edward Browne characterizes Bahār's poem as a remarkable *mostazād*, bearing resemblance in both form and metre to Ashraf Gilāni's renowned poem, *Dard-e Irān bi davāst* (Iran's Pain Has No Cure). According to Browne, the poem was composed and published during the 'lesser tyranny' (June 1908–August 1909), when the poet was involved with a clandestine newspaper called *Khorāsān*.[33] For Browne, the poem 'was designed to arouse in Khorasan sympathy with the efforts put forth by Azerbaijan, Gilan and

---

[31] Rancière, p. 4.
[32] Loraine, and Matini, (para. 11 of 14).
[33] 'Lesser Tyranny' (*estebdad-e saghir*) refers to the short period of Mohammad-Ali Shah's reign before the capture of Tehran and his deposition by the conquerors of Tehran in July 1909.

Isfahan'.³⁴ In other words, the poet composed the poem as a realization that he needed to establish a means of communication between his politically committed poetry and the general public. He therefore experiments with freer, yet simultaneously conventional, literary language and templates in order to publicize the hidden and suppressed words of the people:

با شه ایران ز آزادی سخن گفتن خطاست / کار ایران با خداست
مذهب شاهنشه ایران ز مذهبها جداست / کار ایران با خداست
شاه مست و میر مست و شحنه مست و شیخ مست / مملکت رفته ز دست
هر دم از دستان مستان فتنه و غوغا بپاست / کار ایران با خداست³⁵

Talking to the Iranian Shah about freedom is a mistake / Just God can save Iran
The Shah's religion (manner) is different from all religions / Just God can save Iran
The Shah is drunk, the governor is drunk, the sheriff is drunk, and the preacher is drunk / The country is lost
Every moment the hands of these drunkards cause new agitations and turmoil / Just God can save Iran

Colloquial phrases, such as '*Kār-e Irān bā khodāst*' and '*Mamlekat rafteh ze dast*', are placed into a classical context where the poet denounces the authorities, '*Shahneh*', '*Mir*', '*Sheykh*', and '*Shāh*', for being drunk. The recurring motif of inebriated authorities, rendered impotent in their oversight of society, finds its echoes throughout classical poetry. However, in this poem the theme is further developed by colloquial words and phrases alongside the conventional language and imagery. In addition, the tone of the poem is similar to that of folk *nowheh* poems, which are typically sung collectively by crowds in *Husaynias*. While some staunch purists of literature may not perceive this reformulated structure as a subtle literary form, it nonetheless signifies the initiation of a communal practice within the aesthetic regime of Persian poetry, engaging both the poet and their readers.

In order to poeticize the general, political concerns of society, Bahār needed to refashion the politics carried by the poetry itself. By using a freer language and template, the poet democratically redistributes to all components of the poem the right to exist, regardless of whether their roots are elite or common. He dismantles the hierarchy of values among the components of the classical form and confers upon all components the right to appear in the poem on equal terms.

---

³⁴ Edward G. Browne, *The Press and Poetry of Modern Persia* (Cambridge: Cambridge University Press, 1914), p. 260.
³⁵ Mohammad Taqi Bahār, *Divān-e Malek al-Sho'arā Bahār* (Tehran: Negāh, 2008), p. 124.

On the other hand, Bahār has some contradictory terms and conditions which he practises in the colloquial form. He is open to structural changes in his poetry, in so far as the content allows him, as long as these changes do not violate the principal rules of classical poetry. Ideally, he would like to harmonize the politics of his text with the political issues of the real world with which he is engaged. However, he does not want to sacrifice the aesthetic excellence of his poetry at the expense of radicalism. In his poetical criticism of contemporary poets, Bahār says:

گر نو آید در نظر شعر کسی / اختراعی نیست در شعرش بسی / هست فکرش نو رسی ...
نکته دیگر کنم بهرت بیان / شاعر اندر هر زمان و هر مکان / هست شاگرد زمان
هر زمانی فارسی یک طور بود / شاعر آنطوریکه صحبت مینمود / شعرهایی میسرود ...
سبک هندی گرچه سبکی تازه بود / لیکن او را ضعف بی اندازه بود / سست و شیرازه بود
فکرها سست و تخیلها عجیب / شعر پر مضمون ولی نا دل فریب / وز فصاحت بی نصیب
از پس مشروطه نو شد فکرها / سبکهایی تازه آوردیم ما / شد جراید پر صدا
بدعت افکندند چندی ز اهل هوش / سبکهایی تازه با جوش و خروش / لیک زشت آمد به گوش ...
بود ایرج پیرو قایم مقام / کرده از او سبک و لفظ و فکر وام / عارف و عشقی عوام ...
من خود از اهل تتبع بوده ام / جانب تقلید را پیموده ام / وز تعب فرسوده ام
لیک در هر سبک دارم من سخن / پیرو موضوع باشد سبک من / سبک نو سبک کهن
نوترین سبکی که در دست شماست / بار اول از خیال بنده خواست / دفتر و دیوان گواست
بود در طرز کهن نقصی عظیم / رفع کردم نقص اسلوب قدیم / با خیال مستقیم[36]

If someone's poetry seems new / there are not many innovations in his poem / but rather it is his thoughts that are novel
Let me make another point to you / A poet in any time and any place / is a follower of his age.
The Persian language has not always been the same / Poets have composed their poems / as they speak ...
Although the Hindi style used to be a novel one / it had lots of flaws / it was weak and arbitrary.
Thoughts were loose, and imageries were strange / The poems were full of diverse themes, but not pleasant / and not eloquent either
The Constitutional Revolution was followed by new ideas / We came up with new styles / and newspapers found the chance for a colourful presence.
Some brilliant figures achieved some breakthroughs / They adopted new styles vigorously / but they did not sound pleasant ...
Iraj was a follower of Qā'em Maqām / and borrowed his style, language and thoughts / Also, Āref and Eshqi were common men ...
I have been an imitator myself / I have copied others in poetry / and I became exhausted

---

[36] Bahār, pp. 881–4.

> However, I have composed poems in various styles / My style matches the subject / whether it is new or old.
> The newest style you know now / was first invented by myself / One can confirm it by seeing my poetry collection and *Divān*
> There was a tremendous flaw in the classical style / I modify that flaw / by proposing a direct imagery.

The poet states that the poetic innovations of constitutional poetry were a consequence of the new political ideas of the time rather than independent aesthetic experimentation. This point of view resembles what Bloom terms 'the school of resentment', where literary critics exaggerate the role of sociopolitical activism in fashioning the arts.[37] This perspective politicizes every aspect of poetry at the expense of aesthetic creativity and the politics of poetic work. Bahār devalues the individual subjectivity of constitutional poetry by relating it to the automatic alignment of literary works with the changes of the time. Then, he denounces the aesthetic achievements of poets who are his contemporaries as vulgar and immature, while introducing his own work as both pioneering and perfected.

In the last verse, Bahār reveals his revisionary approach towards classical Persian poetry. He states that he has spotted a significant shortcoming in classical poetry and has rectified it through 'direct imagery'. This term is probably created to differentiate between Bahār's practices in the new style of colloquial poetry and those of others. It means that in his poetry Bahār, unlike his contemporaries, not merely has used colloquial language but has also been able to remodel the imagery of Persian poetry through changing the whole system of poetic signification.

Bloom terms this revisionary position towards the literature of the past as '*tessera*'. He defines this term as an antithetical completion of the precursors' work. In this relationship, the newcomer poet tends to retain the old terms, but 'mean[s] them in another sense as though the precursor had failed to go far enough'.[38] Bahār, in this verse-essay, declares that the literary language of the past has always been close to everyday language, and that one should not see this as an achievement of the constitutional era. He then refers to the idea of direct imagery and the simplification of language in Persian poetry as a way of regaining the glory of classical poetry, which was lost in the Hindi style. Bahār intends this term to be an antithesis of the Hindi style, and also to be a way of completing the pre-Hindi style poetry. In other words, this idea is antithetical; it suggests simplification in order to emancipate Persian poetry from indirect and complicated language and imagery, while also striving to contribute to the more classical formats

---

[37] Bloom, pp. xi–xiii.
[38] Bloom, p. 14.

by offering a more sociopolitically engaged outlook and a more engaging tone in order to gain wider audiences.

In practice, however, Bahār is not always loyal to the idea of direct imagery and its consequential revisionary perspective. Although the politics of Bahār's poetry in his semi-colloquial works are more in line with the democratization of literature, he has an entirely different approach in his classical, politically engaged *qasidehs*. The politics of literature, as Rancière defines it, is 'the egalitarian principle of indifference to the hierarchical law of the old regime'.[39] That is to say, democracy in a literary work should be more than the mere representation of it as a genuine social state. Although in his topical *qasidehs* his critical views towards the despotism of the time were reflected in the content, Bahār has failed to democratize the form. The democracy of colloquial poetry is 'a specific regime of speaking whose effect is to upset any steady relationship between manners of speaking, manners of doing and manners of being'.[40] It is in this sense that the democratic form of Bahār's semi-colloquial poetry opposed the hierarchical regime represented in the poet's classical *qasidehs*.

The colloquial form is a democratic regime which intervenes in the unequal relationship existing between the components of poetry. The intricate language and masterfully constructed structure naturally exclude incompatible components, thereby maintaining a cohesive and harmonious composition. One way to formulate a democratic form based on the equal status of components is to reconfigure the regime of literary evaluation which divides all subjects and objects into literary and non-literary. Rancière cites Flaubert's prose as an example of a democratic work of literature, not for its sociopolitical commitment but for its indifference towards any hierarchy of values among things, concepts, and people. Unlike Jean-Paul Sartre, who comprehends commitment as the political act of literature, Rancière believes that being indifferent to the 'distribution of sensible' (or the accepted) rules of the relationship between things, concepts, and people is at the core of the politics of literature.[41]

Sartre's understanding of commitment as the political act of literature resonates with Bloom's concept of the 'School of Resentment'. This notion finds embodiment in early twentieth-century academic studies of Persian literature, where scholars trace the origins of aesthetic changes to contemporary social and political activism. Notably, they attribute the emergence of constitutional poetry to the proliferation of political journals during that era. The desire for a simplified language in journalism is widely regarded as the primary catalyst for linguistic and lexical transformations

---

[39] Rancière, p. 14.
[40] Rancière, p. 14.
[41] Rancière, p. 12.

in Persian literature, ultimately giving rise to colloquialism in poetry. Ali Gheissari asserts that the surge in political newspapers and journals prompted poet-journalists to engage in professional journalism, leading to an adaptation of their poetic language to align with the sociopolitical orientation of their respective publications. Consequently, this linguistic alignment shaped a new literary language that was non-religious and non-courtly in nature.[42]

Bloom characterizes this ideologically biased perspective as a manifestation of the 'anxiety of influence', whereby scholars and critics are apprehensive about the influence exerted by innovative authors.[43] Through an ideological lens, this group of scholars infused literary studies with a charged perspective, proclaiming any form of aesthetic eminence as inherently opposed to resistance, unless they could portray it as a conduit for revolutionary propaganda. However, they failed to recognize the potential of individual aesthetic achievements in fostering the democratic ideals of the Revolution within the realm of the arts. Therefore, they demarcated colloquial poetry as part of a natural trend, which resulted in significant shifts in literature and in people's literary taste. Contrarily, some scholars discerned the roots of colloquial poetry's democratic and emancipatory spirit in the literature of folklore and the performative arts.

---

[42] Ali Gheissari, *Iranian Intellectuals in the Twentieth Century* (Austin: University of Texas Press, 1998), p. 16.
[43] Bloom, pp. xi–xiii.

2

Constitutional poetry and the performative arts

Constitutional poetry finds its roots in folk comedic plays, particularly musical ones, which traditionally possessed the freedom to satirize the upper social classes, including the authorities, in private parties and social gatherings. These plays often featured sections with memorable lyrics that could be sung repeatedly, easily retained by ordinary people. Āriānpur contends that the language of colloquial poetry has specifically evolved from the language employed in these lyrics.[1]

Furthermore, the act of singing and vociferously expressing the people's demands in the public sphere establishes a connection between constitutional poetry and the performative arts. Some of the most well-known constitutional poets composed works which functioned as slogans and revolutionary songs in demonstrations during and after the Revolution. For instance, people were singing Bahār's poems in the demonstrations held following the victory of the Revolution, Sayyed Ashraf asked people to sing his poems in public places, and Eshqi composed anthems for demonstrations. Streets had become a new space for spreading ideas through the collective recital of poems.

Constitutional poets incorporated traditional performances into their new experiences in political action, while also extending the borders of poetry, taking it outside courts, houses, and private meetings and changing its form and function by using it as a weapon against the dominant power. Āref Qazvini, whose works will be analysed exclusively in the following section, undertook many experiential projects utilizing his experiences

---

[1] He also mentions itinerant mystic lyrics which had traditionally played a major role in motivating people to rebel against sociopolitical oppression ever since the Safavid era (1501– 1736). Yahyā Āriānpur, *Az Sabā tā Nimā*, 2 vols (Tehran: Frānklin, 1976), p. 29.

in performative arts, public protests and revolutionary literature. It can be argued that Āref's amalgamation of all these elements, along with his public performance of aesthetically and politically radical works in public parks, constituted the most impactful stride in the literary revolution of that era. Moreover, experimentation with folk performances and the newborn Persian drama transformed the poetry of young experimental poets such as Mirzādeh Eshqi, whose oeuvre will be discussed in the last section. Dramatizing poetry and composing poetic dramas changed the form and function of constitutional poetry and separated it from the established literary traditions in ways that reverberated with the other goals of the revolutionary forces, including, but not limited to, the aspiration to educate ordinary people.

One might argue that for constitutional poets, the allure of the folk comic play format stemmed from its historical role as a medium for the subaltern stratum of society to publicly express their suppressed thoughts. According to Rashid Yāsemi, some of the entertainers hired by the court had remarkable critical authority, in that they could even criticize the actions of state officials and courtiers.[2] Such comic plays have multiple forms and structures and were performed on various occasions. Due to their relatively free structures, they were also compatible with the circumstances and the location of the performance. Using the term '*tamāshā*' to refer to the majority of such plays, Bahrām Beyzā'i writes:

> *Tamāshā* was the umbrella term for all public entertainments. [...] The later significant entertaining forms were all rooted in the plays and practices of solo actors called *dalqak* and *maskhareh*, or *nowruzi khān*, the groups involved in such carnival forms as 'Mocking the Beardless Guy', 'Mocking *Mir-e Nowruzi*' (The Lord of Misrule) and 'Mocking Omar', and especially the plays of both itinerant and ceremonial *motrebān* (musical entertainers). This process continued until the Safavid period, during which plays with stories similar to the present *taqlid* (mime) and *mazhakeh* (farce) evolved from the musical plays of the *motrebān*, without losing their tendency to involve dancing and singing.[3]

These kinds of plays evolved mainly during the eighteenth century, becoming more public and more commonly seen in the private parties and ceremonies of various social classes. According to Willem Floor, *tamāshā* (which was a kind of slap-stick comedy) and *taqlid* (which was mostly mime or danced mimes) 'gradually became a general designation for comical improvisatory

---

[2] Gholām-Rezā Rashid Yāsemi, *Maqāleh-hā va Resāleh-hā*, ed. by Iraj Afshār (Tehran: Barresi va Gozinesh-e Ketāb. 1994). p. 309.
[3] Bahrām Beyzā'i, *Namāyesh dar Irān* (Tehran: Rowshangarān va Motāle'āt-e Zanān, 2001), p. 157.

drama; it is called *ru-howzi* or *takhteh-howzi* in modern times'.⁴ Sādeq Āshurpur says that these performances were generally played in three different locations: (1) among ordinary people, (2) in the houses of upper-class people, and (3) in court or in the houses of high-ranking officials.⁵ These dramas were entertaining to each social group through the mockery of the different statuses of ordinary people, higher-class figures, and even the host.

Beyzā'i asserts that in a society where open discussion of certain issues is constrained, the artist is compelled to conceal their rebellious stance behind a comic mask. Thus, in this situation, comedic drama is not merely entertainment but a secure means to criticize and even to enact revenge.⁶ In folk plays, critical ideas about the dominant classes were sometimes attached to the performance and had no direct relation to the main story. The act of portraying these allusive parts was significant too. That is, the critical parts could become more radical if viewers responded positively to them during the play. Furthermore, performers could not be condemned by inspectors for their use of strong language to criticize the authorities or the rich, as there was no written script for these plays and all acts and dialogues were improvised. This is the spirit of politics in folk literature which, by its nature, is covert and reliant on anonymity. The performative nature of constitutional poetry as a form of public protest requires that it takes place in the public view but remains protected in a manner which shields the identity of the performers.

The politics of singing

The incorporation of singing, a prominent characteristic of folk performance, was adopted by constitutional poetry to transform poetry from an abstract and isolated art form into a collective mode of resistance. Collective singing was common in some of the most popular traditional performative forms such as *nowheh* (lament), *ta'zieh* (passion play), *tamāshā*, and later *ru-howzi* plays. A principal part of these performances was rhythmic recitation and singing by the performers, requiring, in some cases, the active participation of the spectators. For instance, *nowheh*,⁷ a prevalent form of poetry in the Qajar period, was intended to be performed in the public space and usually included participatory verses that required the audience to contribute to

---

⁴Willem M. Floor, *The History of Theatre in Iran* (Maryland: Mage Publishers, 2005), p. 44.
⁵Sādeq Āshurpur, *Namāyesh-hā-ye Irāni*, 7 vols (Tehran: Sureh-Mehr, 2014), 7, p. 19.
⁶Beyzā'i, p. 157.
⁷Discussed in the first chapter pp. 53–7.

the act of singing. Similarly, folk comic plays incorporated singing and dancing, with the expectation that the spectators themselves would actively participate.

During the Revolution, people experienced another form of collective singing in the streets as an integral part of their demonstrations. This time, singing was no longer religious or purely for entertainment but rather became a political act through which people voiced their demands and grievances in the public space. The experience of making the hidden transcript public through folk performances and shouting in public and semi-public spaces inspired people to create their own chants and rhythmic slogans. The same sort of influence from folk performances can be observed in the works of the pioneer poets of the era. They employed the same prosodic metres, rhyme arrangement, and language that they used for musical parts of the comic plays in the works that they composed for collective performances. Indeed, the idea of reader-performers singing constitutional poems in public spaces led to a significant change in the form and function of Persian poetry.

By adopting the form of folk plays, constitutional poets transformed the function of poetry. It shifted from being a platform solely for expressing personal or religious feelings and ideas to becoming a powerful tool for demanding socio political rights and challenging the authority of the state. Although the following poem, *Tasnif-e Jomhuri* (Song of the Republic), was composed about a decade after the main conflicts of the Constitutional Revolution and is more related to the events leading to Rezā Khān's rise to power, it is one of the best examples of the slogan-like poems of the constitutional epoch. The poem was likely composed collaboratively by more than one poet, most notably Bahār and Mirzādeh Eshqi. It was published and disseminated clandestinely, operating within underground networks.[8] It is composed in the *tasnif* (light song) template, appropriated to be performed in public. For this reason, the prosodic metre is not carefully arranged, and the rhyme does not follow the precepts of any of the specific formats of classical poetry:

دست اجنبی چون کرد، کشور عجم ویران
تخم لق شکست آخر، در دهان این و آن
گفت فکر جمهوری، هست قند هندستان
هاتفی ز غیب، خوش گرفت عیب:
جمهوری نقل پشکل است این
بسیار قشنگ و خوشگل است این
تا تهیه در لندن، شد اساس جمهوری
خود سری تدارک شد، بر قیاس جمهوری
ارتجاع و استبداد، در لباس جمهوری

---

[8] Mohammad Qā'ed, *Eshqi; Simā-ye Najib-e Yek Ānārshist* (Tehran: Māhi, 2015), p. 168.

CONSTITUTIONAL POETRY AND THE PERFORMATIVE ARTS

آمد و نمود، حیله با رنود
جمهوری نقل پشکل است این
بسیار قشنگ و خوشگل است این
شد خزان جمهوری، نو بهار امساله
دست اجنبی بنهاد، داغ بر دل لاله
شد نصیب این ملت، غصه و غم و ناله
بلبل سحر، کرد نوحه سر
جمهوری نقل پشکل است این
بسیار قشنگ و خوشگل است این⁹

When the foreign forces destroyed the non-Arab country (Persia)
It gave a chance to anyone (to invade this land)
He said the idea of a republic is sweet like Indian sugar
An unseen messenger complained fairly:
This republic is a dung nougat
This is so beautiful and pretty
Since the fundamentals of this republic were made in London
Despotism was prepared in the republic style
Reaction and tyranny, in the guise of a republic,
Came and tricked us with the help of wily people
This republic is a dung nougat
This is so beautiful and pretty
The spring turned into the fall of the republic
The tulip's heart is blazed by the foreign forces
Grief and sorrow were the fate of this nation
The nightingale of dawn lamented:
This republic is a dung nougat
This is so beautiful and pretty

The metre of the *tarjiʿ* (refrain) and the last line of each *band* (stanza) do not follow that of the other verses. The *tarjiʿ* line is to be scanned *mafʿulo mafāʿelon faʿulon* (--ᴗ/ᴗ-ᴗ/ᴗ--), while the last hemistich of each stanza is *fāʿelato faʿ fāʿelato faʿ* (-ᴗ-ᴗ/-/-ᴗ-ᴗ/-) and the rest of the poem follows *fāʿelato mafʿulon fāʿelato mafʿulon* (-ᴗ-ᴗ/---/-ᴗ-ᴗ/---).¹⁰ Also, the last hemistich of each stanza has a double metre in which each hemistich consists of two equal halves marked by an internal rhyme. This format facilitates the

---

⁹ Ali Akbar Moshir Salimi, *Kolliyāt-e Mosavvar-e Eshqi* (Tehran: Amir Kabir, 1971), pp. 298–9.
¹⁰ In Persian prosody, known as *ʿaruz*, the foundation of the verse, called *beyt*, is built upon the arrangement of separate and repeated quantities. The *beyt* consists of two metrically similar lines called *mesrāʾ*. Each *mesrāʾ* is composed of *arkān* (feet), which are combinations of short, long, and overlong syllables. In notation, short syllables are represented by (ᴗ), long syllables by (u), and overlong syllables by (-ᴗ). Metres, or *bohur*, are specific arrangements of *arkān* within a line. In other words, they define the rhythmic patterns by repeating the arrangement of feet.

reader-performer in finding the rhythm of the poem and enables them to sing it more effortlessly. Using three different metres, the poet has created a performative poetic form – a form designed to be performed collectively in the public space.

The poet expands the genre by combining it with public singing to change its function from a passive, written, literary work for the elite to an active work of literature resisting despotism unrelentingly. The focal point in this type of composition is that the participants, regardless of their social class, share both the activity and the words themselves. Thus, the act of singing the poem combines the voices of all classes equally to generate a new and shared voice.

However, the essence of equality, as Rancière states, 'is not so much to unify as to declassify'.[11] Equality in this sense is an anarchic concept that suggests a call for illuminating all classification regimes, even those dominant in the arts. In the case of constitutional poetry, singing in the street does not redistribute the power of shouting among the people, but it demolishes the whole regime of distribution. Shouting out constitutional poems in public places, as Peter Hallward explains, is a form of 'disruptive equality against the advocates of an orderly, hierarchical inequality'.[12]

Āref Qazvini stands as one of the paramount poets of the constitutional, wielding unparalleled influence with his works not only resonating during his era but transcending the boundaries of time and being embraced amid the countless political upheavals that have swept through contemporary Iran. Hādi Hā'eri claims that Āref's *tasnifs* were extremely popular even outside of Iran, to such an extent that shortly after he released a new *tasnif*, it was disseminated among the public throughout Turkey, Afghanistan, and Iraq.[13] What makes Āref unique to his audiences is his role not only as a poet within the public sphere but also as a composer and performing musician. He not only creates the poems which are to be sung collectively, but also operates the very act of singing them on the stage.

Āref was born in Qazvin, where he was trained in traditional Iranian music and singing. His father decided to guide Āref towards using his singing skills for religious performances such as *rowzeh-khāni* (martyrdom-recitation). The quality of his voice distinguished him from his peers, and around the year 1898, he was introduced to Mozaffar al-Din Shāh and became a court singer. However, he resigned from this position shortly afterwards and, having stayed in Qazvin for a while, went back to Tehran to join the Constitutional Revolution, which was then in its early stages. During the First World War, when the northern part of Iran was occupied

---

[11] Jacques Rancière, *Politics of Literature*, trans. by Julie Rose (Cambridge: Polity Press, 2011), p. 32.
[12] Peter Hallward, 'Staging Equality', *New Left Review*, 37 (2006), 109–29 (p. 110).
[13] Hādi Hā'eri, *Āref-e Qazvini Shā'er-e Melli-e Irān* (Tehran: Jāvidān, 1985), pp. 21–2.

by Russian troops, Āref joined *Komite Defā'-e Melli* (the National Defence Committee), which formed an alternative government in Kermanshah. In 1916 he migrated to Istanbul along with many of his contemporary intellectuals and the leading members of the committee. After returning to Iran in 1921, he joined Colonel Mohammad Taqi Khān Pesyān (1891–1921) during his uprising in Khorasan against the central state. After Colonel Pesyān's death he became an advocate of the then prime minister, Sayyed Ziā' Tabātabā'i (1889–1969), whose government was known as the '*Kābineh-ye Siyāh*' (Black Cabinet). After a while, he supported Sardār-e Sepah, later called Rezā Shāh (1878–1944), one of Tabātabā'i's opponents who was then trying to change the regime from a constitutional monarchy to a republican state. According to Hā'eri, one of Āref's most overcrowded concerts, held in the Bāqerov Theatre in Tehran, was dedicated to the republicans for their support. However, due to his earlier support of Rezā Shāh's opponents, Āref was not welcome by the Shāh after the latter's appointment as the new monarch by the *Majles-e Mo'asessān* (Constituent Assembly) in 1925. In consequence, Āref moved to Hamedan, where he died, in solitude and poverty, on 21 January 1934, and was buried in Avicenna's mausoleum.[14]

As mentioned before, the major difference between the approach of Āref and that of his contemporaries in remodelling the forms and the functions of politically engaged poetry was the poet's role as a poet-performer. In this instance, every aspect of the performance, even the performer's attire and his behaviour, can be interpreted as an act of resistance. This is the reason for the numerous accounts of Āref's appearance and behaviour, while we barely know anything about that of his contemporaries. For example, Āref in his autobiography describes an occasion when, for the first time after moving to Tehran, he returned to Qazvin on the twenty-first night of Ramadan.[15] According to his account, his outfit, a mixture of Western and traditional clothes, and his unconventional hairstyle, caused a considerable reaction among passers-by, to the extent that some preachers publicly excommunicated him. Āref himself interprets his outfit as an attack on the Muslim community's reactionary outlook towards the prevailing revolutionary mood of the world. He also describes it as a representation of the social changes caused by the Revolution.[16]

Recognizing the profound impact that performance had on his audiences, Āref astutely organized a concert to unveil his significant poems. According to Yaghub Āzhand, the poems *Nāle-ye Morgh* (The Birds' Lament), *Rahm Ey Khodā-ye Dādgar* (O Merciful God), *Jomhuri* (The Republic), and

---

[14] Hā'eri, pp. 17–42.
[15] In Islamic belief *Laylat al-Qadr* (Night of Decree) is the night that the first verses of the Quran were sent to the prophet Muhammad. It is also the night that Ali Ibn Abi Tālib, the first Shia Imam, was killed.
[16] Hā'eri, pp. 71–3.

Mārsh-e Jomhuri (March of the Republic) were performed to an audience for the first time in the Bāqerov Theatre, Grand Hotel, and National Garden of Mashhad, respectively.[17] Shafi'i Kadkani states that although Āref's poems were not as strong technically as those of most of his contemporaries, thanks to his performative talents his works became much more popular. To support this claim, he refers to one of Āref's verses which says:

شب که میگشت آن ترانه بلند / روز طفلان کوچه می خواندند[18]

Every night that a song was sung / the following morning children sang it in the streets.

Shafi'i Kadkani contends that the immense popularity of *tasnifs* can be attributed to their function as a source of entertainment within the daily lives of ordinary individuals, along with their historical association with vocal performances at religious and national events. However, due to the intrinsic connection between *tasnifs* and music, with singers often accompanied by musical instruments during performances, scholars have shown limited interest in preserving and documenting them as professional poetic works. Consequently, *tasnifs* have predominantly thrived in the realm of live performances, rather than being recognized and preserved as literary compositions by academic scholars. Shafi'i Kadkani has written:

> Most *qowls* [and *tasnifs*] have been slightly different from standard poetry in language because [recorded] poetry was composed in the standard language of literature. *Qowl* and *tasnif*, however, have been more or less closer to the language of the masses, who were their main addressees. This [closeness to the masses], in turn, has led to the reluctance of the scholars of previous generations to record these works.[19]

Despite the exclusion of *tasnif* by the literary elite, the constitutional poets, particularly Āref, established this poetic form as an independent genre. *Tasnifs* were published in journals and included in poetry collections by most of the well-known constitutional poets. According to Āriānpur, *tasnif* exhibited a greater degree of flexibility in terms of metre and rhyme compared to other classical templates. As such, because of the ease of expression it allowed for, it had become an accessible template for patriotic and political

---

[17] Ya'qub Azhand, *Tajaddod-e adabi dar dowreh-ye mashruteh* (Tehran: Mo'asseseh-ye Tahqiqāt va Towse'eh-ye 'Olum-e Ensāni, 2006), pp. 127–8.
[18] Mohammad-Rezā Shafi'i Kadkani, *Bā Cherāgh va Āyeneh: dar Jostoju-ye Risheh-ye Tahavolāt-e She'r-e Mo'āser-e Fārsi* (Tehran: Sokhan, 2011), p. 395.
[19] Shafi'i Kadkani, *Bā Cherāgh va Āyeneh*, p. 99.

topics among pioneer constitutional poets.[20] The *tasnifs Morgh-e Sahar* (The Morning Bird) by Bahār and *Az Khun-e Javānān-e Vatan Lāleh Damideh* (The Tulip Has Sprouted from the Blood of the Homeland's Youth) by Āref both became nationalist symbols to the Iranian emancipatory movements and remained part of the continuing classical tradition of Persian music.

Shafi'i Kadkani further argues that Ali Akbar Sheydā (1843–1906) was the soundest composer of romantic *tasnifs*, while Āref excelled as the best composer of political-themed *tasnifs*.[21] Describing Sheydā's poem as the 'soundest' and Āref's as the 'best' illustrates Shafi'i Kadkani's ideologically biased standpoint towards the poetry of this period. Shafi'i Kadkani, who can be counted as a member of 'the school of resentment' in Iranian academia, prioritizes Āref's *tasnif* over that of Sheydā, not because of its aesthetic excellence, but because it is 'political'. He comments on these two poets by using a hierarchical system of evaluation. That is, although he believes in the mastery of Sheydā in this genre, he prefers Āref because of the value attributed to his favouring of a democratized system.

However, one may argue that the democratic aspect of Āref's work is part of the poet's endeavour to ensure that a vulgar subgenre such as *tasnif* is considered just as valuable as other classical, literary forms. Ahmad Karimi-Hakkak states that Āref is a 'far more public figure as a poet', someone who constantly searches 'for ways of breaking through existing poetic borders'.[22] The exclusion of *tasnif* from classical poetic forms by men of letters relegated this genre to an uncategorized form. Although Persian poetry has been associated with music and performance from its very beginnings, *tasnif*, which shares many characteristics with both poetry and music, has always been treated as an out-of-literature poetic form. Peter Hallward states that the Rancièrian concept of equality 'is not the result of a fairer distribution of social functions or places so much as the immediate disruption of any such distribution; it refers not to place but to the placeless or out-of-place, not to class but to the unclassifiable or out-of-class'.[23] Āref does not attack the hierarchy of literary forms in order to include *tasnif* in it – rather, he attempts to destroy the whole hierarchy of literary forms altogether. He concentrates on *tasnif* as a point of departure in order to tackle the entire hierarchical regime of aesthetics in classical poetry. Indeed, he chooses *tasnif* for this mission because the informality of this form allows him to experiment freely with its semantic and formal aspects.

According to Margaret Caton, Āref's *tasnifs* drew upon traditional symbols and themes, 'sometimes altering them to suit their purposes, and

---

[20] Ārianpur, 2, p. 152.
[21] Shafi'i Kadkani, *Bā Cherāgh va Āyeneh*, p. 99.
[22] Ahmad Karimi-Hakkak, *Recasting Persian Poetry: Scenarios of Poetic Modernity in Iran* (London: Oneworld, 2012), p. 88.
[23] Hallward, p. 110.

made open propaganda in ways not at all in accordance with the tradition of veiled allusion'.[24] This approach is in line with Bahār's notion of 'direct imagery', in which he encourages the poet to avoid convoluted and abstract classical imagery. Indeed, one can find Āref's *tasnifs* composed of more concrete images, unlike the ambiguous metaphors and the abstractness of analogies of classical poetry. Caton states that in his political *tasnifs* Āref 'left the world of veiled allusion and classical turn of phrase to address current issues and conditions directly'.[25] For example, in the following poem, the poet leaves no ambiguity about the reference of the metaphors:

ننگ آن خانه که مهمان ز سر خوان برود (حبیبم)
جان نثارش کن و مگذار که مهمان برود (برود)
گر رود شوستر از ایران رود ایران بر باد (حبیبم)
ای جوانان مگذارید که ایران برود (برود)
بجسم مرده جانی
تو جان یک جهانی
تو گنج شایگانی
تو عمر جاودانی
خدا کند بمانی...[26]

Shame on the home (host) whose guest unfed does from the table rise!
Sacrifice your life for him, and don't let him go
Should Shuster go from Iran, Iran will be lost:
O young men of Iran, let not Iran thus be lost!
You are life for the dead body
You are the life of the world
You are the unique treasure
You are the eternal life
I pray to God that you stay.[27]

In the first verse, the words '*khāneh*' (home) and '*mehmān*' (guest) are two metaphors which are decoded immediately in the second verse. Āref clarifies that '*khāneh*' is mapped onto Iran and that the '*mehmān*' refers to William Morgan Shuster, an American civil servant serving the Iranian parliament after the Constitutional Revolution as a financial consultant.[28] In addition

---

[24] Margaret Caton, 'Tasnif', in *Encyclopaedia Iranica* http://www.iranicaonline.org/articles/tasnif-music-term [accessed 9 March 2016] (para. 13 of 23).
[25] Caton (para. 13 of 23).
[26] Edward G. Browne, *The Press and Poetry of Modern Persia* (Cambridge: Cambridge University Press, 1914), p. 252.
[27] For another rendering of the words in English, see Browne, p. 252.
[28] Shuster was forced to resign under the pressure of British and Russian forces in December 1911.

to specificity of imagery and clarity of references, Āref has attempted to substitute some of the conventional motifs of classical poetry with new ones. He changes the regular tenor of metaphors to the ones associated with a specific historical event: Shuster's resignation.

Āref's exploration of the formal aspects of *tasnif* and his endeavours to disrupt the established structure of classical poetry serve as further manifestations of the political dimension in his work. In the following *tasnif*, the poet adeptly utilizes the inherent flexibility of *tasnif* to manipulate prosodic metres, effectively dismantling the confines of traditional poetry's structure:

ز عشق تو ای شوخ شنگول
شد عقلم چو سلطان معزول
چه خوش خورد از اجنبی گول
یار مقبول عقل معزول
قدرت عشق عجب پا گرفته
دشت و کهسار و صحرا گرفته
همچو مشروطه دنیا گرفته
همچو مشروطه دنیا گرفته ...[29]

Because of your love, O you witty and mirthful one,
My wisdom was dethroned like the king
How it was deceived by strangers
The sweetheart was approved, and wisdom dethroned
The vigour of love has achieved such power
It has conquered the plains, mountains and deserts
Like the Constitutional Revolution it has conquered the world.
Like the Constitutional Revolution it has conquered the world.

In this *tasnif*, the poem intentionally deviates from a uniform metre across its hemistichs. Instead, it dynamically shifts its rhythmic patterns, showcasing the deliberate exploration of different prosodic structures within the composition. The first three hemistichs should be scanned as *mafā'ilo maf'ulo fa'lon* (∪--∪/--∪/--), while the fourth hemistich is *fā'elāton fā'elāton* (-∪--/-∪--). Moreover, the final four hemistichs are in different metres and should be scanned as *fā'elāton fa'ulon fa'ulon* (-∪--/∪--/∪--).

The fluctuation of the lines between different prosodic metres is the first step towards polyphonic poetry, in which various voices can be equally present, and Āref arranges the order of words in order to endow his work with the capacity to give voice to the voiceless. Breaking the monotony of classical poetry, he attacks the solidified order of classical prosody. He disruptively intervenes in the hierarchical prosodic system of Persian poetry

---

[29] Hā'eri, p. 363.

and obliterates its solidity in an anarchistic manner. In the subsequent example, while each verse adheres to a consistent prosodic metre, it is the seamless compatibility of these verses with the accompanying music that sets it apart from classical prosodic poetry. As Caton elucidates, *tasnif* intricately coordinates its sectional divisions, line lengths, rhyme schemes, and metric arrangements with the underlying musical theme, establishing a harmonious fusion of poetic and melodic elements.[30]

چه شورها که من بپا ز شاهناز میکنم
در شکایت از جهان به شاه باز میکنم
جهان پر از غم دل از (جهان پر از غم دل از)
زبان ساز میکنم (میکنم)
ز من مپرس که چونی دلی نشسته به خونی
ز اشک پرس که افشا نموده راز درونی
(نموده راز درونی نموده راز درونی نموده راز درونی)
اگر که جان از این سفر بدون درد سر
اگر بدر برم من، به شه خبر برم من
چه پرده های نیرنگ زشان به بارگاه شه درم من
(زشان به بارگاه شه درم من)[31]

What ecstasies/excitements (*Shour*) I create by *Shahnaz*.[32]
I open the gates of complaining about the world to the Shah
I fill the world with the grief of my heart with the tongue of my instrument
Do not ask me how I am. A heart drenched in blood.
Ask tears which have revealed the inner secret
If I survive this travel without trouble
I will inform the Shah
I will tear the curtains in the court of the Shāh to show him their treacherous acts, I will tear the curtains.

Unlike the majority of classical poems, this *tasnif* derives its strength from its utilization of diverse metres and rhyming arrangements. The first three hemistichs are composed in a 'repetitive metre' with four similar feet, and should be scanned *mafāʿelon mafāʿelon mafāʿelon mafāʿelon* (∪-∪-/∪-∪-/∪-∪-/∪-∪-). However, the metre of the fourth and fifth hemistichs changes into an 'alternate metre', scanned *mafāʿelon faʿalāton mafāʿelon faʿalāton* (∪-∪-/∪∪--/∪-∪-/∪∪--). The second-to-last and final hemistichs turn into *mafāʿelon*

---

[30] Caton (para. 13 of 23).
[31] Hā'eri, pp. 382–3.
[32] '*Shour*' is one of the major modes of Iranian classical music, and '*Shahnaz*' is one of the major pieces of *Shour*.

mafā'elon mafā'elon fa'al (ᴗ-ᴗ-/ ᴗ-ᴗ-/ ᴗ-ᴗ-/ᴗ-). This metre has a shorter foot at the end of the hemistich and is frequently used in folk poetry.

The rhyme arrangement, too, is in accordance with the musical theme. Despite the first three hemistichs, which are rhymed in relation to each other, the remaining verses are rhymed individually. The hemistich '*Agar ke jān az in safar bedun-e dard-e sar*' does not rhyme with any other verses, and the ninth and tenth hemistichs are distinguished by an internal rhyme. In this *tasnif*, the poet breaks the lines and repeats parts of, or the entirety of, certain hemistichs, thus harmonizing the poetic text with the musical theme. In traditional poems, it was not customary to include specific instructions for the singer or audience regarding repeated words or phrases.

The aesthetic achievement of Āref's experimentation with the form of *tasnif* was to break the monotony of prosodic metres, as well as to introduce a more natural and freer musical system by altering fundamental elements of classical prosody. Releasing poetry from the stipulations of traditional poetry, Āref exposed the words he used to the tools of a freer form of art, which resulted in its perception as non-literary in the minds of the men of letters. As Karimi-Hakkak states, these changes were too technical and were 'not visible to the naked eye or immediately perceptible in other ways'.[33] The readers of constitutional poetry did not see Āref as a groundbreaking poet, and his poetic innovations were ultimately overshadowed by the politically engaged topics of his poems.

Mirzādeh Eshqi, however, was the first poet of this era whose work drew the readers' attention to his significant attempts to create a 'new style'. Mohammad-Ali Sepānlu states that Eshqi, as the foremost rival of Nimā Yushij, could have played a more significant role in the process of literary modernization, had he not been assassinated just three months after the publication of his masterwork, *Se Tāblo; Maryam* (The Three Tableaux; Maryam). Sepānlu posits that Eshqi's exceptionally radical approach to literature and politics had the potential to elevate his popularity even beyond that of Nimā Yushij.[34]

Theatrocracy in Mirzādeh Eshqi's dramatic poetry

Mohammad-Rezā Mirzādeh Eshqi was born in Hamedan on 11 December 1894. He studied in two European-style schools, Olfat and Alliance, where he learned French, before leaving Hamedan to pursue his education in

---

[33] Karimi-Hakkak, *Recasting Persian Poetry*, p. 234.
[34] Mohammad-Ali Sepānlu, *Chahār Shā'er Āzādi* (Stockholm: Baran, 1993), p. 202.

Tehran. However, he left school at the age of seventeen and joined a group of intellectuals who, after the occupation of the north-western provinces by the Russian forces during the First World War, migrated to Istanbul.[35] This probably took place in 1914 when Eshqi was twenty years old and had published three issues of his own newspaper, *Nāmeh-ye Eshqi*, in Hamedan.[36] Some scholars claim that he attended classes in the Social Sciences and Philosophy Division of Bāb-e Ali University. Mohammad Qā'ed, however, states that there is no evidence of Eshqi pursuing his education during his three-year stay in Istanbul. Nevertheless, the composition of his most famous operatic verse dramas, *Rastākhiz-e Shahriyārān-e Irān* (The Resurrection of the Persian kings) and *Kafan-e Siyāh* (Black Shroud), could feasibly have been inspired by operas which he had the opportunity to see in Turkey.[37] After his stay in Turkey he returned to Iran, where he began composing and drafting various radical critical writings, which led to his assassination on 3 July 1923. In addition to a number of politically engaged literary texts, he delivered several public lectures and several critical articles against the authorities of the time, publishing them in newspapers such as *Shafaq-e Sorkh* and *Siyāsat*. Eshqi's political ideas reached their apex in articles published in his own weekly newspaper, *Qarn-e Bistom*, from May 1921 to June 1923, in which he propagated the anarchistic idea of '*id-e Khun* (Blood Feast).[38]

Eshqi authored several theoretical texts, primarily as prefaces to his own works, where he expounded upon the idea of a literary revolution and offered his unique perspective on the concept of modernity. In his foreword to *Se Tāblo; Maryam*, Eshqi writes that in creating work which best exemplifies the poetic revolution, he has benefited from the failed experimentation of others yet reemphasizes the same ideas.[39] That is to say, he asserts that his work represents the culmination of efforts initiated by his contemporaries and predecessors, positioning his contributions as a necessary continuation and progression of their endeavours. He then states that if 'these tableaux were the product of some other talent, I would praise them even more, for never before has there been such a composition in the Persian language'.[40] He confidently praises his own work over any other innovative attempt of

---

[35] Moshir Salimi, pp. 4–5.
[36] Qā'ed, p. 34. Karimi-Hakkak implies that Eshqi probably had contact with Āref during his stay in Istanbul as Sa'id Nafici 'recalls a gathering, perhaps in 1919, in which the poet Āref introduced Eshqi to him as "one of our friends of the migration" to Istanbul'. Ahmad Karimi-Hakkak, 'Eshqi, Mirzādah', in *Encyclopaedia Iranica* http://www.iranicaonline.org/articles/esqi-mohammad-reza-mirzada# [accessed 19 January 2012] (para. 6 of 10).
[37] Qā'ed, pp. 40–1.
[38] Karimi-Hakkak, 'Eshqi, Mirzādah', (para. 8 of 10).
[39] Karimi-Hakkak, *Recasting Persian Poetry*, p. 217.
[40] Karimi-Hakkak, *Recasting Persian Poetry*, p. 218.

his age, firmly believing that his poetry is the antithesis of the various other novel approaches attempted by his contemporaries and precursors.

One could argue that Eshqi's approach towards the works of his precursors is similar to one of the Bloomian revisionary terms: '*tessera*'. Bloom states that, in this, the poet tries to complete the endeavours of previous poets antithetically. Bloom employs the term 'antithetical' in its rhetorical sense, referring to the deliberate placement of contrasting ideas within balanced or parallel structures, phrases, or words.[41] The poet reads the parent poetry in order to redefine its main concepts and notions, while still retaining the general sense of them. Eshqi says that he 'began to correct poetic ideas in an unprecedented way (*shekl-e newzohur*), and [he] thought to [himself] that the literary revolution of the Persian language must be carried out in some way'.[42] Indeed, the new poet perceives his innovations as being aligned with those of his precursors, while simultaneously believing that they failed to go far enough.

In his second foreword to *Se Tāblo; Maryam*, Eshqi states that he is aware of shortcomings in his work, yet he is hopeful that the future generation of poets will be guided by him and will go on to 'complete' his new, poetic manner of articulation.[43] In suggesting that the next generation should apply the same revisionary approach that he has implemented in his readings of the works of previous poets, Eshqi reveals his own point of view regarding the process of revising these past poets' achievements. According to Bloom, the notion of completion here represents the endeavour of the new poet to persuade himself and his readers that 'the precursor's Word would be worn out if not redeemed as a newly fulfilled and enlarged Word of ephebe'.[44]

The first manner in which Eshqi ventured to redefine conventional concepts and complete the innovative works of other constitutional poets was through his experimentation with the formal features of Persian poetry. Karimi-Hakkak summarizes Eshqi's experiments as follows:

> ... his solitary attempts to break through the constraints of poetic diction and to liberalize the concepts of rhyme and metre were recognized as well. There was also some consciousness of the fact that Eshqi experimented with variations on generic forms and alternative systems of rhythmic expression such as syllabic verse, and that he used a variety of strophic forms of the classical genre known as the *mosammat*.[45]

---

[41] Bloom, *The Anxiety of Influence*, p. 65.
[42] Karimi-Hakkak, *Recasting Persian Poetry*, p. 218.
[43] Karimi-Hakkak, *Recasting Persian Poetry*, p. 218.
[44] Bloom, *The Anxiety of Influence*, p. 67.
[45] Karimi-Hakkak, *Recasting Persian Poetry*, p. 210.

Qā'ed claims that Eshqi liberated Persian poetry from strict rules of prosodic metre and conventional rhyme arrangements before Nimā Yushij.[46] One of Eshqi's most radical attempts in this regard appears in the poem *Barg-e Bād Bordeh* (The Windblown Leaf). Eshqi, in a very short foreword to this poem, writes that 'these verses were composed in a new style when I was in Istanbul ... [this poem is composed] based on my ideas and reflections on the Persian literary revolution and its new [aesthetic] regime'.[47]

به گردش در کنار بوسفور اندر مرغزاری نگاهش دیده افروز
چه نیکو مرغزاری طرف دریا در کناری ره افتاد دیروز
درختان را حریر سبز بر سر زمین را از زمرد جامه در بر
به هر سو با گلی راز
نموده مرغی آغاز[48]

I was wondering around alongside the Bosporus in a field Its perspective was uplifting to the eyes
What a meadow with the coast on the side That was on my way yesterday
Trees wore green silk on their heads The ground had on an attire of emerald
In every corner a bird
Was saying his secrets to a flower.

This work is a stanzaic poem, with an unequal length of hemistichs and an unconventional rhyme arrangement. One may argue that this poem is a type of *mosammat-e mosamman* (eight-hemistichs *mossamat*) with structural modifications to its rhyme and metre. *Mosammat* is a stanzaic and strophic verse form that typically employs a rhyme pattern to connect the stanzas through a recurring refrain. In the traditional *mosammat*, all lines except for the refrain rhyme, while the refrains of the poem rhyme independently. For instance, in a traditional *mosammat-e mosamman*, rhymes are arranged as (aaaaaaab). However, in this poem, the rhyme arrangement in each stanza reads as (ababccdd).

The poem also pushes the boundaries of traditional prosodic metres. In each stanza, the first and the third hemistichs are scanned as *mafā'ilon – mafā'ilon mafā'ilon fa'ulon* (∪---/ ∪---/ ∪---/∪--) while hemistichs two, four, seven and eight are *mafā'ilon fa'ulon* (∪---/∪--) and hemistichs five and six are *mafā'ilon mafā'ilon fa'ulon* (∪---/∪---/∪--).[49] Eshqi in this poem tries to

---

[46] Qā'ed, pp. 137–8.
[47] Moshir Salimi, p. 306.
[48] Moshir Salimi, *Kolliyāt-e Mosavvar-e Eshqi*, p. 306.
[49] This metre (هزج مسدس محذوف) is a very popular prosodic metre in Persian poetry and is also known as the metre of *dobeyti*.

vary the length of hemistichs by disregarding the traditional obligation to have an equal number of prosodic feet in each hemistich. Lifting the troublesome rule of the corresponding prosodic value of parallel hemistichs in turn naturalizes the poetic expression as it harmonizes the rhythm with the content of the verse. However, in practice, Eshqi does not completely free his poem from the metrical constraints of classical poetry. Instead, he replaces an old template with a new one, still operating within the framework of established prosodic structures. This refined template gives him more space to freely express himself, yet it limits the tone of the poem in some ways. However, one could argue that Eshqi's experimentation with varying the number of prosodic feet in each hemistich can be considered the early seeds of a new style, which would later come to be recognized as *Nimāic* poetry.

According to Karimi-Hakkak, Eshqi tried to redefine the concept of rhyme in his poetry, concerning himself with 'the auditory function' of the letters, rather than their visual forms. Karimi-Hakkak provides the example of the poem *Noruzi-Nāmeh* (Book of New Year's Day) in which the poet rhymes the words '*gonāh*' (گناه) with '*qadah*' (قدح). Despite being based on the traditional rules of rhyme, this is considered as a flaw, termed *ekfā* (homology). In his foreword to this poem, Eshqi writes that 'it is obvious that the distinction [between the two] and the perception of the balance conveyed through rhyme is a function of the ear. I have no doubt that today we hear *gonāh* and *qadah* as rhyming'.[50] He also breaks other rules associated with the traditional concept of rhyme, such as *qāfiyeh-ye maʿmuleh* (feigned rhyme), by rhyming the words '*mikhāham*' and '*ham*', as well as '*tekrār-e qavāfi*', effectively repeating the rhyming words within the same poem. It can be argued that Eshqi's reconfiguration of the concept of rhyme aligns with the notion of collective singing as a new function for poetry. In the context of a public space where a poem is sung by a crowd without the reliance on written text, the distinction between two letters with different written forms that create the same sound becomes irrelevant.

Collective singing in order to give voice to the subaltern in the public scene can be considered the central pillar of the politics of Eshqi's work. Eshqi's intention appears to be creating a sense of equality for suppressed voices and thoughts by harnessing the performative potential of his poetry. Peter Hallward states that the Rancièrian concept of politics begins with a demonstration or manifestation by the subaltern. This demonstration happens in the public space, in order to get 'the world of [their] subjects and [their] operations to be seen'.[51] In his poems, Eshqi endeavours to construct a stage that allows for the equitable presence of all individuals. Qā'ed refers to

---

[50] Karimi-Hakkak, *Recasting Persian Poetry*, p. 312.
[51] Hallward, p. 117.

the foreword of a little-studied poem by Eshqi, *Kolāh-Namadi-hā* (Felt Hats), in which the poet asks his readers to perform the poem in a public space. In this short text, he urges readers to recite these verses 'in cafés and streets in order to enlighten the addressees of the poem', that is, the working class.[52]

شهر فرنگ است ای کلاه نمدی ها / موقع جنگ است ای کلانمدی‌ها
بنده قلم دستم است و دست شماها / بیل و کلنگ است ای کلانمدی‌ها
خصم که از رو نمیرود، تو ببین روش/ آهن و سنگ است ای کلانمدی‌ها
فکر چه کارید ای کلانمدی‌ها
دست در آرید ای کلانمدی‌ها
ما دگر این مرد را قبول نداریم / رای بر این خائن عجول نداریم
گر نرسیده بگوششان سخن ما / هست از این ره که ما فضول نداریم
حرف من و دوستان من همه حق است / این گنه ما بود که پول نداریم
گوش بدارید ای کلانمدی‌ها
دست در آرید ای کلانمدی‌ها ...

It is the city of wonders, O felt-hats (peasants) / This is the time of war, O felt-hats!
I have a pen in my hand / And you have shovels and pickaxes
The enemies have no shame, look how shameless they are / They are like iron and stone, O felt-hats!
What ponders your minds, O felt-hats?
Take action, O felt-hats!
We no longer trust this man / We do not want this hasty traitor
If they have not heard our words / That is because we have no snitch among us
My words and those of my friends are all correct / Our only fault is that we do not have money
Listen, O felt-hats!
Take action, O felt-hats!

The poem explicitly calls for a demonstration by the working-class in order to show their objection to the prime minister, Ahmad Qavām al-Saltaneh (in office 1921–22). Eshqi even justifies the presumed violence of the street protests as being for the democratic cause of overthrowing the corrupt prime minister. Indeed, the poem encourages the subalterns to publicize their hidden, suppressed wishes for change in the public space. The poem invites the *Kolāh-namadi-hā* ('felt-hats' or peasants) to stage their discontentment by coming out onto the streets and reciting the poem collectively. Eshqi's call, as Rancière puts, is a 'claim to visibility, a will to enter the political realm of appearance, the affirmation of a capacity for appearance'.[53]

---

[52] Qā'ed, p. 166.
[53] Hallward, p. 117.

This assumption might stem from the position of theatre as a communal means of education in the eyes of the constitutional intellectuals and their successors. For instance, Gholām-Rezā Rashid Yāsemi believes the theatre to be the space for publicly illustrating the advantages of modernity and the disadvantages of adhering to illogical traditions. Rashid Yāsemi also argues that educating people through 'plays and entertainment' during the constitutional period was 'more practical compared to direct education by preachers or speakers'.[54] This group of intellectuals refer to anti-superstition works such as *Rastākhiz-e Shahriyārān-e Irān* and *Kafan-e Siyāh* in order to explain how dramatic poetry and poetic drama were able to provide educational content in the interest of the general public.

One can argue that these intellectuals are referring to a part of Eshqi's career in which he still obeyed the moral imperatives of 'the ethical regime of images'. In this kind of work, Eshqi sees his readers as spectators at a theatre, with no agency and no ability to intervene in the performance that they are watching. Gabriel Rockhill and Philip Watts outline the Rancièrian notion of the ethical regime as an artistic creation system that originated from Plato's concept of distributing images that would effectively align with the ethos of the community. The ethical regime in this sense is 'preoccupied with distinguishing true art – meaning art that is both true to its origin and to its telos of moral education – from artistic simulacra that distance the community from the truth and the good life'.[55]

However, Eshqi, in his innovative poems, has tried to shift from the ethical regime to 'the aesthetic regime of art', where he can demolish the hierarchical relationship between the poet as the teacher and the audience as the student. The aesthetic regime of constitutional poetry, particularly in the performative works of Eshqi, blurs the line between the elite and ordinary people. In other words, as Hallward explains, in the aesthetic regime, the teacher attempts to blur the line between himself and the student.[56] Karimi-Hakkak conceptualizes this aspect of the aesthetic regime in Eshqi's poetry as an 'interactive environment' in which the poet and reader are positioned in a 'near equal subjectivity'. He writes:

> Rhetorically at least, the poet places himself, as well as his reader, in the position of an onlooker subject to the vicissitudes of the narrative. What makes this posture modernistic in conception as well as in execution possible is the conceptualization of the speaking voice not as a master moralist but as an accidental observer of the scene, or reporter of the

---

[54] Rashid Yāsemi, p. 309.
[55] Gabriel Rockhill, and Philip Watts, 'Jacques Rancière: Thinker of Dissensus', in *History, Politics, Aesthetics: Jacques Rancière* (London: Duke University Press, 2009), p. 9.
[56] Hallward, p. 121.

story, or presenter of the idea which he then takes it upon himself or herself to share with the reader. As poet, he or she then considers it a duty to report the findings accurately and realistically.[57]

The equality of subjects in Eshqi's works envelops the formal aspects of the poetry, to the extent that the text becomes indifferent to the hierarchical structure of genres and literary rules. This indifference may appear in the form of the dissolution of traditional literary genres and the alteration of rhetorical rules. The literary revolution of Eshqi is that which blurs the lines between poetry and non-poetry in the same way that his poetry declassifies the relationship between the established elite and the placeless subaltern. For instance, Ali Akbar Moshir Salimi, the editor of Eshqi's *Kolliyāt*, places the poem *Se Tāblo; Maryam* in the drama section alongside other poetic and non-poetic pieces by the author. On the other hand, experimenting with the existing poetic template of *mosammat*, as well as implementing the direct and verisimilar imagery of constitutional poetry, affiliates this work with its contemporary context of the project of poetic modernization. In other words, *Se Tāblo; Maryam*, as the literary manifestation of Eshqi, despite all of its historical and political functions, is out-of-place and incapable of categorization.

Eshqi seeks to replace the orderly hierarchies of both society and literature with a disruptive and anarchic form of equality. His attempts in this regard are embodied in his experimentation with the concept of theatrocracy in poetry. Indeed, Eshqi wants to break the aristocratic system of classical literature, a system in which the reader has nothing to do with the text. By designing his poetry to be performed in a public place, and by giving a voice to ordinary people in his poems, he lets the subaltern conquer the stage, seeking an equal power of speech to that of the conventional speaking voice within Persian poetry. For example, in *Se Tāblo; Maryam*, the poet demonstrates this theatrocratic equality by demoting the narrator to a casual observer of the scene. The poem opens with a long *bara'at-e estehlāl* (poetic introduction) where the narrator sets the stage by observing the village in which the subsequent story will unfold:

اوایل گل سرخ است و انتهای بهار
نشسته ام سر سنگی کنار یک دیوار
جوار دره دربند و دامن کهسار
فضای شمران اندک ز قرب مغرب تار
هنوز بد اثر روز بر فراز اوین
نموده در پس که آفتاب تازه غروب
سواد شهر ری از دور نیست پیدا خوب

---

[57] Karimi-Hakkak, *Recasting Persian Poetry*, p. 230.

جهان نه روز بود در شمر نه شب محسوب
شفق ز سرخی نیمیش بیرق آشوب
سپس ز زردی نیمیش پرده زرین[58]

It's the start of the rose, the end of spring.
I am seated on a rock, next to a wall
on a sloping hillside near Darband's dell.
Shemran's horizon dimmed from the dusk;
yet above Evin some traces of the day remained.

The sun has now set behind the mountain,
the city's silhouette is only half visible from afar;
in reckoning, this moment counts as neither day nor night:
the dusk resembles half a banner of revolt in redness;
the other half is yellow, like a golden drape.[59]

Mas'ud Ja'fari suggests that the narrator's realistic depiction, serving as a storyteller in the narrative, is a direct response to the neoclassicism of *Bāzgasht-e Adabi*.[60] Eshqi's poems embody an emancipatory spirit, giving rise to more natural and realistic modes of poetic expression. To liberate his poetry from the artificial and abstract poetic expression found in *Bāzgasht-e Adabi*, Eshqi recognized the necessity of fundamentally transforming the entire system of poetic signification. In *Se Tāblo; Maryam*, nature is not a vehicle for a metaphor, or an analogy for other images; mountains, the rose, the rock, the sun, and so on in this poem, as elements of direct imagery, represent their own identity and function. Qā'ed states that before Eshqi, the voyeurism of the narrator-reporter and his description of himself watching others engaged in sexual activity had no precedent in classical poetry.[61] Following the introductory section, the narrator-reporter delves into reporting his observation of the intimate encounter between the two lovers, Maryam and the young man, as they rendezvous and engage in lovemaking within the woods. In this depiction, the poet deliberately avoids obfuscating the scene with abstract metaphors, similes, or other rhetorical elements, opting instead to portray the meeting of the lovers in a vivid and realistic manner.

Another dimension of Eshqi's naturalized and realistic poetic expression appears in the dialogues. The poet attempts to free dialogues from the restricted format of *monāzereh* (poetic debate) in classical narrative poetry and to arrange them in a more fluid structure. Eshqi offers the names of

---

[58] Moshir Salimi, p. 174.
[59] Karimi-Hakkak, *Recasting Persian Poetry*, pp. 214–15.
[60] Mas'ud Ja'fari, *Seyr-e Romāntism dar Irān; as Mashruteh ta Nimā* (Tehran: Markaz, 2007), pp. 65–68.
[61] Qā'ed, p. 157.

the characters, followed by a segmental colon at the beginning of their respective speaking parts. Despite the conventional format of *monāzereh*, in this poem the length of each oration is not limited to the length of the line. Indeed, each persona can talk for the length of, or less than, a full line or hemistich, since the other persona's words can start anywhere in the line. Also, the persona's names in parentheses are not counted in the prosodic metre of the verse; thus, regardless of where in the verse they are placed, the rhythm is unaffected:

(جوان): سلام مریم مهپاره (مریم): کیست ایوائی! / (جوان): منم نترس عزیز، از چه وقت اینجائی؟...
دگر بقیه احوال پرسی و آداب / به ماچ و بوسه به جا آمد، اندر آن مهتاب
خوش آنکه بر رخ یارش نظر کند شاداب / لبش نجنبد و قلبش کند سوال و جواب
(عشقی) برای من بخدا بارها شدست چنین[62]

(Young man): Hello gorgeous (Maryam): Who is this! O my god! / (Young man): Don't be afraid, dear, how long have you been here? ...
Then there were greetings and attention / And then kissing under the moonlight
Blessed is the one who looks at his beloved's face passionately / Whose lips remain still, yet asks questions and answers in his heart
(Eshqi) Swear to God, it has happened to me many times

In the second and third verses, the narrator describes two lovers greeting each other with heartfelt affection. In the final hemistich, the voice of the narrator emerges as one of the personae within the poem, offering commentary on the preceding description of the lovers' encounter. In the later part of the poem, particularly in the final section, the narrator enters the village and engages in a direct conversation with another character, an elderly individual. This intentional distribution of speech power between the narrator, the young Tehrani man, the village girl, and the working-class old man reflects the poet's endeavour to achieve equality and balance in the voices represented within the poem.

It can be argued that the deliberate pursuit of a balanced representation of voices serves as a structural mechanism to evade the imposition of authority by concepts and contents in Persian poetry. Within the aristocratic regime of classical poetry, the elite poet assumes a position of superiority when addressing the audience. However, in Eshqi's theatrocratic works, this hierarchical relationship is subverted, and the poet assumes the role of just one of the personas within the dramatic poem.

The Rancièrian concept of theatrocratic equality does not emerge from a re-evaluation of the system of distributing functions and positions. Rather, theatrocracy represents a disruptive and violent deviation from

---

[62] Moshir Salimi, p. 176.

any established system of orderly distribution. Most scholars considered *Se Tāblo; Maryam* as a radical outburst against the corruption of the ideals of the Constitutional Revolution. The poem, in fact, was composed in response to a query by Iranian intellectuals in the journal *Shafaq-e Sorkh* (Red Dusk) regarding their vision for the future of the country. Shāhrokh Meskub states that Eshqi, in *Se Tāblo; Maryam*, has crafted a metaphorical depiction of the failure of the Constitutional Revolution. Within this dramatic poem, the characters of Maryam, representing the lower class, and her father, symbolizing the oppressed freedom fighter, become victims of an opportunistic and dominant force. In other words, Meskub proposes that this narrative should be interpreted as an allegory for the political climate of the country during that period, highlighting the struggles and challenges faced by the nation as a whole.[63] At the end of the poem, Eshqi reveals his idealized vision which, as Karimi-Hakkak describes, is a call for 'an annual bloodbath in retaliation for the treachery that has diverted that Revolution from its original path, causing its demise'.[64]

The anarchic bloodbath that Eshqi has conceptualized in other texts, such as *'id-e Khun* (The Blood Feast), provides an illuminating dimension to his theatrocratic concept of equality. According to Hallward, theatrocratic equality should be defined as 'a pure supposition that must be verified continuously – a verification or an enactment that opens specific stages of equality, stages that are built by crossing boundaries and interconnecting forms and levels of discourse and spheres of experience'.[65] *'id-e Khun* is also a continuous verification happening in the form of an annual cleansing ceremony, in which 'the people, while singing songs, would head for the houses of those public officials who during the previous year had committed treason against their public trust, and, levelling their homes, would cut the traitors up into pieces'.[66]

Most scholars denounced Eshqi's encouragement of the public towards vandalism and perceived the notion of the bloodbath in *Se Tāblo; Maryam* and the *'id-e Khun* articles to be in contradiction with the other democratic dimensions of the poet's political thoughts. However, Kamrān Sepehrān states that the idea of *'id-e Khun* is not a call for genuine violence. Eshqi, inspired by the ideas reflected in folk rituals and plays such as *Mogh-koshi* (Killing the Magus), *Kuseh-Barneshin* (Hairless Ride) and *Mir-e Nowruzi* (The Lord of Misrule), offers a metaphorical solution in order to emphasize the need for structural changes within both culture and the political system, so as to create checks and balances against abuses of power. Like *'id-e Khun*,

---

[63] Shāhrokh Meskub, *Dāstān-e Adabiyāt va Sargozasht-e Ejtemā'* (Tehran: Farzān-e Ruz, 2007), pp. 115–17.
[64] Karimi-Hakkak, *Recasting Persian Poetry*, p. 213.
[65] Hallward, p. 111.
[66] Moshir Salimi, pp. 125–6.

all of these folk performances are created based on the idea of an annual, temporary overthrow of the system. Sepehrān also spots some concepts analogous to Western culture, such as those in '*serate futuriste*' (futurist evenings), early twentieth-century theatrical poetry recitals conducted in a public space, which incited the audience to riot. [67] Eshqi himself, in the last stanza of the poem, clarifies the figurative sense of anarchy in his work:

در این محیط که بس مرده شوی دون دارد / وزین قبیل عناصر ز حد فزون دارد
عجب مدار اگر شاعری جنون دارد / بدل همیشه تقاضای عید خون دارد
چگونه شرح دهم ایده آل خود به از این؟ [68]

In this milieu where there are a lot of lowly corpse-washers / and even more breeds of similar things
Do not wonder if a poet is insane / and constantly wishes for a blood feast
I cannot explain my ideal better than this?

The verses imply that '*id-e Khun* and its poetic presence in *Se Tāblo; Maryam* represent the literary manifestation of theatrocratic equality. Eshqi aims to convey his personal experiences as a political activist and express his aspirations for a liberated society through the medium of a performative literary piece.

Comprehending the significance of the politics of literature, Eshqi, in line with Bahār, Āref, and some other pioneer poets of this era, upholds the ideals of the Constitutional Revolution in the form of an aesthetic revolution within the realms of poetry. This aesthetic revolution on the one hand appeared to be the cohabitation of new and old, as well as representing gradual changes to the fundamental elements of classical literature, as seen in the works of Bahār and his advocates. On the other hand, poets such as Āref and Eshqi confronted the traditional poetic frontiers by demolishing the conventional systems of signification and presentation embedded in Persian poetry. There is no doubt that both of these revisionary approaches towards the literary traditions formed the principal politics of literature in the constitutional era, thus laying the groundwork for the more comprehensive movements of literary modernization in the succeeding decades.

---

[67] Kamrān Sepehrān, *Te'ātrokerāsi dar 'asr-e Mashruteh, 1285–1304* (Tehran: Nilufar, 2008), pp. 210–11.
[68] Moshir Salimi, p. 193.

3

The left wing of the poetic revolution and constructive misreading of the literary tradition

As argued in the previous chapters, constitutional poetry was divided into two, each employing different revisionary strategies to drive the literary revolution. These revisionary approaches served as the theoretical foundation for the political act of poetry in this era. The right wing of constitutional poetry, including Bahār and his advocates, endeavoured gradually to reform structural elements of classical literature while introducing new standards to be implemented in the context of classical poetry. The more progressive group involved with the poetic revolution, however, included Āref and Eshqi, who strove to deconstruct the conventional system of signification and some of the main formal conceptions of Persian poetry. The antithetical revisionary approach of this group, which aspired to complete the works of their precursors, was the embodiment of their political radicalism in the realm of poetics. Although one can spot significant traces of figurative innovations such as colloquialism and freer poetic forms in some of Bahār's colloquial poems, Āref's *tasnifs*, and Eshqi's dramatic poems, the majority of constitutional poets understood literary revolution as a thematic and elemental change rather than a deconstructive reformulation of the whole poetic system.

The emphasis placed by constitutional poets on thematic modernity and current issues has led Persian literary scholarship to diminish the achievements of this era to mere 'political engagement in subject matter'. This perspective is exemplified by Hamid Dabashi, who, in his conceptualization of sociopolitical commitment in the literature of this period, undermines the significance of the constitutional and post-constitutional literary revolution, perceiving it solely as a reflection of ideological shifts and a radical restructuring of power dynamics within society. According to Dabashi, in contrast to European Romanticism, which challenged established aesthetics in favour of nature and intense emotions, the Persian literary revolution adopted ideological positions and re-established traditional models of authority. This allowed the emancipated spirit of Persian intellectuals to strive for the highest expression of their calling.[1]

Persian literary scholarship, as an embodiment of the Bloomian concept of 'the school of resentment', overemphasizes the thematic engagement of literary works with politics at the expense of its aesthetic achievements. Thus, it assumes that the lifespan of literary movements depends on the persistence of the sociopolitical situation which has influenced them. Dabashi, describing the constitutional and post-constitutional period as 'a faithless age of shifting patterns of authority', states that the poets of this era 'could only achieve tormented disloyalties to a glorious past' and 'half-hearted devotions to a revolutionary present'.[2]

However, one may argue that 'disloyalty' to the aesthetic values of the precursor's works and an antithetical approach to the work of contemporaries suggest that the leading post-constitutional poets had a more proactive revisionary approach towards both classical poetry and their immediate tradition. In contrast with the right wing of the literary revolution which promoted a gradual programme for literary modernization, another group of literary activists, the left wing, were much more radical in their approach to literary change. The leftist group of the poetic revolution in this era, particularly Taqi Raf'at (1889–1920), Abolqāsem Lāhuti (1887–1957), Shams Kasmā'i (1883–1961), and Ja'far Khāmene'i (1886–1983), were the first generation of modernists to embark upon a process of severely disputing and attempting to correct the works of classical masters. Furthermore, they endeavoured to conceptualize and employ innovative poetic forms that eventually became integral to Persian poetic conventions. Indeed, although pre-constitutional intellectuals such as Fath-Ali Akhundzādeh (1812–1878) and Aqā Khān Kermāni (1854–1897) started the project of reconsidering the values of classical masterpieces,[3] this group of poets developed similar

---

[1] Hamid Dabashi, 'The Poetics of Politics: Commitment in Modern Persian Literature', *Iranian Studies*, 2/4 (1985), 147–88 (p. 181).
[2] Dabashi, p. 181.
[3] Akhundzādeh wrote his groundbreaking treatise called *Irād* (Objection) in 1863 in the style of Western literary criticism. This treatise included critical ideas on the reactionary nature of the traditional style of Rezā-Qoli Khān Hedāyat's writing in *Rowzat al-Safā* (The Garden of Purity). Later, in 1867, he wrote another treatise entitled *Qeritiqā* (Criticism), analysing one of Sorush Esfahāni's *qasidehs*. Dissemination of these texts among the intelligentsia started a long-lasting

arguments in their creative and critical writings. Also, in choosing an antithetical approach, they accomplished the mission of constitutional poets by experimenting with multiple dimensions of poetic form in order to erect a new aesthetic system for Persian poetry.

To establish the foundational principles of this emerging aesthetic regime, the group (commonly referred to as *Tajaddod* poets throughout this chapter due to their affiliation with the newspaper *Tajaddod*) had to articulate their position regarding the prevailing literary traditions. One can mark a twofold approach towards literary traditions in the theory and practice of poetry in this group. First, they undertook a series of alterations in the content, form and function of Persian poetry, which will be analysed in the following sections, to perform a counter-sublime role corresponding to the sublime works of the classical poets. This revisionary approach, characterized by Harold Bloom as '*daemonization*', manifested in their endeavours to dismantle the hierarchical regime of subject matter prevalent in classical literature. Their aim was to transform Persian poetry from a realm of divine themes into one grounded in earthly matters. As Mohammad-Reza Ghanoonparvar states, in pre-modern Persian poetry the text is 'centred around the divine and the supernatural'; however, the modern poets centre their literary world around the reality of their own lives and that of 'individuals of modern society' and their 'unique characteristics, sensibilities, conflicts and aspirations'.[4]

In addition, the left wing of the poetic revolution implemented another revisionary approach, not merely to reform the poetic traditions as constitutional poets did but to discontinue the literary heritage of classical poets in their works. They experimented with either original or borrowed metres, rhyme arrangements, and imagery systems to substitute the whole figurative and semantic system of classical poetry with one which was more compatible with the characteristics of the modern world. Bloom refers to this revisionary approach as '*kenosis*' and describes it as an act of emptying one's poetry of the characteristics associated with the classical masters. According to Bloom, by emptying the poem of the spirit inherited from the poetic predecessors, the poet is freed from the constraints of

---

dispute on the impact of traditional literature on the process of modernization and the necessity of the Westernization of literature and literary criticism. These ideas were later developed by Aqā Khān Kermānī, who, in his uncompleted *Resāle-ye Reyhān* (Reyhan's Treatise), scrutinized literary traditionalism and encouraged Persian writers and poets to remodel their perspective on literature. He also composed a poem criticizing the despotism of the time, as an example of Westernized poetry for the younger generations. Māshāllāh Ajudānī, *Yā Marg yā Tajaddod; Daftari dar She'r va Adab-e Mashruteh* (London: Fasl-e Ketāb, 2002), pp. 63–81; Abdolhoseyn Zarrinkub, *Naqd-e Adabi*, 2 vols (Tehran: Amir Kabir, 1983), 2, pp. 637–8.

[4] Mohammad-Reza Ghanoonparvar, *Prophets of Doom: Literature as a Socio-political Phenomenon in Modern Iran* (Maryland: University Press of America, 1984), p. 25.

continuity. This liberation enables the poet to avoid replicating the 'precursor's afflatus or godhood'.[5]

Exercising these revisionary approaches, *Tajaddod* poets strove to revolutionize both the subject matter and figurative aspects of Persian poetry. In theorizing the politics of their poetic revolution, and in confronting the representations of autocratic regimes in classical literature, *Tajaddod* poets embarked upon conversations with other frontiers of poetic modernization. For instance, disputes between Rafʿat and Bahār on the value of the classical masters' literary heritage in modern Iran, which will be analysed in the following paragraphs, were a revolutionary effort. These debates shed light on the undemocratic nature of classical literature and set the stage for innovative proposals concerning the formal and generic structures of Persian poetry.

This chapter opens with a very brief account of Taqi Raʿfat's life and career as the leading figure of the *Tajaddod* group. It goes on to explore the theoretical dimensions of long-lasting disputes between *Tajaddod* poets and the *Dāneshkadeh* association on their different perceptions of the conception of literary revolution. The next section starts with a short overview of Abolqāsem Lāhuti's life and oeuvre. It then moves on to a narrative of his transition from conventional mystical subject matters to sociopolitically committed, counter-sublime ones, before studying figurative transformations in his poetry before and after his emigration to the Soviet Union and his acquaintance with Soviet socialist realism. At the end of this section, the experiments of the poet in poetic forms, particularly innovative rhythmic systems and unconventional rhyme patterns, will be discussed.

The third section examines the improvisations of *Tajaddod* poets, mainly Shams Kasmāʾi, in generating poetic forms, as well as adopting novel rhyme patterns inspired by French and Russian sonnets. Although one cannot see these experiments as constructively theorized poetic forms, they should be perceived as a significant break between classical and modern Persian poetry. The final section discusses the role of these practices in developing a new conception of the stanza in Persian poetry, which in turn led to the introduction of a new poetic form called *chārpāreh* (four-liner). This poetic form, on account of its roots in both European and Persian poetry, has a hybrid nature which soon turned it into the most popular poetic form among different groups of poets. At the very end of this chapter, the role of *chārpāreh* in changing the classical generic classification system will be identified.

---

[5] Harold Bloom, *The Anxiety of Influence: A Theory of Poetry* (New York: Oxford University Press, 1997), pp. 87–8.

The Ra'fat era: From deconstruction to construction

Mirzā Taqi Khān Ra'fat was born in 1889 in Tabriz, where he undertook his primary studies before moving to Istanbul to pursue his education at higher levels. He worked in Turkey as the head of *Maktab-e Nāseri-e Irāniān* (the Iranian Nāseri School) until 1917, before returning to Tabriz after the occupation of Turkey by Russia in the First World War. During the last years of the 1910s and the early 1920s, he taught French in high schools and composed poems in support of *Hezb-e Demokrāt-e Āzarbāyjān* (the Democratic Party of Azarbaijan). He published his poems frequently in a newspaper called *Tajaddod* (Modernity) between April 1917 and August 1920, and later a magazine named *Āzādistān* (Land of freedom), for which he also acted as chief editor. Both of these journals aimed to propagate the rebellion of Tabriz against the central government. *Tajaddod* was the official organ of the Democratic Party of Azarbaijan and Sheykh Mohammad Khiyābāni's rebel government, and *Āzādistān*, which was published in just four issues during 1920, was the educational and cultural organ of the party.[6] The last issue of *Āzādistān* was in the printing house when the central government entered Tabriz and defeated Khiyābāni's forces, eventually killing Khiyābāni in September 1920. Ra'fat, who was a comrade of Khiyābāni during his uprising, hid in a small village for a few days before ending his life.[7]

Ra'fat was a prominent innovative poet and a significant reader of the poetry of his time. He not only sought an alliance with his contemporary radical poets but also initiated several groundbreaking reconsiderations of the forms and functions of literary modernization in his correspondence with moderate modernist literary figures. During his short life, Ra'fat devoted himself to writing critical articles, manifestos, and poems. Additionally, he took the initiative to establish one of the earliest professional associations of critics and poets. Their collective goal was to challenge and resist the autocratic literary establishment of their era. Ra'fat was the leading writer of *Tajaddod* and had a regular column in which he promoted his ideas about the different angles of literary modernity. He turned this newspaper and its successive magazine, *Āzādistān*, into a stronghold for leftist forces of the literary revolution such as Shams Kasmā'i and Ja'far Khāmene'i.[8]

Ra'fat's critical ideas about literary conventions initiated several debates between the radical and gradualist modernists of the time. Although both

---

[6] Yahyā Ārianpur, *Az Sabā tā Nimā*, 2 vols (Tehran: Frānklin, 1976), 2, p. 230.
[7] Ārianpur, 2, p. 452.
[8] Nassereddin Parvin, 'Tajaddod', in *Encyclopaedia Iranica* http://www.iranicaonline.org/articles/tajaddod [accessed 31 March 2018].

sides of these debates believed in some sort of a revolution as the only path towards literary modernity, they had fundamental disagreements on the corrective paths that the new poets should undertake in confronting traditional literature. In fact, the similarities between what most of these groups conceptualized as literary modernity or literary revolution were numerous, yet their suggested paths for achieving the goal were different. Some groups, such as *Anjoman-e Dāneshkadeh*, *Anjoman-e Adabi-e Irān* (*Iran Literary Association*), and the *Kāveh* journal, argued for gradual and moderate modifications in classical poetics in order to modernize Persian literature. The *Tajaddod* group, however, promoted the idea of radical change through adopting and reformulating the figurative and thematic aspects of these modern literary traditions, while innovating new poetic forms. For instance, the manifesto of *Anjoman-e Adabi-e Irān* states that the primary objective of this group is to safeguard prose and poetry from losing the valuable qualities of classical literature. At the same time, they express their openness to embracing the characteristics that the modern world can bring to literary texts.[9] *Tajaddod* poets, however, argued that the only way of modernizing Persian literature was to follow an 'international doctrine of arts'.[10] As Karimi-Hakkak puts it:

> Varying degrees of tolerance for rupture, the search for innovation beyond established thematic and generic boundaries, and particularly the linkage between aesthetic value and the presentation of socio-political issues signal the leap from elemental to structural changes. Of the two tendencies illustrated here, the gradualist position would not initiate formal and generic violations of the traditional poetic system, whereas the more radical position might do so to redress what it sees as a lack in the native tradition.[11]

In a manifesto published on 17 November 1919, Ra'fat states that *Tajaddod* poets rectify classical poetics on three levels: form, language, and style. One could find this somewhat confusing, as he offers no further explanation about these levels and the means of remodelling poetry. However, characterizing these levels as *Tajaddod's* points of departure from literary traditions implies a form of corrective movement in the works of this group. The call for reconsidering all elements of poetry was tantamount to emptying poetry of the old elements and forging a discontinuity with the aesthetic regimes of classical poetry.

Bloom sees a poet's promotion of discontinuity with his precursors as a defence mechanism by which the new poet resists the imitation of his poetic

---

[9] Zarrinkub, p. 641.
[10] Ārianpur, 2, p. 452.
[11] Ahmad Karimi-Hakkak, *Recasting Persian Poetry: Scenarios of Poetic Modernity in Iran* (London: Oneworld, 2012), p. 116.

fathers. New poets, such as *Tajaddod* poets, seek to be contemporary and topical; therefore, they go through a process of 'undoing' the achievements of their poetic fathers in their works.¹² Indeed, unlike moderate modernists who were eager to reform and rebuild the traditional system of aesthetics at a rational pace, *Tajaddod* poets intended to empty or release their poetry from the old structures and to construct an entirely new aesthetic system based on modern conceptions of form, language, and style.

Although Ra'fat's theoretical articles were much more coherent than those of other groups, they were still too destructive and were unable to illustrate the structural changes in poetics suggested by *Tajaddod* poets. As a result, a high level of ambiguity entered the discourse of literary change put forward by *Tajaddod* poets in their debates with other frontiers of literary modernity. As Ahmad Karimi-Hakkak writes:

> In short, the language of the debate on modernity in the Persian poetry of the early twentieth century is intricate and opaque, subject to a variety of interpretations that come ultimately to depend on the interpreter's own ideology and vision of modernity. As a result the poetic discourse that emerges begins to throw all cultural products into two antithetical poles: the old and the new.¹³

In his articles, Ra'fat constantly claims that traditional literary forms are incompatible with the requirements of modern life. Nevertheless, he is unable to articulate his ideas in the form of explicit rules for a new style. Even in his manifesto, Ra'fat does not highlight the poetic forms or techniques that distinguish the works of *Tajaddod* poets from those of other groups. However, one may explain some of the statements of this manifesto based on the poetic practice of some of the *Tajaddod* poets and Ra'fat's other theoretical writings.

One can argue that this manifesto's call for the remodelling of poetic forms indicates the writer's enthusiasm for demolishing the system of traditional templates, rhyme schemes, and prosodic metres in order to formulate alternative conceptions. Moreover, *Tajaddod* literary language is neither as colloquial as that of constitutional poetry nor as belletristic as that of the Literary Return Movement. The poetic language of this group contains a considerable number of foreign words and grammatical structures which entered into the Persian language through political discourses of the time.¹⁴

---

¹²Bloom, p. 87.
¹³Karimi-Hakkak, *Recasting Persian Poetry*, p. 105.
¹⁴*Kāveh* journal condemns *Tajaddods* for being Westernized and using a blended and unnatural language in their prose and poetry. *Kāveh* assumes that this language is influenced by Westernized immigrants who returned from Turkey to Iran after the Constitutional Revolution. See Karimi-Hakkak, *Recasting Persian Poetry*, pp. 459–60.

Ra'fat asserts that *Tajaddod* poetry defines itself as a form of attack against 'the literary and political forts of reactionary forces and tyranny' and the language of this poetry should correspond with 'the noise of gunfire in public protests'. Therefore, the belletristic language of classical literature is unable to reflect that situation.[15] The discourse of public protest and street fights was even more apparent in Ra'fat's theoretical texts. This language was used by *Tajaddod* poets to fight against both political and 'literary despotism'. Indeed, Ra'fat utilized this discourse to denounce the advocates of both traditionalism and gradualism by aligning them with political autocracy.[16]

According to Rezā Barāhani, Ra'fat believed that a poem adhering to the style of the classical masters falls short in capturing the contemporary and distinctive thoughts of modern Iranians. Therefore, he attempts to establish the concept of 'revolution' as an essential element of any contemporary work of literature. He calls for using a 'rebellious style' to reflect the anxious mind of his society in encountering the modern world.[17] The new style that the *Tajaddod* manifesto proposes as an ideal form is the result of the indigenization of certain elements of a wide range of European poetic styles. However, one can see the masters of French revolutionary romanticism (and perhaps poets who emulated their style in the Ottoman context) as the focal points of *Tajaddod* poets. The key to this intercultural dialogue is, of course, the similar application of the politics of literature in the works of French and Turco-Persian poets. For instance, referring to Victor Hugo, Ra'fat describes the literary revolution as the 'supplement and conclusion' to the political revolution.[18]

In addition to the contents of the manifesto, Ra'fat's articles written during his correspondence with *Dāneshkadeh* members, the representatives of gradualist modernization, functioned as a means of declaring the *Tajaddod* poets' corrective approach towards the Persian literary tradition. These disputes started when a member of *Dāneshkadeh* published a poem in a style resembling that of the Persian classical master Sa'di (1210–1292). Ra'fat criticized the *Dāneshkadeh* association for publishing a traditional poem despite their support for literary modernity. Although *Dāneshkadeh* apologized for the controversy surrounding the behaviour of its member, shortly thereafter, Ra'fat penned an article titled *Maktab-e Sa'di* (Sa'di's School) in which he launched an attack on the literary legacy of Sa'di, as well as the members of *Dāneshkadeh* whom he deemed as contemporary followers of Sa'di.[19] This was the outset of a critical correspondence within

---

[15] Karimi-Hakkak, *Recasting Persian Poetry*, p. 440.
[16] Karimi-Hakkak, *Recasting Persian Poetry*, p. 111.
[17] Rezā Barāhani, *Kimiyā va khāk; Moqadameh-i bar Falsafe-ye Adabiyāt* (Tehran: Morgh-e Āmin, 1985), p. 30.
[18] Ārianpur, 2, p. 451.
[19] Ārianpur, 2, pp. 437–8.

which Raf'at defended and Bahār denounced the opinions of the writer of *Maktab-e Sa'di*. These articles brought about one of the most significant discussions among constitutional intellectuals about the ethical and educational advantages and disadvantages of the classical masterpieces. First and foremost, it forced the two sides to clarify their revisionary approaches towards traditional literature.

In April 1918, less than two years before the publication of the *Tajaddod* manifesto, *Dāneshkadeh* released the first issue of a journal with the same name, including their literary manifesto under the title of *Marām-e Mā* (Our Creed). The text was drafted by Mohammad Taqi Bahār, the head of the association.[20] In this manifesto, Bahār highlighted the necessity of reforming the practice of poetry in the post-constitutional era and suggested a 'gradual and smooth' change in the traditional aesthetics of Persian poetry. This reformist approach was in fact 'to repair the old mansion of the ancestors' and 'to build a new one beside it' in a rational manner.[21] In essence, the Dāneshkadeh manifesto perceived traditional elements as ideal monuments that, at most, necessitated reorganization to align with the new aesthetic regime. In response, Raf'at published an article in May 1918 in which he ridiculed the conservative tone of the manifesto and highlighted the writer's controversial approach to the notion of literary modernity:

> In the above lines, you admit a few things. First, that you are afraid [to venture out], preferring to continue to live in your ancestral home. Second, that structure is in need of repair and that you shall undertake such repair. Third, that next to the structure mentioned above, you shall erect newer structures. No mason or architect devises a plan of this sort. Such a thought will condemn you to failure.[22]

Later in the same article, Raf'at accuses *Dāneshkadeh* of hypocrisy and fear of change. He warns his contemporary poets against surrendering to the past and repeating the works of their poetic fathers. He underscores the metaphor of buildings, initially employed by Bahār, to illustrate the deconstructive essence of the literary revolution. He clarifies the controversy in repairing the hierarchical and absolute structure of traditional poetry while building an emancipatory poetic system at the same time. Bloom sees this situation as a different side of '*kenosis*' or repetition mood, where

---

[20] *Dāneshkadeh* members reflected the contents of the manifesto in a series of essays published in the journal from the first issues, including *Tārikh-e Adabi* (Literary history) by Abbās Eghbāl Āshtiāni (1896–1956) and *Enteqād-e Adabi* (Literary criticism) and *Bozorgān* (The Great) by Gholām-Rezā Rashid Yāsemi (1896–1951). *Dāneshkadeh* journal was published for ten issues from April 1918 to February 1919.
[21] Ārianpur, 2, p. 450.
[22] Karimi-Hakkak, *Recasting Persian Poetry*, p. 112.

the ambivalent behaviour of the new poet leads him to misdirect his battle against the traditional regimes of art and 'falls or ebbs into a space and time that confines him' in the past, even if he intended to have 'undone the precursor's pattern by a deliberate, willed loss in continuity'.[23] As a result of this ambivalence, the stance of the newcomer poets towards the politics of their poetry appears to be the same as that of their poetic fathers. Nevertheless, the meaning of the stance might not be the same.

Thus, although Bahār's manifesto portrays *Dāneshkadeh* poets and critics as advocates for literary revolution, their continuity with the classical masters in fundamental poetic conceptions impacts negatively on the relevance of their work to the needs of their contemporary society. While terrified of destroying the traditional poetic rules which represent the autocratic social order, in line with the intelligentsia of the time, they express their fascination with the political changes of the modern world. However, as Terry Eagleton articulates, the creation of modern aesthetic conceptions is inseparable from 'the construction of the dominant ideological forms' among the intelligentsia as well as the 'new form of human subjectivity' based on the new social order.[24] Thus, one can argue that, by failing to harmonize the politics of their poetry with the reality of society, *Dāneshkadeh* members could not form a modern aesthetic conception of form, language, and style as it appeared in the *Tajaddod* manifesto.

Some scholars, however, criticize Raf'at for politicizing the domain in which Persian poetry was crafted and for disregarding the accomplishments of traditional literature in favour of topicality. For instance, Karimi-Hakkak states that Raf'at formed a mode of discourse on Persian poetry in which both traditionalists and gradualists were analogized to 'undesirable political elements'. He blames Raf'at for the 'interlocking of the literary and political discourses of modern Iran', which is 'still a feature of the literary culture'.[25] However, one can argue that legitimizing cultural changes by interlocking them with sociopolitical issues is a characteristic of revolutionary periods in general. As explored in Chapter 1, nearly all poets of this era, including those with religious or mystical inclinations, crafted poems addressing revolution-related themes. They believed that the assessment of their works would be influenced by their connection to the prevailing sociopolitical concerns of the time. Hamid Dabashi states that politicizing the literary innovation sphere is a peculiar characteristic of modern Iranian literati. Indeed, Iranian modernists see politicization as a way of transfiguring literature.[26] Even Bahār, in his response to Raf'at's criticism of the *Dāneshkadeh* manifesto entitled *Enteqādāt dar Atrāf-e Marām-e Mā* (Criticisms Concerning Our

---

[23] Bloom, p. 90.
[24] Terry Eagleton, *The Ideology of the Aesthetic* (Oxford: Blackwell, 1990), p. 3.
[25] Karimi-Hakkak, *Recasting Persian Poetry*, p. 111.
[26] Dabashi, p. 152.

Creed), predicted major changes in poetic forms, language, and expressive devices, acknowledging them as effects of the revolutionary atmosphere on the evolutionary process of literature.[27]

By politicizing the environment of modern Persian poetry, *Tajaddod* poets embarked upon a democratic revisionary movement towards personalized and counter-sublime subject matter. Politicizing is a reaction to the sacredness of the traditional poetics and sublime subject matter used by the classical masters. This corrective action often happens through the newcomers' breaking of the values of the hierarchical regime and abandoning the highly appreciated themes of classical literature. Politicizing the poetic sphere drove poets of this era to disturb the traditional autocratic order of subject matter and cover subjects which stemmed from their own lives and/or their immediate environment. In other words, the new aesthetic regime which *Tajaddod* poets proposed was against the hierarchy of subject matter and instead expanded the field of literature to take everything as a subject of art. They broke down the classical hierarchy of values in Persian poetry and equalized the values of subject matter relating to the everyday life of ordinary people with traditionally sacred ones. As Ghanoonparvar puts it:

> No longer are the kings praised for such attributes as bravery and ancestry, nor is this poetry any longer a medium for the poet to engage in worshipping the almighty, and the classical image of the beloved as a moon-faced beauty ... In the philosophical sense as well, the poet no longer concerns himself with mysticism and fatalism ... instead of writing a poetry centered around the 'divine' and the spiritual, the poet now writes of a universe cantered around humankind, about a society inhabited by individuals.[28]

It can be argued that if politicization is limited to the domain of subject matter and does not extend to the form of the poem, ultimately, the poem may end up reproducing the hierarchical relationships of the old regime. For example, most constitutional poets devoted their career to the change of subject matter; however, they were not able to demolish other hierarchical orders, such as classical expressive devices, the prosodic system, and poetic templates. In this sense, when a poet worships his homeland or freedom instead of God, a patron, or his beloved in a classical poetic form, in emancipating the poem from the hierarchical regime of subjects, he simultaneously creates a new hierarchical order. In fact, because of the autocratic formal ground of the poem, the subject matter has been changed, but the new subject forms the new sublime.

---

[27] Ārianpur, 2, pp. 450–1.
[28] Ghanoonparvar, p. 25.

Tajaddod poets conceived deviation from classical formal rules as a counter-sublime movement against the structural despotism of Persian poetry. They intended to alter the sacred order of classical poetry in a way that secured the interrelation of emancipatory subject matter with a free aesthetic system. Ghanoonparvar describes this system as 'a democratic order in which every poem determines its own form and shape'.[29] *Tajaddod* poets' conception of aesthetic revolution illustrated that they were prepared to go further than the thematic changes of gradualist poets such as Dehkhodā and Bahār, and the elemental changes of experimenters such as Āref and Eshqi. From *Tajaddod* poets' point of view, even the experiments of these poets in poetic forms were insufficient for remodelling Persian poetry. Therefore, they focused on revolutionizing the formal aspects of poetry and refused to accept the autocratic aesthetic regime of classical poetry as a guide to action and a source of meaning. Karimi-Hakkak writes:

> The changes initiated by poets like Dehkhodā and Āref [...] tend to convey the message that the existing system can be expanded to serve new purposes, here the perception of a previously existing ideology shared between the poet and the reader gives rise to the perception of a common need to alter, rather than expand, the system of poetic signification and communication.[30]

Abolqāsem Lāhuti was probably the most inspirational poet of this approach to poetic renovation. Lāhuti's endeavours 'to alter, rather than expand' both the thematic and formal aspects of Persian poetry paved the way for more thorough changes in the poetry of the following generation of modernists. The emancipatory nature of Lāhuti's poetry and its politically charged themes required 'new systems of poetic expression, presumably privileging greater artistic allegiance to socio-political causes'.[31]

Major Lāhuti: Persian socialist realism and the aesthetic revolution

Abolqāsem Lāhuti was born in Kermanshah on 12 October 1887. On account of his family's financial problems, he did not obtain a formal primary education until a local masonic society called *Jāme'eh Ādamiyat* (the Society of Humanity) sent him to a school in Tehran. After some time, amid the upheavals of the Constitutional Revolution, Lāhuti aligned himself with the

---

[29] Ghanoonparvar, p. 26.
[30] Karimi-Hakkak, *Recasting Persian Poetry*, p. 202.
[31] Karimi-Hakkak, *Recasting Persian Poetry*, p. 201.

revolutionaries and became actively involved in the movement.[32] Following the restoration of the Constitution in 1911 he joined the gendarmerie force, but after a clash, the details of which are unclear, he became a fugitive and for a time lived between Istanbul and Kermanshah. During the First World War, Lāhuti revealed his inclination towards Germany. Like many other Iranian nationalists, he regarded Britain and Russia as Iran's foremost enemies, especially after they united over their exploitation of Iran in the Anglo-Russian Entente of 1907, which divided Iran into spheres of influence. In 1914, in the context of the conflicts between pro-German Iranians and the British and Russians, he attempted to form a group of revolutionary men to fight against Russian and British forces. He failed and was sentenced in absentia to death for subversion, but he managed to escape to Turkey.

In 1916 Lāhuti returned to Kermanshah, where a provisional government with pro-German sympathies had been established. During this period, he served as one of the editors of *Bistun*, a newspaper with clear militant tendencies. It is plausible that during this period of his life, especially after the 1917 Russian Revolution, Lāhuti's political ideology underwent a transformation from a form of socialist nationalism to communism. Eventually, he became involved in the establishment of *Hezb-e Ferqeh-ye Kārgar* (the Workers' Faction Party), which was formed by pro-Soviet activists in Kermanshah in 1917. With the withdrawal of the Russian Army in 1918, however, he had to escape to Istanbul again where he was mostly associated with the *Ahmadiyeh* school in various capacities. Lāhuti collaborated with the essayist and playwright Hasan Moqaddam (1897–1925) to publish a few issues of the bimonthly literary journal *Pārs*.

Lāhuti returned to Iran towards the end of 1921 and was reappointed into the gendarmerie force. In January 1922 he organized another revolt against the state and occupied Tabriz for eleven days with the help of some of his gendarmerie's comrades and the former followers of Khiyābāni. As with other military revolts of the early 1920s, Lāhuti's was crushed by the army in February 1922, and consequently he sought refuge in the Soviet Union. In 1923, in Moscow, he was appointed as a compositor and literary assistant in the Central Publishing House. After a year, he moved to Tajikistan, where he held some governmental positions and contributed to Tajik literary modernization.[33] In the last years of his life, Lāhuti moved back to Moscow, where he passed away on 16 March 1957.

---

[32] Ārianpur, 2, p. 68.
[33] Most scholars consider Lāhuti as one of the founders of Soviet Tajik poetry. He became a significant member of the Union of Tajik writers in the early years of his presence in Tajikistan. His poems soon became popular and were published in the Latin and Cyrillic scripts. He also composed 'the libretto of the first Tajik opera', *Kāveh-ye Āhangar* (Kaveh the Smith), as well as the Tajik Soviet anthem. See Jiri Becka, 'Two Iranians in Modern Tajik Poetry', *Oriente Moderno*, 1 (2003), 29–35, (pp. 30–1).

Lāhuti's oeuvre reflects the vicissitudes of his life, ideas and his reactions to his immediate environment. His early poems are mostly composed in classical forms with mystical content. These poems were influenced by his father, Mirzā Ahmad Elahāmi (1848–1907), a relatively well-known provincial poet. Lāhuti's early poems are mystical and celebrate the *Ne'mat-Allāhi* order of mysticism. The mastery of the young poet in classical poetry convinced the editors of some prestigious journals such as *Habl-al-Matin*, *Tarbiyat*, and *Irān-e Now* to publish Lāhuti's poems when he was in his early twenties.

Despite his early success, in the 1910s Lāhuti introduced into his poetry a counter-sublime revisionism and substituted the sacred themes of mystical poetry with those relating to the situation of his contemporary society. Mohammad-Rezā Shafi'i Kadkani perceives the counter-sublime movement of Lāhuti to be a misunderstanding of the ideology that the poet actually advocated for. He argues that there were traces of 'heresy' in Lāhuti's earlier poetry, suggesting a move from mysticism to atheism which set the stage for his superficial interpretation of communism.[34] However, there appears to be a parallel between Lāhuti's counter-sublime approach, the inclination to challenge the long-standing conventions of classical poetry, and the introduction of fresh subject matter in Persian poetry of the early twentieth century.[35]

The initial stage of this counter-sublime movement primarily involved thematic changes within the framework of classical aesthetics. In this sense, Lāhuti replaced conventional themes in his poetry with modern subject matter, while maintaining a traditional form. As Lāhuti states in his autobiography, this transition was inspired by listening to 'the speeches of the liberals, especially Malek al-Motekallemin', and encountering the social reality of his age. He continues that he composed his first sociopolitically engaged poems in about 1909 and recited them to some of the literary men of Kermanshah.[36] Lāhuti names these works as 'labour poetry'; this was a common term in constitutional and post-constitutional poetic discourse referring to politically committed poems centred on working-class issues. Sorour Soroudi states that the first of these labour poems was probably *Ey Ranjbar-e Siyāh-Tāle'* (O Black-fortuned Labourer, November 1909).[37]

---

[34] Mohammad-Rezā Shafi'i Kadkani, *Bā Cherāgh va Āyeneh: dar Jostoju-ye Risheh-ye Tahavolāt-e She'r-e Mo'āser-e Fārsi* (Tehran: Sokhan, 2011), p. 420.
[35] Karimi-Hakkak, *Recasting Persian Poetry*, p. 191.
[36] Sorour Soroudi, 'Poet and Revolution: The Impact of Iran's Constitutional Revolution on the Social and Literary Outlook of the Poets of the Time: Part I', *Iranian Studies*, 1/2 (1979), 3–41 (p. 245).
[37] Soroudi, p. 246.

ای رنجبر سیاه طالع
بیچاره پا برهنه زارع
ای رنجبر ستم کشیده
جز زهر ز دهر ناچشیده
ای آنکه جهان زندگانی
بی تو همه صورت و تو جانی[38]

O unfortunate toiler
Poor barefoot peasant
O suppressed toiler
You haven't tasted anything but poison in this universe
O you are such a person that the world of life without you
is entirely a corpus and you are its soul

The theme and the language of this poem are aligned with the colloquial poems of the constitutional era. The poem is composed in the *masnavi* template, which is a traditional template with independently rhyming verses following the aa/bb/cc rhyme scheme. The prosodic metre employed by Lāhuti in his poetry is *hazaj-e mosaddas-e akhrab-e maqbuz-e mahzuf* (--ᴗ/ᴗ-ᴗ-/ᴗ--), which is inspired by *Leyli va Majnun*, a renowned Persian narrative *masnavi* written by Nezāmi Ganjavi (1141–1209). Lāhuti also composed some labour poems in other traditional forms and styles such as *ghazal* and *robā'i*. At the same time, he aimed to carry forward the accomplishments of constitutional poetry, such as simplicity of expressive devices and relatively more realistic imagery:

دهقان خوراک و فعله جهان را بپا کند
بیجا گمان مبر تو که این را خدا کند
بی شک و شبهه نیست خدائی، اگرکه هست
مظلوم را مسخر ظالم چرا کند؟
الله و شاه آلت صنف ستمگرند
زاهد ربا پرستد و کار ریا کند.[39]

Peasants provide the world with food and labor
Do not believe in vain that these are God's doing.
Doubtless there is no God; if there is,
Why does he turn the oppressed into the hands of the oppressors?

---

[38] Muhammad Abbāsi, ed., *Divān-e Ash'ār-e Abolqāsem Lāhuti* (Tabriz: Helāl-e Nāseri, 1941), p. 1.
[39] Abbāsi, pp. 38–9.

Allāh and the Shah are playthings in the hands of the tyrant
And the devout worships usury and on hypocrisy feeds.[40]

Regarding the template, this is a part of a *ghazal* in the metre *mozāre' mosamman-e akhrab-e makfuf-e mahzuf* (--ᴗ/-ᴗ-ᴗ/ᴗ--ᴗ/-ᴗ-), which is a commonly used prosodic metre in this poetic form.[41] On the other hand, in comparison to the previous example, the content has taken on a more radical tone in its critique of the sublime aspects of traditional culture. In this poem, Lāhuti portrays the reality of his society where the subordinates struggle with enormous financial problems while the upper class, including officials and clergy, live a prosperous life. While critique of the clergy is not a new theme in Persian poetry, Lāhuti distinguishes himself from many of his contemporaries by exhibiting pronounced anti-religious inclinations in his poetry. He explicitly states that religion is a means of suppression used by the upper class against the masses to take advantage of the fruits of their labour.

Although Lāhuti's poetry in this phase does not show any interest in formal changes in traditional orders, one can see the counter-sublime approach in subject matter as a path towards a revolution in the figurative dimensions of poetry. According to Karimi-Hakkak, the importance of such conversion of subject matter lies in the fact that confronting and confirming traditional forms at the same time disturbs and disconnects the existing relations between form and content. In this sense, the poet breaks 'the stylized conventions' of solidified and sacred subject matter confined in specific traditional templates, and pushes 'the system of poetic signification further toward new conventions'.[42] Abandoning classical subject matter is, in turn, the start of a generic corrective movement towards the conventional aesthetic system, which can be followed by more radical changes in classical poetics.

Kāveh Bayāt suggests that Lāhuti's oeuvre, after his transition from mystical to politically engaged poetry, can be divided into at least two parts: before and after his emigration to the Soviet Union. In the first of these two phases, which spans from the final years of the First World War until his coup d'état in Tabriz in 1922, he shows strong nationalist and socialist tendencies in his poems. This part of his poetry, as discussed, is mostly in line with the formal characteristics of constitutional poetry. In his later phase, however, he portrays himself as a genuine advocate of communism, and the Soviet Union as a utopia for all revolutionaries. His poetry in this period can be distinguished by his experiments with the figurative dimensions of socialist realist poetry. Stephanie Cronin sees Lāhuti's transformation from

---

[40] Translation is taken from Soroudi, p. 246.
[41] This metre is the third most widely used prosodic metre in Hāfez's *divān*.
[42] Karimi-Hakkak, *Recasting Persian Poetry*, p. 201.

a 'militant populist Nationalist' to a 'committed communist' as a common trajectory witnessed among many intellectuals in Iran who were influenced by the turbulent events of the Constitutional Revolution and the First World War. She contends that this leftward shift is shared by 'the Democrat wing' of the constitutional movement.[43] One could argue that Lāhutī's ideological transition and the political commitment of his poetry in both of these periods are key to the politics of his corrective approach to the traditional aesthetic system and the regime of expression.[44]

Lāhutī is a prototype of a sociopolitical committed poet in the modern sense of the term. Dabashi defines the concept of commitment (ta'ahhod) in modern Persian poetry as 'a preconceived notion of responsibility to supraliterary concerns'. He states that the committed poet intends to 'convey an idea, propagate an ideology, convert an audience, defend a cause, or mobilize a mass' through his poetry.[45] Lāhutī, in the first phase of his oeuvre, attempted to convert the traditional clichés and motifs of Persian poetry to nationalist subject matter. In the second phase, he tried to create a direct conversation with his audience in order to convey the message of communist ideology. In so doing, he not only simplified the system of expression and imagery, as colloquial poetry did, but also incorporated elements of his ideology to educate his intended audience. For instance, in the following poem, he writes:

من دشمن شاه و شحنه و خان هستم
من منکر اهریمن و یزدان هستم
هرگز نخورم فریب روبه صفتان
من شیر پرولتار ایران هستم[46]

I am the enemy of the Shahs, the sheriffs and the feudal lords
I deny *Ahrīman* (the devil) and *Yazdān* (the god)
I will never be deceived by vulpine people
I am the lion of the proletariat.

In these *robā'i*, the poet denounces two principal sublime classes of his society: the authority and the clergy. He also portrays himself as a revolutionary who fights against both the political and religious dominant ideologies. Calling himself 'a lion of the proletariat', Lāhutī also establishes the concept of the proletariat for his readers. He utilizes the rousing energy of poetry to incite people against the dominant power and to educate them

---

[43] Stephanie Cronin, *Soldiers, Shahs and Subalterns in Iran: Opposition, Protest and Revolt, 1921–1941* (New York: Palgrave Macmillan, 2010), p. 101.
[44] Kāveh Bayāt, *Koudeta-ye Lāhutī* (Tehran: Shirazeh, 1997), p. 8.
[45] Dabashi, p. 150.
[46] Abbāsi, p. xi.

through the terminology of Marxism. Cronin states that while in the Soviet Union, Lāhuti acquainted himself 'systematically with the ideas of socialism'. Since then, his poetry reflected what he thought was the 'radical economic and social transformation of Soviet society'. The inspiration from Soviet communism was so significant in his poetry that he earned the soubriquet '*Adib-e Sorkh*' ('Red Writer').[47] In his poem *Ma Zafar Khāhim Kard* (We Will Succeed, 1930), Lāhuti goes even further and suggests that the only means of emancipation from the tyrannical Iranian regime is to establish a communist system and align with the will of Soviet Union leaders:

الصلا ای توده زحمت کش روی زمین
صاحبان پینه دست و عرق‌های جبین
ای رفیقان ستالین، ای محبان لنین!
شد به ضد ما مسلح قوه قانون و دین
این جهان میدان جنگ رنج و استثمار شد،
داس و چکش روبرو با مسجد و دربار شد.
ما اصول سوسیالیستی مهیا میکنیم
عالم بی صنف و استثمار بر پا میکنیم
خواجگی را جمله کالیکتیو و یکجا میکنیم
چون وصایای لنین را خوب اجرا میکنیم
پیشرفت ما به چشم بورژوازی خار شد،
مرگ خود با دیده خود دید و چون سگ هار شد[48]

Greetings! O you toilers of all lands!
You with sweat on brows, with swollen hands!
O friends of Stalin! Comrades of Lenin!
Armed against us have law and religion been.
This world is a battlefield; against agony and slavery we clamour.
The court and the mosque are face to face with sickle and hammer.
The principle of socialism we shall finally establish
A classless world slavery we shall abolish
All mastership we shall make collective
Since we shall practice Lenin's directives.[49]
Our progress became a thorn in the eyes of the bourgeoisie,
They saw with their own eyes the coming of their death and got angry like a rabid dog.[50]

---

[47] Cronin, p. 126.
[48] Abbāsi, p. 118.
[49] Dabashi, p. 173.
[50] The first verse of the semi-final stanza can be translated as: We strive to lay the foundations of socialism / creating a world free from classes, a prism. In addition, the translation of the last verse is mine.

These two stanzas are a part of a long *tarkib-band*,[51] which consists of thirty-five stanzas. The poem does not deviate from the conventional rules of a traditional *tarkib-band*. In terms of metre, also, the whole poem is composed in one of the most popular prosodic metres called *ramal-e mosamman-e mahzuf* (-ᴗ--/-ᴗ--/-ᴗ--/-ᴗ-). However, the propagandistic subject matter and the language of the poem, which is charged with many political terms, distinguish it from a classical *tarkib-band*.

One can argue that this poem serves as a clear manifestation of Lāhuti's inclination towards Soviet socialist realism, which was the official literary method and theory of Soviet literature.[52] Katerina Clark examines the primary theoretical sources of socialist realism and identifies specific features that a socialist realist literary text should contain or abandon. She argues that each literary work created in the system of Soviet realism had to use proper, puritanical and straightforward language and sound, orderly structure 'in accordance with the de facto master-plot'. Through these features one could create a literary work which was both party-minded and true to social reality.[53]

The previous example, like Lāhuti's other labour poems, shows the passion of the poet to educate, inform, and talk directly to the proletariat, whom he considered as his foremost readers. He uses a puritanical and straightforward language to make the poem more informative and communicative. Moreover, acknowledging and addressing the masses and toilers directly in the first and the third hemistich devises intimacy between the poet and his audience. Lāhuti develops this socialist-realist feature more vividly in his narrative works, especially in his characterizations. Indeed, instead of using imaginary characters, he creates exemplars inspired by the life of real revolutionary martyrs and ordinary people. Then, he builds a narrative based on these exemplars' class-life.[54] For instance, the poem *Be Shālla'i va Fiurest* (To Shālla'i and Fiurest, 1932) is an elegy for two

---

[51] 'Tarkib-band consists of a number of stanzas built up by couplets, but in this form each stanza is followed by a different couplet.' Gabrielle van den Berg, 'Stanzaic poetry', in *Encyclopaedia Iranica*, https://iranicaonline.org/articles/stanzaic-poetry [accessed on 5 May 2019] (para. 2 of 52).

[52] This literary school was formed 'after a decree as promulgated in April 1932', based on which all independent literary organizations were to be disbanded and merged into the Union of Soviet Writers. However, soon after Stalin's death in 1953, young writers broke the hegemony of social realism and experimented with new literary styles. See Katerina Clark, 'Socialist Realism in Soviet Literature', in *From Symbolism to Socialist Realism: A Reader* (Boston: Academic Studies Press, 2012), pp. 419–20.

[53] Clark, p. 431.

[54] Evgeny E. Berthels, in his introduction to a selection of Lāhuti's poems titled *Hezār Mesra'* (One Thousand Lines), identifies such features in Lāhuti's poetry as the result of the poet's Marxist education (*tahsilāt-e mārksisti*) gained over the years. Abolqāsem Lāhuti, *Hezār Mesra'* (Moscow: Nashriyāt-e Kargarān Khāreji dar Ettehād-e Showravi, 1935), p. 9.

Hungarian revolutionaries executed by the dictatorial state. Similarly, in the poem *Yatimān-e Jang-e Jahāngir* (Orphans of the World War, 1931) Lāhuti draws inspiration from his observations of the devastating impact of the Nazi invasion on children in the Soviet Union during the Second World War.

In the following example, the poet has avoided the language of the upper class which might not be accessible to the lowbrow crowd. According to Clark, socialist-realism aimed to 'avoid all approaches and language that might not be accessible to the masses'.[55] Therefore, Lāhuti attempted to compose his poems in a language which did not require any specialized knowledge of classical literature in order to be understood. Furthermore, one can interpret Lāhuti's utilization of a counter-sublime and anti-elitist language as a deliberate attempt to break away from the hierarchical regime of literary language. The semi-colloquial language, driven into the poem by political factors, in turn generates a democratic form within the poem in which all kinds of words from different origins can stand beside each other and expand the ranges of words used in poetry:

شیر گرمی که در آن قوطی کنسرو سیاه
به من آن روز خوراندید و تبسم کردید،
وقت تحریر همین قصه به یاد آمدم ... آه،
پیش چشمم همه تان باز تجسم کردید.
گویی اکنون بوَد آن حادثۀ آن روزی
که یکیتان به چه سختی و تعب جان می داد،
دیگری، بر سر بالین وی، از دلسوزی،
بی ثمر، لیک صمیمانه به او نان می داد.
خاطرم هست که با پارچه ای از شیشه
میتراشید گریگور، سر محی الدین را.
من از این عشق مقدس به چنین اندیشه
که پدرهای شما کاش ببینند این را[56]

That warm milk in the black can
which you fed me while smiling,
I remembered when I was writing this story ... Oh,
I see you all standing before me,
As if that day's events are unfolding anew,
when one of you was dying in severe pain and distress.
Another one, on his bed, out of compassion,
futilely, yet warm-heartedly fed him with bread.
I remember with a piece of glass
Gregory was shaving Mohi al-Din's head.

---

[55] Clark, p. 419.
[56] Abbāsi, p. 144.

I thought, affected by the sacred love,
May your fathers see this!

In addition to the straightforward semi-colloquial language of the poem, Lāhuti's realistic imagery and less complicated expressive devices, in comparison to classical poetry, form the other aspects of his socialist-realist style. The poem consciously avoids the subjective figurative devices of classical poetry, particularly metaphors, in order to maintain its connections to social reality. In doing so, the poem benefits from a direct system of signification in which all words signify a tangible object, person, or situation in the real world. For instance, elements such as '*shir-e garm*' (warm milk), '*quti-e konserv*' (can), and '*shishe*' (glass) neither function as metaphors nor represent other abstract concepts in some other ways. Moreover, images such as children feeding their dying friend and shaving each other's head should be seen as the poet's presentation of his surrounding world through the direct treatment of the objects. Indeed, this poem, and most of Lāhuti's socialist-realist poems, can be described as collections of interrelated direct images which are bound by social reality.

Some scholars tend to root the realistic system of expression and imagery in Lāhuti's poetry in the works of his precursors. Āriānpur states that the conception of realism in Lāhuti's works was built upon Ashraf Gilāni's translations of Mirzā Ali Akbar Sāber's (1862–1911) critical poems from Azeri Turkish. He also refers to Lāhuti's letter on 17 June 1954 to the author of Sāber's biography, in which the poet describes his role model's works as 'popular' (*khalqi*), 'simple and straightforward' (*sadeh va ravān*), and at the service of 'emancipating toilers'.[57] This letter suggests that Lāhuti was aware of the realistic qualities present in Sāber's poetry and indicates that he may have been receptive to the influence of Sāber's work during his initial phase as a poet. However, despite Lāhuti's initial exploration of a realistic system of expression and imagery in the early stages of his career, his exposure to socialist realism during his time in the Soviet Union profoundly influenced his artistic approach. Lāhuti incorporated and theorized the figurative techniques and achievements of socialist realism to effectively convey the ideological messages of communism as a committed Persian poet. Highlighting the priority of the message over formal aspects of a text in socialist realism, Greg Carleton states:

> Subordinating concerns for genre to the reification of topoi ensures that the constitution of textual function occurs at an antecedent and higher axis than genre per se. [...] This system's reversal of meaning production,

---

[57] Āriānpur, 2, pp. 169–70.

however, does not eliminate the value of generic distinction. Rather, it assumes a different role: the formal properties of a given genre (the imagery, language, characters, plot and so forth that are specific to novel, story, poetry, etc.) function more as auxiliary factors conditioning the accessibility and comprehension of the text.[58]

In other words, Lāhuti's experimentation with semi-colloquial literary language, a realistic system of expression, and direct imagery (mostly in his post-emigration poetry) were to make his text more accessible to its target audience. However, despite what Carleton says about socialist realism, the aesthetic changes in Lāhuti's poetry are not merely the effects of his ideological inclinations. Constant changes to figurative aspects of Lāhuti's poems demonstrate that he discerns change as the politics of his poetry, the path he has taken to correct the hierarchical regime of classical literature. Lāhuti fights for the emancipation of Persian poetry on two fronts: first, on the battlefield of content, by replacing democratic subject matters with authoritarian ones, and second, in the realm of aesthetics, by demolishing the solidified and autocratic order of classical poetics.

The most perceivable dimension of Lāhuti's aesthetic revolution is his experiential approach to modifying the conception of the rhythmic system. Most scholars refer to *Sangar-e Khunin* (The Blood-Covered Trench, 1923) and its unconventional rhythm and rhyme arrangement to give precedence to Lāhuti over Nimā in terms of refashioning traditional poetic forms. This poem is indeed one of the most successful attempts (before the rise of *Nimāic* poetry) to free Persian poetry from the traditional prosodic system, through the creation of uneven lines in terms of the number of prosodic feet in each hemistich. However, as this poem is an adaptation of a poem by Victor Hugo,[59] most scholars assert that Lāhuti's experiments in poetic form should be examined in the context of modern French and Russian poetics. Prejudices about the European origin of this poem overshadowed all of Lāhuti's experiments in prosody, even those with other alternative rhythmic systems, such as syllabic verse. For instance, Mehdi Akhavān Sāles refuses to discuss Lāhuti's experiments with syllabic verse because he sees them as fruitless imitations of French and Russian poetry.[60] Similarly, Shafi'i Kadkani attributes Lāhuti's use of syllabic verses to his excessive engagement with Russian poetry.[61]

In one of his more notable experiments with conventional poetic forms, Lāhuti replaces the traditional system of prosodic metres (*aruz*) with syllabic

---

[58] Greg Carleton, 'Genre in Socialist Realism', *Slavic Review*, 4 (1994), 992–1009 (p. 1004).
[59] Abbāsi, p. 54.
[60] Mehdi Akhavān Sāles, *Bed'at-hā va Badāye'-e Nimā* (Tehran: Zemestān, 1997), p. 161.
[61] Shafi'i Kadkani, *Bā Cherāgh va Āyene*, p. 425.

verse.⁶² Finding an origin for this syllabic verse has provoked much debate among scholars of modern Persian literature. Most scholars, as discussed, tend to link Lāhuti's experimentation with syllabic metres to French and Russian poetry, while others root these experiments in marginalized forms of poetry in Persian and other Iranian languages. Parviz Nātel Khānlari represents the first group of critics, who argue that Lāhuti's syllabic verses were merely blind imitations of Russian poems. He explains that Persian word stresses are not as apparent as those of most European languages, and therefore, syllables cannot serve as the foundation for a rhythmic system in Persian poetry.⁶³ However, Nasrin Ali-Akbari and Ali-Nazar Nazari argue that Lāhuti's syllabic verses might be rooted in some little-studied poetic traditions in traditional Kurdish poetry. Studying twenty-eight syllabic poems by Lāhuti, they illustrate the similarities between the number, quality, and arrangement of syllables in these poems and in some of the most popular Kurdish syllabic metres. In thirteen poems, Lāhuti has created ten-, eight-, or seven-syllable verses comparable to the rhythm of two ten-syllable poems that he composed in Kurdish (probably before his emigration to the Soviet Union in 1922).⁶⁴ The following example is a *masnavi* in a ten-syllable metre.⁶⁵ This type of syllabic verse is also similar to decasyllabic couplets, or heroic couplets, which are defined as ten-syllable, 'iambic pentameter lines rhyming in pairs':⁶⁶

لاله‌ها، از اول سیه بودند / یک لاله نو، ناگه زد لبخند
در صحرای لولی ها آنقدر / لطیف بود و خوشبوی و خوش منظر

---

⁶² The first attempts at composing syllabic verse in this period appeared in the works of Yahyā Dowlatābādi (1869–1939), who composed a few syllabic poems in response to Edward Browne's question about the possibility of composing a Persian poem without using the Arabic prosody. Dowlatābādi composed *Sobhdam* (Dawn) and *Sabk-e Tāzeh* (New Style) in about 1911. In the first poem, each stanza consists of a ten-syllable tercet and an eight-syllable couplet. The second poem consists of four sestets with internal rhyme in each line. Dowlatābādi later gathered together his experiential works, along with some translations from French poetry, in a collection of poems entitled *Ordibehest* in 1925. See Bozorg Alavi, *Tārikh-e Tahavol-e Adabiyāt-e Jadid-e Irān* (Tehran: Negāh, 2007), pp. 185–6; Mohammad Shams Langrudi, *Tārikh-e Tahlili-e She'r-e Now*, 4 vols (Tehran: Markaz, 1998), 1, p. 612.
⁶³ Parviz Nātel Khānlari, 'Dar Vazn-e She'r-e Fārsi', in *Dowreh-ye Majaleh Sokhan* (Tehran: Sokhan, 1954), pp. 859–60.
⁶⁴ See Nasrin Ali Akbari, and Ali Nazar Nazari, 'Barresi-e Janbe-ha-ye Nowgarā'i dar Vazn-e She'r-e Abolqāsem Lāhuti va Mansha'-e Ān', *Fonun-e Adabi*, 4 (2016), 143–56. One of these poems is in the third volume of *Hādiqeh-ye Sultāni* in the format of a friendly letter, and the other one is a poem about the Fatherland, addressing Iranian Kurds.
⁶⁵ Syllabic couplets are one of the most popular metres in traditional Kurdish poetry. This is the rhythm of the long couplet poem called *Konz al-Erfān* by Lāhuti's spiritual guide, Sayyed Sāleh Heyrān Ali Shāh. In addition, *Saranjām*, the holy book of the *Ahl-e Haq* or the *Yāri* sect, is a collection of Kurdish poems composed in ten- and eight-syllable metres.
⁶⁶ Meyer Howard Abrams and G. Harpham Geoffrey, *A Glossary of Literary Terms* (Boston & Mass: Thomson Wadsworth, 1999), p. 341.

که دیگران، از خجلت پیش او / یکسره داغدل شدند و سرخ رو
لاله سیاه از آن وقت، یکتاست / لاله سیاه، تاج لاله هاست[67]

The tulips were black from the beginning / A fresh tulip smiled suddenly
In the desert of bohemians / she was so delicate, fragrant and lovely that she humiliated them by her charm / so with their hearts branded, their faces turned red.
Since then, the black tulip is inimitable / the black tulip is the crown of tulips.

The Kurdish syllabic system is solely based on the number of syllables in each hemistich. However, in the *aruzi* system, syllables must correspond in terms of length with their parallel syllables in all hemistichs of the poem. For instance, if the first syllable of the first hemistich is long, there is a corresponding restriction on the first syllable of the second hemistich. It cannot be a short or overlong syllable, ensuring a consistent rhythmic pattern between the two hemistichs. In the previous example, on the other hand, the second line starts with '*dar*', which is a long syllable (-), while the parallel hemistich starts with the short syllable '*la*' (ᴗ). The second syllable of the same line is a long one (*sah*: -), which has been paired with an overlong one (*tif*: ᴗ-). The less restrictive rules of the syllabic metre in terms of pairing uneven syllables allow the poet to use a broader range of words in the text. In so far as the number of syllables in each hemistich matches the quantitative limitation of the metre, any word, regardless of the length of its syllables, can be used. This feature expands the lexicon of the poetry in a way which broadens the potential sources of the poet's word choice:

- انبار ما را تو سوزاندی؟
- من.
- کی این را به تو فرمان داد؟
- میهن
فاشیست از غضب لب را میجود
دل دوشیزه شادان میشود
- تو تلفن را بریدی؟
- آری.
- آفرین، راستی و رستگاری!
- جای پارتیزانها؟
- نمیگویم.
- تازیانه
- حالا؟
- نمیگویم

---

[67] Ahmad Bashiri, ed., *Divān-e Lāhuti* (Tehran: Amir Kabir, 1979), p. 158.

- برهنه روی برف دوانیدش
اگر بیفتد بکشانیدش[68]

- Was it you who burned our armoury?
- I.
- Who ordered you to do this?
- Homeland.
The fascist bites his lips out of anger,
the young lady's heart exults.
- Did you cut the phone cable?
- Yes.
- Bravo! You are honest and blessed!
- The location of the partisans?
- I will not speak.
- (Whipping)
- Now?
- I will not speak.
- Make her run naked on the snow.
If she falls, drag her.

The relatively liberal system of rhythmic expression in this poem allows the poet to use some non-literary and even non-Persian words such as *'telefon'* (phone), *'pārtizān'* (partisan), and *'fāshist'* (fascist). However, in contrast to the previous experiences of adopting non-literary words in traditional contexts, the new lexicon in this poem does not sound out of place and forms a natural interrelation with other elements of the poem. Indeed, political terms in this poem are in line with the informative and educative nature of socialist-realist poetry. Other words relating to technology are also from the everyday language of the masses and correspond with Lāhuti's desire to achieve a counter-sublime and straightforward language. In terms of rhythm, none of the words require an alteration to their pronunciation in order to fit the metre. For instance, due to the more relaxed rules of syllabic verse with regard to the length of corresponding syllables, the word *'fāshist'*, which is scanned (∪--), can be paralleled with *'del-e'*, consisting of two short syllables (∪∪). That is, if one desires to equalize these two hemistichs, based on the *aruzi* metres, one should shorten the long vowel *Ā* (in *fashist*) to a short vowel and also shorten the extended syllable *'ist'* to *'i'* or *'es'*. In other words, to arrange the metre based on prosodic rules, the reader needs to pronounce the word *'fāshist'* as *'fashi'* or *'fāshes'*.

Additionally, the rhyming words at the end of every ten syllables show that the poem was, in fact, composed following a conventional ten-syllable

---

[68] Bashiri, pp. 402–3.

metre. However, to separate the different sides of the dialogue and the voice of the narrator, and to reflect the visual pattern of the drama, verses are broken into uneven lines. Shortening the lines towards the end of the stanza also accelerates the rhythm of the poem and consequently reflects the tension of the scene. Indeed, in such a rhythmic system the poet is not obliged to confine the speech of different personas within a pre-determined length of hemistich and fixed rhyme patterns. The idea of creating verses with unequal length and freer rhyme patterns in order to achieve a natural tone of speech, which will be discussed in the following paragraphs, was one of the primary goals of all *Tajaddod* poets in the process of poetic revolution.

Remodelling the poetic forms: Prosodic metres and rhyme schemes

Shams Kasmā'i is another poet associated with the *Tajaddod* group whose politics of literature was to change the existing undemocratic and monotonous poetic genres through revolutionizing traditional rhythmic systems and rhyme arrangements.[69] Examining her poetry reveals that she had two distinctive periods in her career. Like Lāhuti, in her first phase she introduced new sociopolitical subjects in standard poetic templates. However, in her second phase, she experimented with synchronizing content and template, incorporating novel poetic forms, rhyme patterns, and rhythmic systems.

In the poem *Mā dar in Panj Ruz Nobat-e Khish* (In the Five Days of Our Turn, 1920), Kasmā'i demonstrates a pronounced inclination towards aligning the arrangement of rhymes and stanza length with the demands of speech. By disregarding the formal constraints of classical rhyme schemes and poetic templates, she develops poetic forms that are rooted in the natural rhythm of spoken language. In this particular poem, Kasmā'i departs from

---

[69] Shams (Shams-e Jahan) Kasmā'i (1883–1961) relocated to Azerbaijan and then to Turkmenistan in 1918 because of her husband's job. There she started corresponding with periodicals outside and within Iran. Shams's son, Akbar Arbabzadeh, who was a dissident painter and poet, joined the Jungle Movement and fought alongside Haydar Khān Amo-oghli's (1880–1921) troops in Rasht, where he was killed in about 1920. Lāhuti composed an elegy, *Omr-e Gol* (Life of the Rose, 1921), about the death of the young man, using an innovative template with a syllabic metre. After the suppression of Khiyābāni's revolutionary movement, Raf'at's suicide, and Lāhuti's escape to the Soviet Union, Shams lived in Tabriz, Yazd, and Tehran until she died in 1961 and was buried in Qom. Kasmā'i was the first Iranian woman to be involved in changing the practice of poetry in Iran. However, her collection of poems was lost after her death, and there is no access to her whole oeuvre. See Kāmyār Ābedi, *Be Raghm-e Panjereh-hā-ye Basteh: She'r-e Mo'āser-e Zanān* (Tehran: Nāder, 2001), pp. 18–19; also see Rahim Ra'isniyā, 'Shams Kasmā'i', *Chistā*, 246–247 (2008), 450–8.

the monorhyme systems prevalent in classical poetry, opting instead for a more liberated form that allows for the use of multiple rhyme schemes within a single composition:

ما در این پنج روز نوبت خویش
چه بسا کشتزارها دیدیم
نیکبختانه خوشه‌ها چیدیم
که ز جان کاشتند مردم پیش.
زارعین گذشته ما بودیم
باز ما راست کشت آینده
گاه گیرنده گاه بخشنده
گاه مظلم گهی درخشنده
گرچه جمعیم و گر پراکنده
در طبیعت که هست پاینده
گر دمی محو، باز موجودیم.⁷⁰

In the five days of our turn
We saw so many fields
Luckily we picked many ears of wheat
Which past people had planted.
We were the past farmers
And we must plant for the future
Sometimes receiver and sometimes giver
Sometimes darkened and sometimes illuminating.
If together or scattered
In nature which is lasting
We will exist even if we disappear.

While the rhyme pattern in this poem, abba-bcccccb, may draw inspiration from French and Russian rhyme patterns, it does not precisely mirror any specific poetic forms found in European poetry. This poem consists of a quatrain with the rhyme scheme abba and of an irregular septet with the rhyme scheme bcccccb. This irregular pattern is similar to that of another poem entitled *Medāl-e Eftekhār* (The Medallion of Honour, 1920), in which the poet creates a template consisting of a quatrain with the rhyme scheme abba and two tercets with the pattern ccb. Metrically, however, the poem is still loyal to the fundamentals of traditional prosody, and the deviation is limited to the rhyme arrangements. *Mā dar in Panj Ruz Nobat-e Khish* is composed in the metre *khafif-e makhbun-e maqtuʿ* (-ᴗ--/-ᴗ-/--) and *Medal-e Eftekhār* is scanned *mozāreʿ mosamman-e akhrab-e makfuf-e mahzuf* (--ᴗ/-ᴗ-/ᴗ--/-ᴗ-).

---

⁷⁰Ārianpur, 2, p. 456.

In another poem called *Parvaresh-e Tabi'at* (The Nurture of Nature, 1920), published a few months after the previous two, Kasmā'i sought a freer rhyme scheme, resulting in an experiment with an innovative rhythmic system and a more colourful rhyme arrangement in a poem with uneven lines. In this poem, the poet employs as many prosodic units in each hemistich as necessary to accommodate the natural flow of speech. In this sense, *Parvaresh-e Tabi'at* is comparable to Lāhuti's experimentation in *Sangar-e Khunin*:

ز بسیاری آتش مهر و ناز و نوازش
از این شدت گرمی و روشنایی و تابش
گلستان فکرم
خراب و پریشان شد افسوس
چو گل‌های افسرده افکار بکرم
صفا و طراوت ز کف داده مأیوس ...
یکی، پای بر دامن و سر به زانو نشستم
که چون نیم وحشی گرفتار یک سرزمینم
نه یارای خیرم
نه نیروی شرم
نه نیرو نه تیغم بوَد، نیست دندان تیزم
نه پای گریزم
از این روی در دست هم جنس خود در فشارم
ز دنیا و از سلک دنیا پرستان کنارم
بر آنم که از دامن مهربان سر برآرم[71]

Due to the fire of love and caressing
From the intensity of passion and light and radiation
The glory of my thought
Was, alas, ruined and wasted
My novel thoughts, like withered flowers
Lost their clarity and sparkle, and with disappointment
Alone, I sat, hugging my legs, my head on my knees
Just like a half-wild creature, I'm captive in a land
Not able to do something good
No power to do evil
I don't have the strength or sword, nor do I have any sharp teeth
Nor the ability to run away
That is why, I am here oppressed by my peers/species
I am detached from the world and the world-worshipping people
I am willing to emerge in the lap of the compassionate one.

---

[71] Ārianpur, 2, pp. 457–8.

The rhythmic system of the poem is based on a conventional *monfared* (single) metre consisting of the sequence of the foot *fa'ulon* (◡--). However, in contrast with the classical prosodic system, the number of feet in the hemistichs is not equal: the poet has crafted lines with varying numbers of feet to suit the requirements of each hemistich. The shortest line of this poem consists of two feet, while the longest is made of six feet. In terms of rhyme patterns, *Parvaresh-e Tabi'at* consists of a sestet with the rhyme scheme aabcbc and an irregular nine-line stanza with the rhyme pattern ddeeffggg. Although Kasmā'i knew Russian and Turkish,[72] her poetic forms were not merely adaptations of European templates. Indeed, she was emancipating her poetry from the old formal regimes of Persian poetry by means of an inspiring dialogue with what Raf'at called in *Tajaddod's* manifesto 'the international doctrine of art'. Thus, like her most successful successor Nimā Yushij, she created new rhythmic systems and rhyme patterns based on the fundamentals of classical prosody and rhyming rules.

In this sense, Kasmā'i shows a kind of ambiguity in the politics of her poetry. She creates anti-traditional poems with unprecedented poetic forms but places her work as an extension and completion of traditional poetic practices. Kasmā'i's ambivalent revisionary movement towards her precursors can be explained by the concept of '*tessera*', the second of the Bloomian revisionary ratios. In this, the newcomer locates his/her work as both the completion and antithesis of the poetic father's work. Kasmā'i 'antithetically' changes some aspects of the conventional rhythmic system and rhyme arrangements, not to demolish the old orders but to 'complete' the traditional aesthetic regime of Persian poetry. Although she did not find a chance to propose an alternative poetic form, the irregular arrangement of rhymes and uneven prosodic lines in her poems, alongside Lāhuti's experiments in *Sangar-e Khunin*, are the most tangible example of the *Tajaddod* poets' break with classical poetry.

The poetic templates used by Kasmā'i in her works were not all improvised. Most of these patterns were indeed inspired by encountering rhyme patterns used in European poetry (particularly French and Russian). Karimi-Hakkak spots the first adaptations of Petrarchan and Shakespearean sonnets in poems composed by Raf'at and Khāmene'i.[73] Raf'at, in the *Tajaddod* manifesto, stresses the 'conformity' of the poetic style to the standards of the 'international doctrine of arts'.[74] Indeed, most of the constitutional and post-constitutional poets saw the formal properties of European poetry as an aspect of technical modernity such as the train or the telephone. Accordingly, *Tajaddod* poets defined their literary revolution as a

---

[72] Ārianpur, 2, p. 457.
[73] Karimi-Hakkak, *Recasting Persian Poetry*, pp. 201–5.
[74] Ārianpur, 2, p. 452.

movement which was corrective of the literary past and exposed indigenous forms to the intercultural world of poetic art.

In addition to subjective improvisations, modernists of this period embarked upon a process of indigenization and appropriation of the formal properties of 'the international arts', starting with the most common rhyme templates in French and Russian poetry at the time. Hoseyn Bakhshi argues that these poets modelled their innovative templates on three different types of rhyme schemes, namely alternate rhyme, enclosed rhyme, and chain rhyme. Alternate rhyme, also known as abab rhyme, has been used by most of the Iranian pioneer poets of the period. Although one may find rare examples of this pattern in classical poetry, Dehkhodā was probably the first modernist to use it in his famous poem *Yād Ār* (Remember, 1909). However, Dehkhodā's innovation was limited to substituting a new rhyme scheme for the minimally altered traditional template called *mosammat-e mosamman* (chained octave/octet stanza poem).[75] Although alternating pattern is regularly used in quatrains, Dehkhodā implemented this pattern in octets with an extra line as a refrain at the end of each stanza (ababababc). Bakhshi states that even traditionalists like Parvin E'tesāmi and other gradualists such as Mohammad Taqi Bahār, probably influenced by Dehkhodā, used alternate rhymes as well.[76]

One can also find other examples of this rhyme scheme in the works of radical constitutional modernists. For instance, Eshqi used the pattern abab in one of his little-studied pioneer poems entitled *Sargozasht-e Ta'asor Āvar-e Shā'er* (The Poet's Pitiful Destiny, 1919), which opens with:

در منتهی الیه خیابان بود پدید / تهران برون شهر خرابه یکی به پای
گسترده مه ز روزنه شاخه های بید / فرشی که تابد، ار که بلرزد همی هوای

It was visible at the end of the street; just outside Tehran, the wreckage of house still remaining.
The moon has spread a rug which is shining through willow branches when the air shivers.

In this poem, too, the alternate rhyme pattern does not appear in its standard quatrain form. Eshqi, in his short foreword to this poem, states that this twenty-six-line poem is, in fact, four stanzas of an incomplete *tarji'-band*.[77] This means that in each stanza he has lengthened the alternate pattern from

---

[75] A poem made of eight-line stanzas, in each of which the first seven lines rhyme and the eighth line rhymes with the eighth lines of the other stanzas.
[76] Hoseyn Bakhshi, 'Barresi-e Se Now'-e Jadid-e Qāfiyeh dar She'r-e Mashruteh', *Adabiyāt Pārsi Mo'āser*, 3 (2014), 1–14 (pp. 4–6).
[77] Ali Akbar Moshir Salimi, ed., *Kolliyāt-e Mosavvar-e Eshqi* (Tehran: Amir Kabir, 1971), p. 316.

the standard form of the quatrain to irregular, overlong patterns. This, too, forms a new variation of the old poetic form of *tarji'-band*, as using the alternate rhyme scheme in a traditional form of this template is, if not unprecedented, very rare. In addition to improvisations in this pattern, one may consider the standard pattern of the alternate rhyme as the most prevalent non-Persian rhyme scheme used by modernists in this era. Almost all *Tajaddod* poets, and even other post-constitutional poets such as Nimā Yushij, composed poems using the quatrain form of this template.

The enclosed rhyme is another distinctive European pattern that one may identify in some of the *Tajaddod* poets' works. In this rhyme scheme, the first and fourth lines and the second and third lines of the quatrain rhyme (abba). Enclosed rhyme quatrains are widely used in early experiments by *Tajaddod* poets with the forms of European sonnets. For example, the first two quatrains of the poem *Nowruz va Dehqān* (Nowruz and the Farmer, 1917) by Raf'at follow the standard enclosed pattern:

نوروز! روزگار تکان میدهد همی
بانوج بخت را شب و روز اندر آسمان؛
یک شب به ماه میرسد اقبال شایگان
روزی در آفتاب هویداست خرمی ...
امسال گفته بود، ندارم دگر غمی
دهقان نیکبین به حفیدان خود نهان
راهی گرفته پیش به دلخواه ما زمان
جبران ماجرا شود از بیش یا کمی
نوروز آمد تو ز اعماق ماورا؛
امید زنده شد، سر افکنده شد فرا؛
دهقان راد زد به کمر دامن قیام
نوروز چون شد اندر ارومی بنات جم
با حکم نینوایی شوریده قتل عام
دهقان آذری ز نو آلفته شد به غم[78]

Nowruz! Times swing fortune's cradle
night and day in the sky;
one night eternal prosperity reaches the moon,
one day sweet well-being is visible in the sun.
'I have sorrow no more', the hopeful farmer
had said to his heirs privately this year,
'times have taken a turn after our heart's desire
the past will be redressed, for less or more.'
Nowruz, you arrived from the depths of beyond,

---

[78] Ārianpur, 2, pp. 461–2.

hope was revived, downcast heads were lifted up,
the upright farmer prepared for an uprising.
Yet, Nowruz, when in Urmieh the daughters of Jam
were massacred on orders from rebellious Ninus
once more the Azeri farmer sank into sorrow.[79]

Nowruz va Dehqān is a Petrarchan sonnet which consists of two combined enclosed quatrains (an octet) with the rhyme scheme abba/abba, and two tercets (a sestet) with the pattern ccdede. Karimi-Hakkak suggests that this particular template corresponds to a popular French variation of the Petrarchan prototype. He further notes that the rhyme pattern in the second part of the poem, which includes an internal couplet in lines 11 and 13 instead of the final line, is more commonly found in English variations of the Italian sonnet.[80] Although this poem's template is based on distinctive European rhyme schemes, its metre is scanned as *mozāreʿ akhrab-e makfuf-e mahzuf* (--ᴗ/-ᴗ-ᴗ/ᴗ--ᴗ/-ᴗ-), which is a highly popular prosodic pattern in the classical Persian *ghazal*. Karimi-Hakkak also mentions an even older sonnet-like poem with enclosed rhyme schemes among the works of Jaʿfar Khāmeneʾi. In his poem *Be Qarn-e Bistom* (To the Twentieth Century, 1916), Khāmeneʾi uses the enclosed pattern exclusively throughout the whole work. This poem consists of five enclosed quatrains, which makes it more comparable to some stanzaic classical templates, particularly *mosammat*.[81]

Lāhuti too, inspired by the poetic form of the sonnet, improvised a more complicated form of enclosed rhyme in *Sangar-e Khunin*. He rhymes the first hemistich with the sixth, the second with the fifth, and the third with the fourth to create an irregular enclosed sestet with the pattern abccba:

اذنم بده به خانه روم تا کنم وداع
با مادر عزیز (به سلطان فوج گفت)؛
الساعه خواهم آمد
عجب حقه ای زدی!
محکوم کیستی اگر اصلاً نیامدی؟
خواهی ز چنگ ما بگریزی به حرف مفت؟
سلطان، نه! داد پاسخ او کودک شجاع[82]

Let me go home and say goodbye
to my mother (he said to the commander of the troop);

---

[79] Karimi-Hakkak, *Recasting Persian Poetry*, p. 206.
[80] Karimi-Hakkak, *Recasting Persian Poetry*, p. 206.
[81] Karimi-Hakkak criticizes Ārianpur for not identifying this poem as a European variation of a sonnet and categorizing the poem under the vague term of *qetʿeh* (fragment or piece). Karimi-Hakkak, *Recasting Persian Poetry*, p. 306.
[82] Abbāsi, p. 54.

I will come straight back
Nice trick!
Who will blame you if you do not come back at all?
Do you want to escape with absurd excuses?
'No commander!' answered the brave kid.

The poetic form proposed in this poem consists of both new rhyme patterns and innovative rhythmic system, which was later developed in the works of Nimā Yushij. The rhythm of the poem is based on the *morakkab* (combinatorial) prosodic metre *mozāreʿ mosamman-e akhrab-e makfuf-e mahzuf* (--ᴗ/-ᴗ-ᴗ/ᴗ--ᴗ/-ᴗ-). This metrical pattern, however, is broken into two or three shorter lines in some stanzas. For instance, a full metrical pattern is split into the third and the fourth line of this example, which are then scanned as (--ᴗ/-ᴗ-ᴗ) and (ᴗ--ᴗ/-ᴗ-), respectively. In fact, like Kasmā'i in *Mā dar in Panj Ruz-e Nobat-e Khish*, the poet has tried to harmonize the length of the line with the natural length of the speech. However, the major difference between Kasmā'i and Lāhuti's experiment is that Kasmā'i has used a *monfared* metrical pattern with repetitive feet, while Lāhuti's metrical pattern is *morakkab*. Thus, the metre of Kasmā'i's poem is naturally less restricted, in terms of lengthening and shortening the lines. Indeed, the prosodic foot *faʿulon* (ᴗ--) can be repeated as many times as the poet wishes, while Lāhuti is obligated to stick to the order and number of prosodic feet in the metrical pattern. Therefore, his intervention in the metre remains limited to breaking conventional metrical lines into shorter pieces. More importantly, Kasmā'i was willing to keep sound and distinguishable rhyme patterns in her poem, so every line in each stanza includes a rhyming word corresponding to the scheme. In contrast, Lāhuti places the rhyming words at the end of the lines in which the metrical pattern is completed. This strategy creates several unrhymed lines in the poem, which, in turn, make the rhyme scheme less recognizable.

The final non-traditional rhyme scheme which appeared for the first time in the works of post-constitutional poets, particularly *Tajaddod* poets, is the chain rhyme. This rhyming pattern is commonly used in the poetic form *terza rima*, which is formed by a sequence of interlinked tercets. That is, 'the second line of each tercet provides the rhyme for the first and third lines of the next'.[83] This template was first formed by Dante's *Divine Comedy* (fourteenth century) and then became popular in other European

---

[83] Chris Baldick, *A Concise Dictionary of Literary Terms* (Oxford & New York: Clarendon Press & Oxford University Press, 1990), p. 257.

literature, mainly English.[84] In Persian poetry, although this pattern was not as prevalent as the last two, it was likewise significant to the new conception of stanzaic poetry in modern poetry. Bakhshi states that Lāhuti is one of the few poets who experimented with the chain rhyme scheme:

قصه ها از حیات حاتم طی
خوانده ام یا شنیده ام بسیار
همگی شاهد فتوت وی
ثروت حاتمی نداشت شمار
مال هم بی شمار می بخشود
به فقیران بی کس و بی کار[85]

I have heard or read so many stories
about Hātam al-Tāi's life,
all of them about his generosity.
Hātam's wealth was uncountable
and he donated a huge amount
to poor, alone and jobless people.

In this example, the middle hemistichs correlate all tercets of the poem and play a significant role in the creation of a unified poetic form. Similarly, in some traditional stanzaic templates the physical interrelation between segments functions in a way that can hold several relatively independent parts together as a whole. For instance, Jalāl al-Din Homā'i describes the stanzaic template *mosammat* as a 'poem or poems' consisting of several smaller segments with the same metrical value and different rhymes. His definition of *tarji'-band* and *tarkib-band* also neglects thematic unity and focuses on the connection of 'different pieces of poetry' (*chand qesmat ash'ār-e mokhtalef*) by the refrain.[86] That is to say, Homā'i, like many other traditionalists, conceived the concept of unity as coherent physical interrelation among lines of the work. Even though one may recognize minimal narratives advancing through different segments in lyrical poems,

---

[84] D. H. Abrams states that Sir Thomas Wyatt first introduced this poetic form in the early sixteenth century. However, because of the difficulty of finding rhymes in this pattern, compared to Italian, it was not a common form in English poetry. However, there are many famous English works composed in this template, such as Shelley's *Ode to the West Wind* (1820). This template was also used in closer dates to *Tajaddod* poets by T. S. Eliot (1888–1965). Abrams, and Geoffrey, p. 341.

[85] Bashiri, p. 478.

[86] Jalāl Al-din Homā'i, *Fonun-e Belāghat va Senā'āt-e Adabi* (Tehran: Tus, 1985), pp. 114–19.

organic unity as a thematic and narrative interrelation among all stanzas cannot be considered as inherent to classical poetry. One could argue that *Tajaddod* poets were to establish the concept of organic unity through their experiments with sonnet-like stanzaic poetry. These attempts later cultivated the idea of refashioning the whole regime of poetic forms by reviving stanzaic poetry and proposing stanza as the new poetic unit instead of *beyt* (verse).

Introducing new rhyme patterns which echoed French and Russian forms instead of traditional monorhyme schemes and preferring sonnet-like stanzaic to non-stanzaic templates in their oeuvre illustrates the willingness of *Tajaddod* poets to free themselves from the limitations of *beyt* as the traditional poetic unit. Shams Qeys Rāzi (thirteenth century), the leading theoretician of Persian classical poetics, states that 'the minimum' that can be called 'a poem', or better to say a poetic statement, is *beyt*. He defines *beyt* as 'a piece of rhythmic language [with a fixed number of metrical units] that the poet is required to accomplish before he begins to compose another unit similar to it'.[87] However, in the templates suggested by *Tajaddod* poets, the minimum for a poetic statement is expanded from *beyt* to stanza. Indeed, the poet is not obliged to confine a statement to *beyt*-long units, and each part of a speech can be spread in a stanza. Nevertheless, under some circumstances, even classical poets were not able to confine their speech within one unit. Thus, they proposed a rhetorical exception called *moquf al-Ma'āni* (dependent meanings) which allows the poet to spread his idea in two or more linked *beyt*s. In addition, Shams Qeys states that the rhyme is an element which signifies the completion of a *beyt* and consequently a statement.[88] *Tajaddod* poets, however, changed the poetic unit from *beyt* to stanza to transfer the role of signifying the completion of a speech from a single or at most couple of rhyming words in one or two lines to the full rhyme pattern in several lines. In other words, the completion of a stanza, as the new unit of Persian poetry, is 'marked by a recurrent pattern of rhyme'.[89] Changes in the regime of poetic forms, such as proposing the stanza as the new poetic unit and developments in the conception of organic unity, caused many disputes about the authenticity and originality of the *Tajaddod* poets' achievements. Most of these debates were focused on the role of literary borrowing and the reformulation of existing traditional templates in the emergence of the *Tajaddod* poets' sonnet-like poems. These debates were also particularly concerned with the creation of a new stanzaic poetic form called *chārpāreh*.

---

[87] Sirus Shamisā, ed., *Al-Mo'jam fi Ma'āyir Ash'ār al-A'jam* (Tehran: Ferdows, 1994), p. 52.
[88] Shamisā, *Al-Mo'jam*, p. 52.
[89] Abrams and Geoffrey, p. 341.

Chārpāreh: A collective drive to poetic modernity

Chārpāreh was formed as an innovative form which combined the experiential spirit of the *Tajaddod* poets' sonnet-like templates, the immediate tradition of experimenting with classical stanzaic poetic forms, and the traditional standards of rhyming and prosodic metres. Due to its hybrid nature and its expressive potential, *chārpāreh* soon became a popular poetic form among both gradualists and radical modernists of the time. It also became one of the most used templates by both the mainstream and marginal poets of the next generation. Despite the ongoing disputes about the authenticity of this new template, which will be discussed later in this section, most scholars agree that *chārpāreh* as an independent poetic form first appeared in the experimental stanzaic poems of this era. Sirus Shamisā argues that Jaʿfar Khāmeneʾi used this template in about 1924 for the first time, with some gradualist modernists continuing his experiments in their works.[90] However, some scholars have found older *chārpārehs* in the works of *Dāneshkadeh* members, such as Rashid Yāsemi's *Havāpeymā* (Aeroplane, 1916) and Bahār's *Afkār-e Parishān* (Distressing Thoughts, 1922) and *Sorud-e Kabutar* (Song of Pigeons, 1922).[91] Shafiʿi Kadkani rejects both these arguments and states that the appearance of the first *chārpāreh* should be dated back to 1909 and the composition of the poem *Vafā-ye be Ahd* (Remaining Loyal to One's Oath) by Lāhuti. He even compares this poem, in some respects, to Dehkhodā's *Yād Ār* (Remember, 1909), which is commonly considered as the first experiment with European templates in Persian poetry.[92] Shafiʿi states that the movement of *Vafā-ye be Ahd* towards breaking the restrictions of classical poetics is more constructive, in that it led to the creation of the new poetic form of *chārpāreh*.[93]

To make matters more complicated, Nur al-Din Maqsudi introduces an older poem published in 1907, *Āzarbāyjān Journal*, as the first published *chārpāreh* in Persian literature.[94] This patriotic poem consists of three quatrains with the same prosodic metres and alternate rhyme pattern. However, the system of imagery and expressive devices applied in this poem

---

[90] Sirus Shamisā, *Anvāʿ-e Adabi* (Tehran: Mitra, 2008), p. 314.
[91] Āmer Tāher Ahmad, 'Peydāyesh-e Chāhārpāreh va Jāygāh-e Ān dar Tajaddod-e Sheʿr-e Fārsi', *Adabiyāt-e Tatbighi*, 2 (2010), 7–31 (pp. 8–10).
[92] Ārianpur argues that Dehkhodā, who probably knew Turkish and was familiar with the works of the Turkish poet and critic Mahmud Rajāʾi-Zādeh (1847–1912), was introduced to this poetic form through Rajāʾi-Zādeh's well-known poem *Vaqtā ke Qulub Bahār* (When Spring Comes). Ārianpur, 2, p. 95.
[93] Shafiʿi Kadkani, *Bā Cherāgh va Āyeneh*, p. 425.
[94] Nur al-Din Maqsudi, 'Dobeyti-hā-ye Peyvasteh', *Jostār-hā-ye Adabi*, 48 (1978), 684–715, p. 697.

are still traditional. For example, the poem is full of dead metaphors such as '*bolbol*' (nightingale), '*sarv*' (cedar), and '*māh*' (moon) and overused images associated with these figurative elements. Thus, although this poem is composed in an early form of the *chārpāreh* template, it is entirely built upon the mechanicalized rhetorics and semantic clichés of classical literature.

Vafā-ye be Ahd, however, is formed by a modernized and organic system of imagery and expression. Objective images in this poem are the result of the poet's realistic approach to his surrounding world. The narrative is also inspired by social reality, and the expression of personal sentiments in a realistic setting is, in turn, conducive to shaping an organic form in this poem. Indeed, unlike earlier experiments with traditional stanzaic forms, in *Vafā-ye be Ahd*, realistic imagery, expression, and narrative play a more significant role in chaining together the different stanzas and providing a sense of organic cohesion than the mere interconnected rhyme schemes:

لختی سر پا دوخته بر قبر همی چشم
بی جنبش و بی حرف، چو یک هیکل پولاد
بنهاد پس از دامن خود آن زن آزاد
نان را به سر قبر، چو شیری شده در خشم:
- در سنگر خود شد چو به خون جسم تو غلتان
تا ظن نبری آنکه وفادار نبودم
فرزند! به جان تو بسی سعی نمودم
روح تو گواهست که بویی نبد از نان

Having stared, for a time, at the grave
Not moving, not talking, like a steel statue
The free-spirited woman, then,
Put the bread on the grave, and roared like an angry lion:
After your body rolled in your blood in your trench
So that you don't assume that I was not loyal,
I swear, my child, I tried hard,
But your soul can testify there was no scent of bread anywhere.

In comparison with the earlier examples of stanzaic poetry proposed as the early forms of *chārpāreh*, this poem has a more elaborate rhyme arrangement. *Vafā-ye be Ahd* consists of four quatrains with an enclosed rhyme scheme and two quatrains at the end with the rhyme scheme abbb and ccca. However, if one considers the last two stanzas as a single octet, the rhyme pattern would read as an extended enclosed scheme (abbbccca). It can also be regarded as an extended variation of a sestet, as with the last six lines of a Petrarchan sonnet. All three rhyme patterns used in this poem are unprecedented in Persian poetry. Metrically, however, all verses (like many other experiential works with stanzaic poetry in this era) correspond to the standard rules of classical Persian prosody.

The obligation of the earlier samples of *chārpāreh* to follow the rules of classical Persian prosody and rhyming system while using distinctive French and Russian rhyme patterns and working with both traditional and European poetic forms makes *chārpāreh* a heterogeneous form of poetry. The ambivalent nature of *chārpāreh* provoked several open-ended disputes about the originality and authenticity of this template among literary critics. Some traditionalist (and even some gradualist) scholars tried to root *chārpāreh* exclusively within traditional Persian literature, but radical modernist critics attempted to explain the emergence of this poetic form as an advanced form of intercultural adaptation in poetry.

The first group propose compound names, like *dobeyti-ye peyvasteh* (connected doublet), *mostazād-masnavi* (increment couplets), and *zu-qāfiatain* (double rhymed poem), to correlate the new template with traditional poetics and to disregard the footprint of French and Russian poetry in post-constitutional poetry.[95] Indeed, they argue that *chārpāreh* is an ingeniously Iranian template formed by a number of *dobeyti* (poem of four hemistichs) poems joined together. They also argue that the deficiencies of *dobeyti*, such as being limited to four hemistichs in specific prosodic metres,[96] and having a limited rhyme pattern, made the template in its traditional form unable to convey the more elaborate message of a modern poet. Therefore, modernist poets extended that template in the form of *chārpāreh* to emancipate it from the bonds of its traditional restrictions.[97]

Some gradualist scholars, however, do not support the idea of rooting *chārpāreh* in poems with four hemistichs. For instance, Shafi'i Kadkani denies the kinship between *chārpāreh* and *dobeyti* and argues that the term *chārpāreh* has come to be used to refer to a kind of 'vertical *masnavi*'. *Masnavi* is one of the few Persian templates which does not follow a monorhyme scheme. Indeed, *masnavi* consists of independent couplets in which each hemistich must rhyme with its parallel hemistich. Similarly, in *chārpāreh* each hemistich rhymes with its parallel, which can be one of the odd or even hemistichs of the stanza.[98] Some others also attempted to differentiate between *chārpāreh* and *dobeyti-ye peyvasteh* as two individual poetic forms. For instance, Ziā' al-Din Torābi suggests that poems that adhere to distinct Persian rhyme patterns can be traced back to traditional templates and referred to as '*dobeyti-ye peyvasteh*'. On the other hand, poems that adopt

---

[95] Maqsudi, p. 714.
[96] The traditional *dobeyti* must be composed in *hazaj-e mosadas-e maqsur or mahzuf* (ᴗ--- ᴗ--- ᴗ--). Sirus Shamisā, *Aruz va Qāfiyeh* (Tehran: Payām-e Nur University, 2004), p. 48.
[97] Maqsudi, p. 689.
[98] Mohammad-Rezā Shafi'i Kadkani, *Musiqi-e She'r* (Tehran: Āgāh, 2010), p. 219.

European rhyme patterns without any connection to Persian poetry should be labelled as '*chārpāreh*'.[99]

A major problem with these arguments is that in all the traditional templates introduced as the origin of *chārpāreh*, the connection between sections is much looser than the link among the stanzas of a *chārpāreh*. Therefore, in traditional stanzaic poetry, each section can stand alone, although it might be linked to the following part through its formal features or storyline. In any case, one may argue that although *chārpāreh* fits in the context of Persian poetic standards and shares many elements with existing poetic forms, it was primarily invented to remedy the absence of an explicit organic unity in classical poetry. The interrelation of formal properties, the dramatic and narrative elements, the new ways of looking at and reflecting social reality, and the simplification of the literary language are some aspects of the experimental poetry of this period which reinforced the organic unity of new stanzaic poems, particularly *chārpāreh*. Indeed, all of these aspects should be conceived as the revisionary response of new poets to the mechanicalized rhetoric and semantic clichés of classical poetic forms.

In addition, attempts to name this new poetic form based on classical terminology reflect the revisionary approach of literary critics towards the traditional regime of classifying poetic forms. Traditionalists and gradualists mostly tend to work the new forms up into the existing standards of classical poetics. Indeed, they find it difficult and unnecessary to redefine the old regime of literary classification. Thus, they attempt to tie new concepts to already established ones. As Ghanoonparvar states, the old orders of classical poetics represent the hierarchy of society in which traditionalist and gradualist critics are placed in a higher rank than their radical counterparts.[100] Therefore, they defend the old orders overshadowing innovations by traditional terminology, because the collapse of the old order means losing their established status at the top of the hierarchy. In this sense, the innovation for traditionalists and gradualists is merely to unite the existing elements to form a new compound within the traditional system.

In contrast, radical critics define the experiential poetry of this era as a progressive deviation from literary tradition and a drive towards a whole new regime of aesthetics. Radical modernists of this era, particularly *Tajaddod* poets, were eager to abandon the whole hierarchical regime of generic classification and called for the formulation of a new poetic genre which mirrored their desired 'doctrine of international arts'. Some argue that *Tajaddod* poets, in their search for an intercultural poetic genre, studied the literary modernization in other countries of the region, too. Bāqer

---

[99] Zia' al-Din Torabi, 'Az Dobeyti-hā-ye Peyvasteh tā Chahārpāreh', *Keyhān Farhangi*, 202 (2003), pp. 57–9 http://Ensāni.ir/fa/article/240242 [accessed 11 Nevember 2019].
[100] Ghanoonparvar, p. 21.

Sardriniyā argues that the initiators of *chārpāreh* encountered this poetic form through *Servat-e Fonun* (Wealth of Arts), a journal published by a group of modernist Turkish writers from 1896 to 1901, under the editorship of Tewfiḳ Fikret (1867–1915).[101] Sardriniyā refers to translations and adaptations by *Servat-e Fonun* poets from French Romantic poets such as Victor Hugo and Stéphane Mallarmé as a source of inspiration for Iranian poets, who were somehow familiar with the late-Ottoman Turkish language or had lived in Istanbul for a while.[102] However, the oeuvre of both radical and gradualist poets, particularly Rafʿat and Rashid-Yāsemi, illustrates that they had considerable knowledge of French and even translated some French literary works into Persian. Thus, one could argue that the inclination of both groups towards this template derived from their own observations of original French sonnets and that the Turkish translations in *Servat-e Fonun* were used, at most, as secondary or introductory material.

Āmer Ṭāher Ahmed argues that both radical and gradualist poets of this era were directly inspired by the original works of the French romantic masters. He states that the competition between these two groups led them to a series of creative adaptations from French poetry, which in turn was conducive to the emergence of *chārpāreh*.[103] He compares the poem *Parvāneh va Gol* (Butterfly and Rose, 1916) by Rashid-Yāsemi with one of Victor Hugo's poems (Number 27 from the collection *Chants du crépuscule*, 1837), showing that the former is a creative adaptation of the latter.[104] Similarities between both poems in their templates, particularly the rhyme pattern and uneven hemistichs, confirm Ahmed's claim. Both poems consist of quatrains with an alternate rhyme pattern. Metrically, however, the French poem is a syllabic verse with twelve – (alexandrine) and three-syllable lines, whereas the Persian poem is composed in a classical prosodic metre.[105] Also, to reflect Hugo's uneven verses Rashid-Yāsemi employs a modified form of *mostazād* (increment poem) in each quatrain. The classical form of *mostazād* is constructed based on the framework of *ghazal* or *robāʾi*, with the distinction that the even hemistichs are shorter in length compared to the preceding ones. In this poem, however, *mostazād* is combined unconventionally with *chārpāreh*. This new combination, in turn, is an innovative attempt at the expansion of both templates. The metre of the short lines of this poem, as

---

[101] The poets who were involved with the publication of *Servat-e Fonun* formed a literary movement named after the journal, which has also been referred to as *Edebiyyāt-i djedīde* (New literature). Çiğdem Balim, 'T̲h̲erwet-i Fünūn', in *Encyclopaedia of Islam* http://dx.doi.org/10.1163/1573-3912_islam_SIM_7529 [accessed 18 June 2020] (para. 1 of 1).

[102] Bāqer Sadriniyā, 'Peydāyesh va Tahavvol-e Chārpāreh Sorāʾi dar Irān', *Fonun-e Adabi*. 12 (2015), 23–32, (pp. 23–32).

[103] Ahmad, p. 10.

[104] Ahmad, pp. 11–20.

[105] *Moteqāreb-e mosamman-e mahzuf*.

in the most common form of *mostazād*, adheres the first and last feet to the full metrical pattern.[106]

Furthermore, both poems exhibit a strikingly similar narrative trajectory, with shared motifs and recurring characters. Nevertheless, the differences in subject matter reflect the dissimilar literary and intellectual traditions behind each of them. Both poems portray a dialogue between a rose and a butterfly. The rose is in love with the butterfly but, on account of its physical limitations, cannot accompany its beloved. In Hugo's poem, according to Ahmed, the separation of the rose and the butterfly, because of their essential differences, is a symbolic image of the social crisis occasioned by class differences after the French Revolution of 1830.[107] However, in the Persian poem the restricted rose can be interpreted as an Iranian woman, trapped by the limitations to her social life. The subject matter in Rashid-Yāsemi's poem is in line with one of the major political agendas of poetry in his age: to emphasize the necessity of incorporating Iranian women into the fabric of society.

Thus, the formation of novel poetic forms such as *chārpāreh*, which was among the first steps leading to the rise of a new aesthetic regime, was the result of a collective attempt to deconstruct and reformulate the hierarchical structure of poetry and society through cultural production. The politics of constitutional and post-constitutional poetry was primarily to demolish the traditional, undemocratic, aesthetic regime, which represented autocracy in the real world. In this sense, Rashid-Yāsemi and other initiators of *chārpāreh* attempted to employ a new system of poetic communication, in dialogue with their own understanding of the so-called 'international poetic arts', as a part of their political agenda for modernizing and liberating Iran.

To attain this modern intercultural genre, *Tajaddod* poets initiated a radical movement of adopting and adapting the styles and standards of French and Russian poetics. As Karimi-Hakkak states, the inclination towards the European poetic forms that they adopted indicates that 'those genres must have been thought of as the systemic equivalent, in the modern world, of certain forms in the classical Persian tradition'.[108] Contrary to this, some gradualist modernists tried to moderate the role of European poetry in the emergence of *chārpāreh*. They perceived *chārpāreh* as an extension of established, classical genres, rather than a fundamental change. The series of Rashid-Yāsemi's articles entitled *Enqelāb-e Adabi* (Literary Revolution, 1918), in which he illustrated the dispute between romantic and classical artists, highlights the endeavours by *Dāneshkadeh* members to convert the

---

[106] The odd hemistichs are scanned as *fa'ulon, fa'ulon, fa'ulon, fa'al* (ᴗ--/ᴗ--/ᴗ--/ᴗ-) and the even ones are *fa'ulon, fa'al* (ᴗ--/ᴗ-).
[107] Ahmad, p. 14.
[108] Karimi-Hakkak, *Recasting Persian Poetry*, p. 18.

perception of *chārpāreh* from a mere literary borrowing to a poetic fusion of tradition and modernity.

Rashid-Yāsemi's *Enqelāb-e Adabi* series has a noticeable effect on gradualists' understanding of the reformulation of poetic forms as a corrective movement towards traditional poetry. For instance, Bahār, who as the leader of the gradualist modernists of the time defended the formal fundamentals of traditional poetry, changed his outlook right after the publication of Rashid-Yāsemi's article and called for the expansion of poetic genres in certain domains:

> If we confine ourselves to the rules set by our ancestors, we will remain trapped within the boundaries of limited possibilities, hindering our progress towards new discoveries, valuable innovations, and substantial advancements. It is imperative that we expand our traditional prosody by incorporating thousands of meters. We must introduce countless new rules into our poetics and rhyming system. Additionally, we should discard any poetic regulations that seem obsolete and ineffective in this era. Let us disregard the criticisms of traditionalists who cling to the legacies of our forefathers. Instead, we must liberate poetry and literature, following the path of the romantic literati.[109]

Bahār recommends adding new elements to – and removing restrictive or absurd elements from – the traditional literary rules. However, he still measures all these changes based on their conformity with the literary past. Indeed, unlike *Tajaddod* poets, Bahār sees literary modernity as an extension of the past rather than breaking away from it. In other words, for Tajaddod poets, the literary past is something to avoid, while for gradualists of Dāneshkadeh, it is something to preserve or, at most, reconfigure. Bahār's concept of tradition, in this sense, aligns with T. S. Eliot's perspective in 'Tradition and the Individual Talent' (first published in 1919), as both view traditional elements as precious monuments from the past that should be modified through the introduction of new works.[110] Indeed, aesthetic rules of classical poetry are those existing monuments which Bahār wishes to preserve and simultaneously to modify and expand with a more global vision. As discussed in the first chapter, Bahār's corrective movement towards tradition falls under the Bloomian revisionary ratio '*tessera*', in which the poet antithetically completes his predecessor's poem. He attempts to retain the fundamentals of traditional aesthetics, while imbuing them with new meaning, which are more compatible with the notion of literary revolution in the contemporary age.

---

[109] Ahmad, pp. 28–9.
[110] T. S. Eliot, 'Tradition and the Individual Talent', *Perspecta*, 19 (1982), 36–42 (p. 37).

Tajaddod poets' experiments with *chārpāreh* and other sonnet-like forms, however, should be perceived as a conscious misreading of literary tradition. Indeed, *Tajaddod* poets represent a part of the literary community who, as Eliot describes, praise the poem which least resembles its precursors' works.[111] This act of intentional misreading or poetic misprision by the new poet, as Bloom states, implies that 'the precursor poem went accurately up to a certain point, but then should have swerved, precisely in the direction that the new poem moves'.[112] Raf'at, in his manifesto, states that modern poetry must revolutionize traditional literature in terms of form, language, and style because this literature has 'deviated from its primary resources'.[113] In another article, he states that the value of our poetic ancestors is in their revolutionary approach towards their immediate traditions and in their having an intercultural understanding of literature, not because they submitted to the established literary standards.[114]

Tajaddod poets' conscious misreading of literary traditions, embodied in their unconventional rhythmic regimes, rhyme schemes, imagery, and systems of signification, led to two significant aesthetic achievements. First, through contributing to the creation of *chārpāreh*, they influenced the formation of a notable part of the mainstream literature of the following four decades. Second, by diverging from the conventional conception of genre in traditional poetry, they paved the way for the major changes in the infrastructure of poetry implemented by the avant-gardes and modernists of the next generation.

Tajaddod poets tried to alter the formal properties of their poems based on the thematic concerns of modern art. In so doing, they needed to abandon solidified poetic templates such as *ghazal*, *qasideh*, and so on. Therefore, they improvised new forms based on the theme and subject matter of each individual poem. In experiential poems such as *Sangar-e Khunin*, *Ma dar in Panj Ruz-e Nobat-e Khish*, and many other experiments in stanzaic poetry, the form of each poem is constructed based on the vital interrelations between every aspect of the poem, such as subject, rhyme patterns, rhythmic system, and even expressive devices. In his analysis of Raf'at's ideas about the 'intrinsic thematic or structural differences' of poems as an alternative to the classification of poems based on their templates, Karimi-Hakkak writes,

> Raf'at's line of division, using subject matter and expressive strategies as bases for classification is an important departure from traditional practice in its own right. This position, expanded into a principle of poetic modernism, played a crucial part in undermining the idea of verse

---

[111] Eliot, p. 36.
[112] Bloom, p. 14.
[113] Ārianpur, 2, p. 452.
[114] Ārianpur, 2, p. 443.

forms altogether as a basis for classifying poetic texts. It led eventually to the new poetry's typology of poems along the lines solely of thematic and expressive features, much like that common in contemporary Western literatures.[115]

One can argue that this new approach to the typology of Persian poetry is the essence of the *Tajaddod* poets' revisionary approach to classical literature. This new classification system is both counter-sublime and discontinuous. It breaks the sacred hierarchical regime of poetic categorization in a way that allows the poet to improvise in various aspects of the poetic form and to harmonize the formal properties of the poem with the requirements of speech. Moreover, it discontinues the pre-arranged and restrictive form of poetic creation within the existing frames of classical poetry.

Tajaddod poets were representatives of a new professional class who consciously opposed the aesthetic regime of classical literature, which they perceived to be a representation of the hierarchies of society and its power relations. Their revolution against the regime of poetic classification was their most notable contribution to the process of literary modernization. Moreover, their revisionary approaches to the regime of poetic signification and imagery, their experiments with both borrowed and original poetic forms, and their disputes with the contemporary literary community functioned as a technical resource for fundamental changes in different aspects of poetics. This eventually led to the rise of the so-called *Nimāic* poetry of the following generation.

---

[115] Karimi-Hakkak, *Recasting Persian Poetry*, pp. 204–5.

4

Modernism and high modernism

It is a widely held view among historians of modern Persian poetry that the role of post-constitutional literary intellectuals was a key factor in shaping the conception of the literary revolution in the first half of the twentieth century. The previous chapter determined two significant elements of literary change, which post-constitutional intellectuals, particularly *Tajaddod* poets, established and passed to the next generation of poets. The first was the use of modern and topical subject matter, which revealed the hidden voice of the lower social classes and reflected the political sentiments of the oppressed. The second was the reconstruction or modification of formal aspects of classical poetry such as literary language and poetic forms in order to revolutionize the very practice of poetry and poets' mentalities. These two elements, however, were intrinsically intertwined to such an extent that one could argue that the formal innovations of post-constitutional poetry were fundamentally connected to the emancipatory sociopolitical movements of the era. It can be suggested that the act of revitalizing literary forms, even in cases where the content was not sociopolitically engaged, served as a platform for the unveiling of the politics of literature.

The essence of this aesthetic revolution becomes clearer when we recognize that, in numerous instances, the act of creating something new is intricately linked to and aids in dismantling the prevailing influence of the solidified old. Thus, analysing the works of pioneer poets who experimented with – and created new forms for – Persian poetry suggests that those attempts were in themselves acts of resistance against the entrenched hierarchies of the dominant culture. By accepting poetic reconstruction as an act of rebellion against the sovereignty of the old, one can offer a framework of categorization within which the analysis of modernity in Persian poetry can be undertaken.

The reconstruction of literary traditions during the first half of the twentieth century was undertaken by three main groups. The first of these groups was the modernists, whose followers can be divided into two subgroups: modern poets who supported a gradual form of literary modernization and high modernists who favoured radical amendments in classical poetics. The former group was influenced by Nimā Yushij's (1897–1960) early experiments with romantic themes and tried to improve neo-classical templates, particularly *chārpāreh* as an achievement of post-constitutional poets, in a way which could contain these themes. The poets of the latter group, however, as followers of Nimā's later works, studied and suggested literary modernism as an alternative version of both classical and gradualist modern poetry. Conventional literary historians name these two subgroups *Chārpāreh-Sorāyān* (Four-liners) and *Nimāic* poets, respectively.

The poets of the second group were experimental artists who might not have confronted the literary mainstream directly, but who had realized the necessity for change in poetic structures. So, they experimented in different ways to achieve a new understanding of poetic form and to suggest new styles to revive poetry for a new age. I have dedicated the fifth chapter of this book to the oeuvre of the most significant experimentalist poets of the 1930s to 1950s, namely Mohammad Moqaddam (1909–1996), Zabih Behruz (1890–1972), and Shin Partow (1907–1997).

The third major group comprised avant-garde poets who called for the destruction of all dominant, institutionalized literary traditions and for the introduction of radical changes in poetic structures and aesthetics to achieve new forms of creativity. The most influential figures of this trend were Tondar Kiā (1909–1987) and Hushang Irāni (1925–1973), who will be studied in the last chapter of this book.

After an introductory discussion about the classification of pioneer poets in this era, the chapter reviews some theoretical debates on the avant-garde and experimentalism. It goes on to analyse the career of Nimā Yushij, the most prominent modernist poet of this period, through a close reading of his poem *Khāneh-ye Sarivoyli* (Sarivoyli's House) as a significant turning point in modern Persian poetry. By dividing Nimā's career into two distinct phases, this chapter tries to show how changes in Nimā's revisionary approach towards the literary tradition and the way he engaged his poetry with politics shaped two major subgroups of modernists in Persian poetry.

Modernism, experimentalism, and avant-garde

One of the primary counterarguments against the aforementioned classification of Iran's poetic movements is that experimentalism can be seen as a common approach adopted by all avant-garde groups. In this sense, experimentalism is not a movement but a constant practice in artistic development. As per Chris Baldick, experimentalism refers to the exploration of new aesthetic concepts using methods that surpass the established conventions of literary tradition. Baldick views experimentalism as a defining feature of twentieth-century literature, where successive avant-garde movements emerged in a continuous response to what they perceived as stagnant or rigid forms of expression.[1]

However, in this conception of experimentalism one overlooks the role of independent experiential works which, unlike those of the avant-garde, did not desire to demolish the whole existing aesthetic regime, but their stylistic innovations played an essential role in setting the stage for the infrastructural changes of the avant-gardes. For instance, although Moqaddam's experiments did not confront the accepted conceptions of the new poetry, his experiments with the formal properties of Persian poetry paved the way for the radical alterations made by the next generation of avant-garde poets in the 1960s. Besides, Persian experimentalists often concealed their conflicts with mainstream modernists. In fact, when comparing their works to those of modernists, especially figures like Nimā Yushij, they would refer to their own creations as amateurish and describe them as insignificant experiments. Furthermore, Iranian experimentalists (unlike avant-gardes) experimented with poetry for the sake of experimentation and did not propose an alternative for current literary styles. In essence, experimentalists can be seen as catalysts for the subsequent developments within the avant-garde movement, which brought about significant advancements in literature. However, their corrective stance towards the literary past and their approach to literary change warrant a distinct category in the history of modern Persian poetry.

An additional argument against such categorization is that there may not be a significant distinction between Iranian high modernists, avant-garde poets, and experimentalists, as all three groups share a common point of departure: the desire to challenge and transform the prevailing literary traditions and conventions of the moderate mainstream. One can differentiate between an experimental/avant-garde work and a high modernist one by highlighting the definition of avant-gardism given by Peter Bürger. He offers a twofold definition in which avant-gardism is described as an attack on institutionalized art and an attempt for the creation of a nonorganic work of art.[2] It is true that high modernism, like other pioneer movements, attacked the institutionalized art of the time at some point. However, in contrast with experimentalism and avant-gardism, Persian high

---

[1] Chris Baldick, *The Concise Oxford Dictionary of Literary Terms* (Oxford & New York: Clarendon Press & Oxford University Press, 1990), pp. 89–90.
[2] Peter Bürger, *Theory of the Avant-Garde* (Minneapolis: University of Minnesota Press, 1984), p. 89.

modernism has continuously emphasized the organic unity of the poem as one of the main elements of modern work.

In an organic work of art, the structural principle governs the parts and unifies them into a cohesive whole.[3] By contrast, in a non-organic work, the parts are significantly more autonomous vis-à-vis the whole. In other words, in an experimental/avant-garde work, elements which construct a totality of meaning in an organic form are replaced with autonomous signs. *Nimāic* poets' emphasis on organic unity and poetic form as a unified whole contrasts starkly with the scrappy poetic pieces of Tondar Kiā. Behruz's experimental poetry also appears as arbitrary, autonomous poetic pieces among the dialogues of his plays rather than complete, structured poems.

In addition, according to Renato Poggioli, the varying approaches to sociopolitical engagement within the literary text serve as another significant factor that distinguishes avant-gardism and experimentalism from other high modernist trends. He refers to the earliest text in which avant-garde has been used as a term with both aesthetic and political connotations. He states that the earliest definitions of the term 'avant-garde' (advance-guard: the front segment of an advancing troop) not only place emphasis on 'the idea of the interdependence of art and society' but also propose 'the doctrine of art as an instrument for social action and reform, a means of revolutionary propaganda and agitation'.[4] Poggioli digs into Charles Baudelaire's personal notebook in which he refers to 'littérateurs d'avant-garde' as 'radical writers, writers ideologically on the left'.[5] These so-called literary leftists soon found themselves rebelling against the autocracy of entrenched literary styles, rather than the autocracy of the powerholders. The term 'avant-garde' lost its visible political indication later and transformed into a solely artistic term towards the end of the nineteenth century. Schulte-Sasse mentions the historical avant-garde of the 1920s as the first movement in the history of art that turned against institutionalized art.[6]

Similarly, in Iran, constitutional and post-constitutional poets (particularly *Tajaddod* poets) exhibited a strong inclination to steer modern Persian poetry towards a medium that allowed them to address contemporary issues. However, subsequent generations of pioneering poets shifted their focus towards criticizing traditional literature as a reflection of the hierarchical sociopolitical system, rather than directly challenging the regime itself. For pioneer poets of the 1930s to 1950s, even modern poetry when it became literary mainstream could be interpreted as institutionalized art against which experimentalism (and then avant-gardism) began to rebel. During

---

[3] Bürger, p. 84.
[4] Renato Poggioli, *The Theory of the Avant-Garde* (Cambridge, MA: Belknap Press of Harvard University Press, 1968), p. 9.
[5] Poggioli, p. 10.
[6] Bürger, p. xiv.

the 1950s and 1960s, when *Nimāic* poetry became dominant in literary journals and forums, the advocates of this movement used their influence to suppress the works of other poets who were simultaneously fighting against gradualist modern poets and traditionalists. In addition to criticizing the unfamiliar aesthetics of experimentalist and avant-garde works, they mainly challenged the approach of these works towards the political engagement of poetry. Indeed, the poetry of high modernists was primarily more directly political in the social sense of the term, while the subject matter in the works of experimentalists and avant-gardes was not directly political as such.

Bürger argues that avant-garde art introduces a new form of sociopolitical engagement that renders the traditional dichotomy between pure and committed art obsolete. Drawing inspiration from Adorno, he asserts that the structural principle of the non-organic possesses inherent emancipatory qualities. According to Bürger, a non-organic structure enables the work to liberate itself from the rigid ideology of the established system. In other words, a non-organic structure, due to the autonomy of its individual parts, allows for the coexistence of political and non-political ideas and motifs within a single work.[7]

In fact, one can argue that the notion of political engagement before and after the emergence of experimental and avant-garde movements should not be considered the same; the political act of Persian avant-garde and experimental poetry is internal rather than external. Modernist and high modernist poets consider the political engagement of poetry as an external element suggested by both the content and the paratext.[8] In contrast, the political act of experimental and avant-garde poets lies in their violation of accepted undemocratic conventions in both literary and social discourse. Working on neglected and, in some cases, forbidden subject matter as well as disturbing the traditional orders of literary properties is, in fact, an act of political resistance within literary works. The political engagement of experimental and avant-garde works depends on the newness of the alternative system which they offer for replacing the hierarchical regime of aesthetics.

The definition of newness in the realm of aesthetics varies between different groups of artists. Renato Poggioli states that avant-garde artists

---

[7] Bürger, pp. 90–1.
[8] Some argue that the recognition of high modernist sociopolitically committed poets is partly influenced by the platforms used to showcase their works. A notable example, as highlighted by Ahmad Karimi-Hakkak, is the fact that periodicals related to the Tudeh Party of Iran facilitated the publication of Nimā's works and that Ehsan Tabari, a prominent member of the party, played an important role in promoting Nimā's poetry in the 1940s and early 1950s. See Ahmad Karimi-Hakkak, 'Nimā Yushij; A Life', in *Essays on Nimā Yushij; Animating Modernism in Persian Poetry*, ed. by Ahmad Karimi-Hakkak and Kamran Talattof (Leiden & Boston: Brill, 2004), p. 54.

see the new 'in terms of a birth rather than a rebirth, not a restoration but an *instauratio ab imis fundamentis*, a construction of the present and future not on the foundations of the past but on the ruins of time'.[9] For Iranian avant-garde poets also, newness does not indicate refreshing the old but rather suggests the creation and reformulation of language through lived experience and cross-fertilization. In the case of Persian experimentalists, however, Bürger's definition might be more relevant, wherein he describes newness as 'variation within the very narrow, defined limits of a genre'.[10] Iranian experimentalists tended to experiment with the style of writing, rather than constructing a new poetic regime.

On the other hand, traditionalist scholars like Hasan Vahid Dastgerdi present a contrasting viewpoint. According to Dastgerdi, genuine innovation can only occur within the domain of content. He asserts that classical poetics serve as a measure of quality and should remain unaltered:

> The act of introducing a new literary style is often associated with a scenario in which a pioneering poet, in response to the prevailing social and historical circumstances, discovers a novel path to guide and inspire the public. In doing so, the poet effectively instils the core values of the nation within the hearts and minds of their audience through the adept utilization of innovative content and refined techniques.[11]

Vahid Dastgerdi's assertion loosely characterizes a well-crafted classical work as a harmonious fusion of existing elements, rather than a completely novel style of poetry. Limiting newness by proposing new subjects and new ways of applying the solidified rules of classical literature does not allow the poet to make any infrastructural change in the body of literature.

Both Iranian gradualist modernists and high modernists developed their definition of newness through antithetically completing the approach of traditionalists such as Vahid Dastgerdi. Although Nimā Yushij's *She'r-e Now* (New Poetry) suggests a new regime of aesthetics, it does not entirely reject traditional poetics. For Nimā and his followers, *She'r-e Now* aims to refashion Persian poetry in both poetic forms and subject matter based on the legacies of classical literature. Nimā's doctrine is to change the classical poetic orders in a way that creates conformity between the old and the new. In this sense, literary newness for Iranian modernists is, at most, the renewal of mechanical literary techniques. According to Bürger, classical poetics is a series of mechanical techniques that can no longer be perceived as form, and therefore it no longer conveys a fresh perspective on reality. Hence,

---

[9] Poggioli, p. 216.
[10] Bürger, p. 60.
[11] Hasan Vahid Dastgerdi, *Enqelab-e Adabi* (Tehran: Vahidniyā, 1956), p. 11.

the modernists substitute it for a set of new technique. The new techniques may accomplish the form until they too become mechanical and need to be replaced.[12]

Nimā Yushij: Self-revision and conscious misreading of oneself

Ali Esfandiyāri (1897–1960), pen name Nimā Yushij, was born in a small village called Yush in Mazandaran Province. In about 1912 he moved to Tehran and began his studies in the famous Marvi Seminary School.[13] Simultaneously, he studied in a French Catholic school called St Louis, where he discovered his interest in poetry. One of his teachers, Nezām Vafā (1887–1965), who was himself a traditionalist poet, encouraged him to pursue his literary interests. The school provided its students with textbooks containing the poems of Alphonse de Lamartine, Victor Hugo, and Stéphane Mallarmé. These works were probably the first encounter of the young Nimā with a form of literature which was clearly different from traditional Persian poetry in both style and perspective.

Karimi-Hakkak states that although the school used French textbooks, the degree of proficiency that Nimā could have gained in the French language has often been exaggerated.[14] Nimā himself states that he owed his curiosity and eagerness for newness to his acquaintance with traditional study methods gained at Marvi Seminary.[15] However, Mahmud Kiānush sees Nimā's exposure to French poetry as the most prominent source of inspiration for his works and aesthetic perspectives. Kiānush claims that Nimā's ambition to refashion Persian poetry was largely inspired by French symbolists, particularly the Belgian poet Émile Verhaeren (1855–1916).[16]

Abolqāsem Jannati Atā'i states that the first poem Nimā published in a journal was called *Beyraq-hā* (Flags), which was published by Mirzādeh Eshqi in his periodical *Qarn-e Bistom*. He became known as a professional poet a few months later when his poem *Ey Shab* (O Night!, 1922) was published in the *Now-Bahār* periodical. However, young Nimā started publishing his works more regularly in the second half of the 1930s. Jannati Atā'i also states that Nimā was one of the poets who attended poetry recitals in Heydar-Ali Kamāli's store along with Mohammad Taqi Bahār, Ali-Asghar

---

[12] Bürger, p. 60.
[13] Kiānush Kiāni Haftlang, 'Nimā va Mardreseh-ye Sant Lu'is', in *Asnādi Darbāreh-ye Nimā Yushij*, ed. by Ali Mir Ansāri (Tehran: Sazmān-e Asnād-e Melli-e Irān, 1995), p. 50.
[14] Karimi-Hakkak, 'A Life', p. 22.
[15] Kiāni Haftlang, p. 50.
[16] Mahmud Kiānush, *Modern Persian Poetry* (London: Rockingham Press, 2004), p. 21.

Hekmat (1892–1980), and other famous literary intellectuals of the time. Participating in these recitals might have been influential in the construction of his reputation as a professional poet.[17] Karimi-Hakkak, however, argues that although Nimā's fame as a pioneer poet had grown steadily since the late 1930s, it was his participation in the First Congress of Iranian Writers in 1946 that strengthened his status as a poet and established his role as a mentor to the younger generation of modernist poets.[18]

Nimā categorically influenced younger poets and subsequent literary movements, delineating two distinct phases: early and late. Nimā's early works reflect his attempts to alter traditional forms of Persian poetry and establish a new style, while maintaining the requirements of classical literature. In his later poems, however, Nimā focused on reinforcing and amplifying the so-called *Nimāic* paradigm. In other words, in his later works Nimā attempted to enrich what he had established as the main current of literary modernism by producing high-quality works that showcased his theories. He grouped a young generation of poets under the title of *Nimāic* poetry and endorsed their practices in his writings. Additionally, Nimā's approach to the politicization of poetry underwent significant changes in his later works.

Manuchehr Ātashi states that Nimā's works with sociopolitically committed subjects were composed in the first phase of his career.[19] Yet, in experimenting with different aspects of modern literature, Nimā found new ways of expressing his political sentiments. Ātashi states that the closer Nimā got to his idea of poetic modernization and establishing the modern aesthetics of Persian poetry, the more he realized that political thoughts should be expressed through symbolism. Ātashi describes this transformation in Nimā's perspective as a transition from the explicit manifestation of political sentiments to the implicit but in-depth expression of political thoughts through symbolism.[20]

If one considers structural changes as a means of resistance against the hegemony of dominant forms, as soon as a poet repeats his old experiences and refines the already existing structures, he falls into conservatism. Although extracting the full potential of one style before moving on to another is also crucial in the process of literary change, refining a poetical paradigm, even if it was a pioneering style at the time of creation, indicates the recognition of the paradigm as a tradition. Enriching the standard by

---

[17] Abolqāsem Jannati Atā'i, *Nimā; Zendegi va Āsār-e Ou* (Tehran: Safi-Ali Shah, 1955), p. 8.
[18] Karimi-Hakkak, 'A Life', p. 60.
[19] *Khānevādeh-ye Sarbāz* (Family of a Soldier), *Mahbas* (Prison), *Ey Shab* (O Night!), *Nāmeh be Yek Zendāni* (Letter to a Prisoner), *Shahid Gomnām* (Unknown Martyr), and *Sarbāz-e Fulādin* (Steel Soldier). Manuchehr Ātashi, *Nimā ra Bāz Ham Bekhānim; Khiyāl-e Ruz-hā-ye Rowshan* (Tehran: Amitis, 2002), p. 101.
[20] Ātashi, *Nimā ra Bāz Ham Bekhānim*, p. 101.

reproducing existing forms in order to solidify its basis is reproducing a new hierarchical regime of power and values. Although Nimā in the second phase of his career sought political engagement in deeper layers of poetry, the dominant notion of refining and enriching his own standards affected negatively the pioneering and emancipatory spirit of his later poems.

Khāneh-ye Sarivoyli (Sarivoyli's House, 1940) was a turning point in Nimā's poetry, marking a change from his early stage of creating an aesthetic system for *Nimāic* poetry to the phase of enhancing the fundamentals of this style. In the 116th letter of *Harf-hā-ye Hamsāyeh* (The Neighbour's Words), Nimā names this poem as his favourite work.[21] Shāpur Jorkesh argues that Nimā highlights *Khāneh-ye Sarivoyli* because it showcased the most crucial aspects of the *Nimāic* style.[22]

In terms of poetic form, *Khāneh-ye Sarivoyli* follows a new system of rhyme arrangement and metrical system known as *Nimāic* poetic form. As Majid Naficy puts it, in the classical rhythmic system 'the poet has to follow a metric pattern throughout his piece, and the number of feet in each hemistich should be equal'. However, *Nimāic* poetry has relaxed the restrictions regarding the length of the hemistich and allows the poet to compose 'poems with variable line length and irregular rhyme patterns'.[23] Sa'id Hamidiyān also underlines the freedom of prosodic metre in this poem in comparison to Nimā's other *Nimāic* works at that time. He states that in *Khāneh-ye Sarivoyli*, Nimā utilizes frequent poetic licence (*ekhtiyārāt-e vazni*) to free his verses from old, unnatural metrical conventions.[24] Also, thematically, the poem is a symbolic narrative of a poet's life in a dramatic mood. According to Hamidiyān, this poem is the first symbolic narrative poem to be composed in free verse form in the Persian language.[25]

Nimā has provided a brief introduction to this unfinished poem, offering a synopsis of the story. According to the summary, the narrative revolves around a poet named Sarivoyli, who resides in a rural house to shield himself from the negative aspects of urban life. The events take place in Sarivoyli's house, located in the village of Sarivoyl. One stormy night, Satan appears and requests permission to stay overnight. Sarivoyli lets Satan into his house and engages in conversation with him. Satan fashions a bed for himself in the doorway using his hair and nails. The following morning, the bed transforms into snakes that swiftly spread throughout the entire

---

[21] Nimā Yushij, 'Harf-hā-ye Hamsāyeh', in *Darbāreh-ye She'r va Shā'eri*, ed. by Sirus Tāhbāz (Tehran: Negāh, 2006), p. 247.
[22] Shāpur Jorkesh, *Butiqā-ye She'r-e Now* (Tehran: Qoqnus, 2004), p. 125.
[23] Majid Naficy, *Modernism and Ideology in Persian Literature; A Return to Nature in the Poetry of Nimā Yushij* (Maryland: University Press of America, 1997), p. 52.
[24] Sa'id Hamidiyān, *Dastān-e Degardisi; Ravand-e Degarguni-ha-ye She'r-e Nimā Yushij* (Tehran: Nilufar, 2004), pp. 211–12.
[25] Hamidiyān, p. 201.

village. The poet endeavours to assist the villagers in ridding the village of the snakes, while the people assume that his son has gone mad and seek the help of magicians to cure him. Amid these conflicts, Sarivoyli's house is destroyed. In the story's conclusion, the 'morning birds' reconstruct his house, and Sarivoyli returns there with his wife and dog. However, his son is absent, the blackbirds no longer sing in his garden, and he remains perpetually melancholic for the rest of his life.[26]

The extant poem is a dramatic poem reflecting an extended dialogue between Sarivoyli and Satan from the opening section of the story. The symbolic dialogue between the two main characters of the story can be easily interpreted as a dialogue between an independent poet (Nimā himself) and the temptation of giving priority to personal interests over those of society. These temptations are illustrated in Satan's words, in which he tries to tempt the poet with money and fame. However, he has deliberately chosen to distance himself from the role of a court poet and instead opts for a life of anonymity and independence. Indeed, in a similar vein to the legend of Faust, Satan stands for elements that bring worldly fame for which the poet does not want to sell his soul. The temptation of power and worldly gain has come to the poet, but the result is that he shifts from more melodic, idyllic, and classical forms to find a kind of poetry which touches upon people's suffering:

سریویلی گفت: «لیکن
من نیم ز آنان که میسنجی
رتبتی آنگونه‌شان والا.
دور از آن نام آوران و آن سخنگویان که از تو دل ربودستند
من ز بانم دیگر است و داستان من ز دیگر جا
به کز آن مردم بکوبی در
آن کج آموزان کج پرور»[27]

Sarivoyli said: 'But
I am not like those with whom you compare me,
I do not have a high rank as they have.
I am far from those remarkable men and those orators who have stolen your heart.
I have a different language, and my story is from another source.
It is better to hit those people's door,
Those who learned wrongly and taught wrongly.'

---

[26] Sirus Tāhbāz, ed., *Majmuʻeh-ye Āsār-e Nimā Yushij* (Tehran: Nashr-e Nāsher, 1985), pp. 332–3.
[27] Tāhbāz, *Majmuʻeh-ye Āsār-e Nimā Yushij*, p. 346.

From another perspective, Hamidiyān interprets Sarivoyli as Nimā, and Satan as an external force intent on preventing his poetry from portraying social reality.[28] So, Satan tries to deceive Nimā by admiring the darker elements of his poems and thus encouraging pessimism, which was widespread among intellectuals during the 1930s:

وآنچنان کندر بلایی سخت میزبید
سوزناک و دلنشین بگرفت نالیدن
»ای سریویلی! یگانه شاعر قومی که با ببرند در پیکار،
و همه مهمان نوازان بنام اند و جوانمردان،
این جهان در زیر طوفان وحشت آور شد.
هر کجای خاکدان با محنت و هولی برابر شد.
خانه را بگشای در
در رسید از راههای دورت اکنون خسته مهمانی ...«[29]

And as it is befitting during a severe disaster,
He began to lament sorrowfully and pleasantly:
'O Sarivoyli! You are the unique poet of a people who fight tigers,
and are all hospitable and chivalrous.
This world has become perilous due to this horrifying storm.
Every part of the earth is filled with fear and hardship.
Open the door
From far away, a tired visitor has arrived for you now ...'

Hamidiyān's interpretation of Sarivoyli as Nimā's poetic persona leaving the city to become closer to nature seems convincing. Majid Naficy also points out several occasions in which Nimā encourages poets and writers to either move to rural areas or 'to shut the door to everybody in town'.[30] Sarivoyli shares some other characteristics with Nimā, such as the continuous references to the bravery of his ancestors. Naficy discusses the roots of the pen name 'Nimā' in the northern Iranian knighthood tradition and investigates Nimā's tendency to link himself to his family's legacy in some of his writings.[31] However, a major problem with Hamidiyān's argument is that Nimā, unlike Sarivoyli, does not defend optimistic poetry. The poem *Khāneh-ye Sarivoyli* itself offers a pessimistic view. As the story's conclusion, although the poet rescues his village and reconstructs his house, his peaceful world is destroyed, and he is destined to live in sorrow for the rest of his life.

---

[28] Hamidiyān, p. 205.
[29] Tāhbāz, *Majmu'eh-ye Āsār-e Nimā Yushij*, p. 347.
[30] Naficy, pp. 44–5.
[31] Naficy, p. 38.

Furthermore, in the aforementioned stanza, Satan endeavours to incite Sarivoyli into altering his perspective on the world. The idea of poetry being inspired by Satan or genies, *Tābeʿah* or *Fereshteh-ye Sheʿr* (Angel of poetry), was a common belief among both pre-Islamic and post-Islamic poets.[32] In this poem, Satan, functioning as the *Tābeʿah* of sociopolitically engaged poetry, reminds Sarivoyli of the chaos of society and asks him to acknowledge its reality by opening the door of his cosy house to the horrifying world.

In addition, the stormy world depicted in this poem could be conceived as a symbol of the literary environment in that era. A variety of signs in this poem illustrate that this story is a narrative of conflicts relating to the literary modernization of the 1930s. The poet and his challenging dialogue with Satan are mapped on to (and mirror) conflicts relating to new poetry at that time. 'Outside' represents society and the darkness that reflects the brutal domination of the state. Satan advocates new poetry and enters into the safe, cosy house of the poet (representative of the established classical literature) with the intention of destroying it. The act of demolishing the house and the village can also be interpreted as the process of the abolition of old poetics to experiment with new ones. Finally, morning birds stand in for young modernist poets, with the reconstruction of the house representing the idea of reforming the classical literature in which *Nimāic* poets engaged. However, the poet is indisputably disrupted by the loss of his son and the calm of the village, which can be interpreted as the loss of traditional roots and the disturbance of the conventional order of the aesthetic regime.

Also, one may interpret this poem as a symbolic narrative of an inner conflict in Nimā's mind about the concept of literary modernization. Sarivoyli and Satan represent Nimā's superego and id, respectively. Nimā's superego attempts to maintain its ties with inherited literature. At the same time, his id is a rebel that sees no other manner of changing the traditional autocracy established in the classical poetic regime than by shattering it and creating something new. Satan is Nimā's energetic, demanding id, which pushes for change and risks everything, and Sarivoyli is his controlling, angelic superego, which prefers classical and idyllic poetry. On the one hand, by allowing Satan into the house, the poet/narrator shows an unconscious willingness to destroy his current situation. On the other hand, struggling with his inner contradiction, the poet's superego inclines towards a moderate trend of modernization. It rejects the id, condemning it with being shallow, irrational, and childish with an extreme life force:

من سخن های بد و نیک همه خامان این ره شنیدستم
آن کسان را کز رسن بالا شده بر سوی بامی،

---

[32] Hoseyn Aqā Hoseyni, 'Fereshteh-ye Sheʿr', *Nashriyeh-ye Dāneshkadeh Adabiyāt va Olum Ensāni Tabriz*, 185 (2002), 73–93, (p. 85).

پس چنان دانند کز آن بر فلک بالا برفتستند، دیدستم.
در درون شهر کوران دردها دارم ز بینایی ...
همچنین هرگز نخواهم در میان بوق بیهوده دمیدن،
تا بدانندم کسان اکنون رسیدستم.
این شتاب خام زیبد کودکان را.
میرسد ز ی منزل خود کاروان یک روز
از پی چه خسته کردن کاروان را؟[33]

I have heard the sound and unsound words (poems) of those who are immature in this way
Those who climbed onto the roof by a rope,
and then assumed that they reached the sky through that [rope].
I suffer in the city of the blind because of my vision ...
Also, I will never blow the horn vainly
To make others realize that I have just arrived.
This immature haste is befitting of children.
The caravan will arrive at his residence in time,
Why wear the caravan out?

Condemning his predecessors as 'immature' in the above stanza, Nimā questions the constitutional and post-constitutional poets' understanding of the political nature of literature. He denies using poetry to propagate political manifestos, so he attempts to write a poem which is itself a political act. Nimā's dramatic poems work as models for democracy by creating dialogues among symbolically significant objects and characters of equal value. In other words, writing a symbolic, dramatic poem in an innovative poetic system is a political act in itself, even if these symbols do not represent the highly valued concepts of democracy in its constitutional sense. Picturing Sarivoyli reciting poetry at the very beginning of the poem, while his ancestors' weapons are hanging on the wall, is one of those situations in which the poet challenges the constitutional notion of political literature:

گاه زیر شمشیر و کمانی کز دلاور پدرانش بد نشانی
و به روی تیره سبز کهن دیواری آویزان،
بود آن خلوت گزیده گرم کار شعر خوانی[34]

Sometimes under the sword and bow that represented his brave fathers,
and were hung on an old dark green wall,
that secluded man recited poetry.

---

[33] Tāhbāz, *Majmu'eh-ye Āsār-e Nimā Yushij*, p. 342.
[34] Tāhbāz, *Majmu'eh-ye Āsār-e Nimā Yushij*, pp. 334–5.

The poet's ancestors, the constitutional and post-constitutional poets, saw poetry as a vehicle for emancipatory ideas and a weapon to be used against the enemies of freedom. However, as these weapons (poems in classical forms) are hung on the wall as antique and sublime objects, they have no political functionality. Seeing poetry as an inflexible, traditional form undermines its function as a means of sociopolitical and cultural criticism and thus turns poetry into a merely decorative art. Indeed, sacralizing and overvaluing the classical poetic form so that no one has the right to change it neutralizes the resistance power of poetry.

Nimā implies that his poetic fathers bent to the tyranny of the classical poetic form, which distorted their poetic vision and expression. They maintained the hierarchical, undemocratic poetic forms of traditional poetry and replaced the earlier highly valued concepts (patron, beloved, God, etc.) with two new concepts (freedom and democracy) at the top of the pyramid. In *Khāneh-ye Sarivoyli*, the poet comes to new discoveries about the significance and function of the new and free poetic forms. Thus, he decides to commence a corrective movement towards his precursors' undemocratic poetic forms to publicize the hidden voices of the ordinary people:

از همین دم می کشم من شعرهایم را
به دگر قالب
من فرو خواهم شدن در گود تاریک نهان بیشه‌های دور
بین مرگ و زندگانی در دل سنگین رویای شبی تیره
که خفه گشته ست در آن مردمان را بانگ،
نقطه های روشن از معنی دیگر ره به دست آورد خواهم[35]

From this moment I will cast my poems in another template.
I will sink into the dark, hidden pits of remote groves
Between death and life, in the hard heart of a dark night's dream
Where the cry of the people is muffled,
I will achieve bright points with different meanings.

Majid Naficy argues that even in his early romantic works, before proposing the *Nimāic* style, Nimā 'had compassion towards the poor and was agreeable to social change'.[36] Consequently, he tried to express his political sentiments, which were in line with the Jangali Movement (1915–20), through slightly adapted traditional templates with a romantic tone. Naficy asserts that in the late 1930s, Nimā abandoned his romanticism and developed a tendency to convey his political ideas through a form of political symbolism.[37]

---

[35] Tāhbāz, *Majmuʻeh-ye Āsār-e Nimā Yushij*, p. 345.
[36] Naficy, p. 62.
[37] Naficy, p. 53.

In this form of social symbolism, referred to by Naficy as 'night poetry', the poem revolves around the imagery of day and night, symbolizing freedom and tyranny, respectively.[38] So, he interprets *Khāneh-ye Sarivoyli* as a dream-like expression of the poet's desire for the end of Rezā Shāh's reign. Naficy suggests that the poem was composed in May 1940, a time when there was hope for change as the allied forces were pressuring the German-oriented Iranian monarch to abdicate the throne.[39]

Nimā's revisionary approach towards his precursors and his perspective on the politics of poetic forms divided the post-Nimā modern poetry into two different subdivisions. One group favoured Nimā's romantic themes and the moderately reformed templates of his early works. They were inspired by Nimā's first experiences in romantic, dramatic poems in slightly modified classical poetic forms, particularly *Afsāneh* (Legend, 1922). Another group challenged the conventional understanding of literary modernization and followed Nimā's innovative poetic system in his second phase. They found their way after the establishment of the *Nimāic* style, which began around 1937 and, as Naficy states, led to 'the years of puberty and full-blooming in Nimā's poetry'.[40]

Parviz Nātel Khānlari describes the first group as those whose mastery in classical poetry was approved by prominent literary figures of the time. They had previously demonstrated their skills in composing poetry in standard templates. However, they soon realized that Persian poetry needed to be rejuvenated thematically. From their point of view, standard templates (including *chārpāreh*) were still suitable for modern contents if one made the necessary amendments to their rhyme patterns:

> In doing so, they created new templates which were not so different from the traditional ones. *Mosammats, mostazāds* and *dobeyti-hā-ye peyvasteh* (attached quatrains or four-line *chārpāreh*) with two sets of rhymes in four hemistichs or just two rhymed hemistichs became popular.[41]

The most prominent advocates of this moderate branch were a number of poets associated with a literary magazine called *Sokhan*. This magazine was established by a group of graduates of *Dāneshsarā-ye Āli* (Supreme College) in May 1943. The chief editor, Parviz Nātel Khānlari (1914–1990), was one of these young graduates.[42] The *Sokhan* magazine soon became a stronghold for poets and academics who supported moderate reforms in the structure of classical literature.

---

[38] Naficy, p. 50.
[39] Naficy, p. 80.
[40] Naficy, p. 49.
[41] Parviz Nātel Khānlari, *Haftād Sokhan*, 4 vols (Tehran: Tus, 1998), 1, p. 247.
[42] Mohammad Shams Langrudi, *Tārikh-e Tahlili-e She'r-e Now*, 4 vols (Tehran: Markaz, 1998), 1, p. 244.

Sokhan poets were the first poets who followed Nimā's experiments with less common classical templates such as *dobeyti-hā-ye peyvasteh* or *chārpāreh*. Mohammad Shams Langrudi names Fereydun Tavallali (1919–1985), 'the second-most prominent figure' of the *Sokhan* magazine, as one of the earliest followers of Nimā after Mirzādeh Eshqi.[43] This group later claimed, especially through Parviz Nātel Khānlari's writings on modern Persian poetry, that their gradualist, moderate trend of modernity was the real path towards literary revolution. Thus, they tried to push *Nimāic* poets – those inspired by the second phase of Nimā's poetry – out of the way by any possible means.

This was, in fact, a revisionary movement directed by *Sokhan* poets against their poetic father, Nimā. They swerved away from Nimā as they considered his later poetry to be a drive towards intolerable radical changes in both theme and poetic form. The conversion of Nimā's doctrine from romantic themes and slightly modified classical templates to sociopolitical symbolic poems with a new system of poetic forms was perceived by *Sokhan* poets to be a distortion of poetic modernization. In his analysis of poetic innovation, Harold Bloom theorizes a corrective approach among new poets termed '*clinamen*', in which they attempt to swerve from their poetic fathers' doctrine through a misreading of their works and intentions. This misreading appears as a corrective movement in their own poetry, 'which implies that the precursor poem went accurately up to a certain point, but then should have swerved, precisely in the direction that the new poem moves'.[44] Tavallali, in his foreword to *Nāfeh* (Musk, 1962), the poetry collection for which he is best known, states that he was a follower of Nimā's style in *Afsāneh* for years, but that Nimā's later experiments with the aesthetic regime of poetry and his deviation from his initial classical disciplines in *Afsāneh* did not lead to a new style, as he had hoped. He goes even further to describe the second phase of Nimā's career as unfruitful and confused.[45]

One might argue that the new poet could only come to write in his poetic fathers' place by either killing them or being overwhelmed by them. *Sokhan* poets separated themselves from their poetic father by eliminating him in various ways as a part of their creative revisionism. This process of separation involved both returning to the original principles of Nimā's poetry and denouncing the style known as *Nimāic* poetry as an illegitimate deviation of modern poetry. For instance, in 1946 Parviz Dāryush (1923–2001) published an anthology of modern poetry entitled *Nemuneh-hā-ye She'r-e Now* (Examples of New Poetry) as an appendix

---

[43] Mohammad Shams Langrudi, *Az Nimā tā Ba'd*, 2 vols (Tehran: Markaz, 1991), 2, p. 35.
[44] Harold Bloom, *The Anxiety of Influence: A Theory of Poetry* (New York: Oxford University Press, 1997), p. 14.
[45] Fereydun Tavallali, *Nāfeh* (Shiraz: [n. pub.], 1962), pp. 2–3.

to the *Sokhan* magazine. In this anthology, there is not a single poem by a *Nimāic* poet, except for Nimā himself. However, the author has included in this volume a considerable number of poems by conservatives and traditionalists such as Mehdi Hamidi Shirāzi (1914–1986), Parvin E'tesāmi (1907–1941), Hoseyn Pezhmān (1900–1974), and Ra'di Āzarakhshi (1909–1999). In the First Congress of Iranian Writers (1946), which was run by Khānlari and Ehsān Tabari, Ali-Asghar Hekmat presented the manifesto of the congress on contemporary poetry but did not even mention Nimā Yushij. Following Hekmat's presentation, Mehdi Hamidi Shirāzi recited a poem that mocked the *Nimāic* style, adding to the disregard shown towards Nimā's poetic approach during the event.[46] Furthermore, Khānlari, the editor-in-chief of *Sokhan* and one of Nimā's early followers, completely denied Nimā's role as the leader of poetic modernization in this era and claimed that he, Khānlari, was the person who had invented the term '*She'r-e Now*'.[47]

Sirus Tāhbāz states that in almost every intellectual periodical published between 1941 and 1953, there is at least one poem or essay by Nimā, but Khānlari refused to publish any of Nimā's works in the *Sokhan* magazine.[48] Iraj Pārsinezhād tries to justify the absence of Nimā's works in *Sokhan* by highlighting Khānlari's emphasis on grammatical errors and the implications they had for a poem's legibility and right to appear in a journal, even if the poet was one of the most prominent poets of the era.[49] Nimā, however, condemned the intentional elimination of his name from the journal and stated that 'this magazine is against the poetry of the day. [...] this young man [Khānlari] does anything to eliminate my name'.[50]

Shams Langrudi compares the polarized literary environment of this period to that of the post-constitutional era. He states that the nature and the results of the arguments between gradualist poets of *Dāneshkadeh* and radical modernists of *Tajaddod* are analogous to the conflict between *Nimāic* and *Sokhan* poets.[51] Shortly after the literary coup d'état of *Sokhan*,

---

[46] Mansur Rastgār Fasā'i, *Parviz Nātel Khānlari* (Tehran: Tarh-e Now, 1999), pp. 116–17.

[47] Khānlari, p. 310. Shafi'i Kadkani supports Khānlari's stance on the development of the new poetry and argues that the poem *Bā ghorubāsh* (With Its Sunset) by Nimā was deeply influenced by one of the Khānlari's works, *Vaghmā-ye Shab* (Plunder of the Night), which was published before Nimā's in 1944. However, Nimā dated his work a few months before that of Khānlari to cover the possibility of having been influenced by *Yaghmā-ye Shab*. See Mohammad-Rezā Shafi'i Kadkani, *Bā Cherāgh va Āyeneh: dar Jostoju-ye Risheh-ye Tahavolāt-e She'r-e Mo'āser-e Fārsi* (Tehran: Sokhan, 2011), pp. 491–4.

[48] Sirus Tāhbāz, 'Kamāndār-e Bozorg-e Kuhestān', in *Yādmān-e Nimā Yushij*, ed. by Mohammad-Rezā Lāhuti (Tehran: Gostaresh Honar, 1989), p. 64.

[49] Iraj Pārsinezhād, *Khānlari va Naqd-e Adabi* (Tehran: Sokhan, 2008), p. 57.

[50] Sirus Tāhbāz, ed., *Daftar-e Yāddāsht-hā-ye Ruzāneh-ye Nimā Yushij* (Tehran: Bozorgmehr, 1990), p. 215.

[51] Shams Langrudi, *Tārikh-e Tahlili-e She'r-e Now*, 1, p. 265.

this journal became one of the most popular literary journals of the 1950s and 1960s. On the other hand, the *Nimāic* poets occupied the so-called intellectuals' media such as the leftist periodicals related to *Hezb-e Tudeh-ye Irān* (Tudeh Party of Iran). This separation resulted in the occupation of a major part of the literary mainstream environment by transitional, gradualist modernists and high modernists, which in turn had a negative impact on the visibility of other forms of experimentation.

Nevertheless it is claimed that although most of the literary attempts aligned with Nimā's first phase are perceived as modern experiences in Persian poetry, categorizing *Sokhan* poets as modernists is not entirely accurate. That is to say, the majority of four-liners by *Sokhan* poets can be loosely defined as post-classical romantic compositions with new imagery. However, some followers of this group argued that the process of modernization run by *Sokhan* was entirely different to that of *Nimāic* poetry. An instance of this can be observed in the views of Nāder Nāderpur (1929–2000), a prominent poet associated with this movement. Nāderpur argues that the stylistic approach advocated by Khānlari and the poets of *Sokhan* cannot be compared to that of Nimā or even the classical masters. Consequently, he categorizes the romantic four-liners of the *Sokhan* group as 'neo-classical' poetry.[52]

The *Nimāic* style, or high modernism in Persian poetry, however, is perceivable in Nimā's second phase as well as in the works of a body of young poets, such as Mehdi Akhavān Sāles (1929–1990), Ahmad Shāmlu (1925–2000), and Forugh Farrokhzād (1934–1967). M. H. Abrams states that high modernism is 'marked by an unexampled range and rapidity of change' and commenced as the second wave of the modernism after the end of the First World War.[53] Similarly, in the case of modern Persian poetry, the term 'high modernism' refers to the second wave of literary modernization. Poets of this wave attempted to implement fast and radical changes within the system of millennium-old literary traditions of Persian poetry. These poets stand between the two poles of literary modernization: gradualist four-liners and avant-garde/experimentalists. Richard Sheppard draws a line between high modernism and avant-gardism, writing:

> ... high modernism is the culmination of a trend [...] which separates art from life and beauty from sensuality. In contrast, the main aim of the historical avant-gardes, notably Dada and Surrealism, is said to be the reintegration of art and life, with 'life' understood as the everyday,

---

[52] Shams Langrudi, *Tārikh-e Tahlili-e She'r-e Now*, 1, pp. 266–7.
[53] Meyer Howard Abrams, and Geoffrey G. Harpham, *A Glossary of Literary Terms* (Boston & Mass: Thomson Wadsworth, 1999), p. 167.

mass culture, the material world, and the energies of the body. Several influential critics have accepted this thesis. For instance, although Calinescu is aware that the avant-garde was not all of a piece [...], he drives a wedge between 'high modernists' like Proust, Joyce, Kafka, Tomas Mann, Eliot, and Pound and the movements that constitute the historical avant-garde(s).[54]

In a similar vein, the Persian high modernist trend departed from the direct political engagement of constitutional and post-constitutional poetry. Instead it focused on poetry which was intent on symbolically representing social reality. Thus, high modernists separated their poems from 'everyday, mass culture' and 'the material world' and chose their subjects from highly valued concepts, such as true love, patriotism, and freedom. Even those *Nimāic* poets who engaged with popular culture such as folk tales and songs in their works used mass-culture motifs as symbols of sublime subject matters.

High modernists attempted to create an aesthetic system through which they could replace the mechanical sensuality that the old literary canon suggests with a personal point of view built upon the poets' lived experience. The *Nimāic* style lays emphasis on interpreting the world, including social reality, from the poets' personal perspective by using modern yet conventional linguistic and literary tools. On the other hand, Iranian avant-garde poets and experimentalists look for idiosyncratic, unconventional formal properties to offer a different interpretation of the world.

Because of the idiosyncrasy of experimental works in this era, one should analyse these poets individually and classify them based on the nature of their experience. Furthermore, the absence of well-established institutions, including avant-garde and experimentalist-oriented literary journals, coupled with the marginalization of unconventional voices by mainstream groups, prevented experimentalists from forming cohesive literary bodies or unified movements. However, some experimental poets such as Mohammad Moqaddam, Zabih Behruz, and Shin Partow, whose poetry will be examined in the following chapter, managed to break the hegemonic dominance of the modernists and disseminate their works in the literary community of their time.

---

[54]Richard Sheppard, *Modernism – Dada – Postmodernism* (Illinois: Northwestern University Press, 2000), p. 6.

5

Experimentalism in Persian poetry between the 1930s and the 1950s

This chapter aims primarily to analyse the works of three significant experimentalist poets of the 1930s–1950s: Mohammad Moqaddam (1909–1996), Zabih Behruz (1890–1972), and Shin Partow (1907–1997). This is the first comprehensive study that examines the life and works of these poets as independent subjects in an academic work. While Moqaddam's linguistic contributions have been referenced in various studies, his career as an experimentalist poet has not been objectively examined before this book. Similarly, there has been no dedicated survey of Behruz's poetic experiences conducted prior to this study. Furthermore, due to Partow's close association with Nimā Yushij, existing research has predominantly portrayed him as a *Nimāic* poet rather than recognizing his individual significance as an independent experimentalist.

First and foremost, this chapter delves into the life and career of Mohammad Moqaddam, who emerges as the preeminent experimentalist poet of this period. The section scrutinizes some of Moqaddam's prose poems to illustrate the quality of his experimentation with the tradition of versification. After analysing Moqaddam's conception of free verse through phrasal, rhythmical, and metrical analysis, the section examines Moqaddam's rhetorical departure from dead metaphors and established symbols to the creation of private ones. Next, Zabih Behruz, the second poet of focus, takes centre stage as his works will be examined in a dedicated section. After reviewing Behruz's early experiments with satirical poems in traditional templates, the section analyses the quality of the free verse in three of his poetic dramas. Finally, a section is dedicated to Shin Partow's experiments with prose poetry in three directions: pushing the boundaries of conventional literary language, employing modern fictional techniques, and developing a rhythmic system for free verse.

Mohammad Moqaddam, a prose poet: Introducing free verse into Persian poetry

Mohammad Eʻtemād Moqaddam, born in September 1908 in Tehran and passed away on 30 July 1996, had an intriguing academic and literary journey. He initially studied at an American college in Tehran before venturing to the United States to continue his studies in New York. However, he did not complete his bachelor's degree and returned to Tehran in 1929, where he worked as a translator at the Ministry of Foreign Affairs for two years. In 1931, Moqaddam went to the United States for the second time and successfully obtained his degree in linguistics. Subsequently, he enrolled in a PhD programme in Oriental Culture and Literature at Princeton University. During his time as a PhD student, he published his debut poetry collection, titled, *Rāz-e Nimshab; Rāhi Chand Birun Az Pardeh* (The Mystery of Midnight; A Few Pieces Out of Tune with the Main Melody), in 1934. According to Seyf al-Din Najmābādi, all the poems in this collection were composed in a single night following a conversation with a friend about experiential means of expressing thoughts through poetry.[1] A few months later, Moqaddam published his second poetry collection, *Bāng-e Khorus* (The Voice of the Rooster), in a limited print run of 150 copies. Finally, in May 1935, he released his final poetry collection in the form of a dramatic poem titled *Bāzgasht be Alamut; Pish-darāmad va Nāmeh-ye Yekom* (Returning to Alamut; the Introduction, and the First Letter). This forty-page collection had only forty copies printed, and each copy bore the inscription 'this is not for sale'.

Upon completing his studies in 1938, Mohammad Moqaddam returned to Iran, a period marked by the struggle of modernist poets to establish their manifestos as the definitive path of literary modernism. However, Moqaddam showed little interest in the turbulent developments of Persian poetry at the time. Instead, he embarked on a career as a lecturer in Ancient Iranian languages at the University of Tehran. In the early 1960s, he ventured to the United States and taught Iranian history and culture at the University of Utah. Later, in 1963, he founded the Department of Ancient Languages at the University of Tehran.

---

[1] Seyf al-Din Najmābādi, 'Ostād Doktor Mohammad Moqaddam', *Journal of the School of Humanities and Literature, University of Tehran; Special issue: Jashn-Nāmeh-ye Doktor Mohammad Moqaddam*, 4 (1977), 1–11 (p. 10).

Aside from his academic pursuits, particularly in establishing academic studies on ancient Iranian languages and conducting extensive research on Persian accents and dialects, Mohammad Moqaddam also made notable contributions to the introduction of prose poetry to Persian-speaking audiences. This innovative poetic style drew inspiration from both modern Persian prose and the non-Persian traditions of blank verse. Although Moqaddam published three collections of poetry in 1934 and 1935, he did not release any further creative literary works throughout his life. Nonetheless, his experiments with prose poetry and unconventional poetic language expanded the horizons of literary innovation during that period.

There is a consensus among critics that Moqaddam drew strong influence from American poetry, particularly the works of Walt Whitman (1819–1892), in his poetic style. Mohammad-Rezā Shafi'i Kadkani argues that Moqaddam's poems were probably also influenced by the prose translations of Western poetry in Iranian journals of the first half of the twentieth century.[2] These translations, primarily from French authors, were published in literary journals such as *Bahār*, *Dāneshkadeh*, *Armaghān*, and *Now-Bahār* during the 1910s and 1920s. They served as a significant means for Persian poets to acquaint themselves with the literary currents and innovations of the West during that time, predating Moqaddam's journey as a poet.

A significant problem with this argument is that reducing the experiments of a poet who studied linguistics and literature in the United States to merely an imitation of translated poetry is too simplistic, if not intentionally disparaging. Furthermore, according to Behnam Fomeshi, there were very few translations of American poetry into Persian before the 1940s, with only one page dedicated to Whitman's work in Persian.[3] Studying at one of the leading American universities of the time required proficiency in English, meaning Moqaddam was potentially self-sufficient enough to avoid being influenced by early Persian translations of Western poetry.

In addition, one should question the intensity of the impact of Walt Whitman's poetic practice on Moqaddam's work. Moqaddam himself states that if he wanted to admit any relation between his poetry and a Western model, 'he would name another American poet, Vincent Miller, as a source of inspiration'.[4] It is possible to argue that by presenting such

---

[2] Mohammad-Rezā Shafi'i Kadkani, *Advār-e She'r-e Fārsi* (Tehran: Tus, 2000), pp. 52–3.
[3] Behnam M. Fomeshi, *The Persian Whitman: Beyond a Literary Reception* (Leiden: Leiden University Press, 2019), p. 64.
[4] Probably Moqaddam or the interviewer (Shams Langrudi) has confused the poet's surname Millay with Miller. In this case, he refers to Edna St Vincent Millay (1892–1950), who was a Pulitzer-winning American poet and playwright known for her feminist activism. See Mohammad Shams Langrudi, *Tārikh-e Tahlili-e She'r-e Now*, 4 vols (Tehran: Markaz, 1998), 1, p. 189.

an argument Moqaddam attempted to misdirect critics from their focus on a leading poet, Whitman, to a lesser-known American poet for Iranian readers. That is, he endeavoured to show that the relationship between his works and American poets was one of dialogue between peers, rather than of his work being influenced by the legacy of American masters. Nevertheless, it also suggests that he was indeed aware of the stylistic qualities of contemporary American poets. In any case, Moqaddam's final product improvises and indigenizes poetic forms such as free verse and blank verse to prepare the path for more experiential subject matters and forms in Persian poetry.

Dialogue with his contemporary Persian prose is the second element which shaped the notion of literary change in Moqaddam's experiments with prose poetry. One can argue that Moqaddam's personal interests in linguistics, ancient languages, and modern literature were all reflected in modern Persian stories written between the early 1930s and the 1950s, particularly in the works of Sādeq Hedāyat (1903–1951). Similar to these contemporary writers, Moqaddam's poetic experiments were inclined towards archaic lexicon, themes, and even literary forms.

As to the use of archaic language, one can detect a considerable number of middle Persian words used in the literary language of this era. This development was the direct result of what some essayists and scholars refer to as the 'purification movement', which encouraged Persian speakers to replace middle Persian words or even new words based on old Persian morphophonemics for words of Arabic, Turkic, and more recently French origin. This trend became evident in Moqaddam's poetry too, as he himself was a linguist who specialized in ancient languages and was a leading supporter of this trend. Besides, Moqaddam's engagement with the purification movement may have derived from his relationship with Zabih Behruz, another essayist, dramatist, and poet who was a leading figure of this movement.

Thematically, also, during the same period, several short stories, novels, and plays which adapted folk stories and historical narratives from the pre-Islamic or early Islamic era were written from a nationalistic perspective. These include some celebrated works such as Hedāyat's plays *Parvin Dokhtar-e Sāsān* (Parvin, Sāsān's daughter, 1930) and *Maziyār* (1933), set in ancient Iran, and a collection of short stories called *Anirān* (Non-Iranian, 1931) by Shin Partow, Bozorg Alavi (1904–1997), and Sādeq Hedāyat.[5] Some of the most famous novels of this period were also set in a pre-Islamic Iran, such as *Shahrbānu* (1931) by Ali-Asghar Rahimzādeh Safavi (1895–1959)

---

[5] This collection is dedicated to Zabih Behruz. Shin Partow and Bozorg Alavi and Sādeq Hedāyat, *Anirān* (Tehran: [n. pub.], 1930), p. 2.

and *Lāzicā* (1930) by Heydar-Ali Kamāli (1869–1936).⁶ Authors of this period also embraced the structural potential inherent in folklore stories and poems. They began incorporating elements of folk poetry, such as syllabic verses, into their modern works.

The growing popularity of folklore and pre-Islamic Iranian language and literature during this period can be attributed to several significant factors that aligned with the cultural policies of the Pahlavi, which sought to combine revivalism and modernization. First of all, scholarly or creative studies in folk literature, particularly *Osane* (Fairy Tales, 1931) and *Neyrangestān* (Trickland, 1933) by Sādeq Hedāyat, and *Vag Vag Sāhāb* (Mister Bow Wow, 1934) by Mas'ud Farzād and Sādeq Hedāyat, became a model for further studies and for the practice of reformulating folk heritage within modern literary works.⁷ Second, the celebration of Ferdowsi's Millennium, which included an international conference in 1934, was conducive to a wave of new editions and translations of Pahlavi texts. Moreover, certain academic endeavours such as *Irānkudeh* (1943–84), a journal of the *Irānvich* Forum at the University of Tehran, affected the literary environment; pioneering writers and poets of the era capitalized on the widespread interest in this retrospective trend to break away from literary clichés and experiment with new aesthetic systems.⁸

In his pursuit of an unconventional and democratic aesthetic regime, Moqaddam ventured into various aspects of Persian poetics, exploring rhyme schemes, rhythmic systems, and diction. In all these aspects Moqaddam attempts to distance his poetry from the accepted tradition of versification. In the realm of rhyme, Moqaddam's poetry embraces scattered rhyme patterns, incorporating rhymes at both the end and the middle of verses. Unlike classical rhyme schemes, which adhere to a specific template, Moqaddam's freestyle rhyme liberates the poem from a rigid structure, injecting a sense of rhythmic variety and breaking the monotony of the poetic rhythm. It was the use of freestyle rhyme that, in time, altered the entire narrative system of Persian poetry and gave distinctive voices to different elements within the

---

⁶Hasan Mir-Ābedini lists a considerable number of celebrated historical novels, short stories, and dramas published during the 1930s and 1940s, most of which were focused on the pre-Islamic and pre-Mongol era. Hasan Mir-Ābedini, *Sad Sāl Dāstānnevisi-e Irān* (Tehran: Cheshmeh, 2001), pp. 40–1.
⁷Jahāngir Hedāyat, *Farhang-e Āmiyāneh-ye Mardom-e Irān* (Tehran: Cheshmeh, 1999), pp. 10–18.
⁸Some of the most well-known writers of this period who had a clear tendency to the trend of archaism in modern literature, such as Sādeq Hedāyat, Mojtabā Minovi, Abdolhoseyn Nushin, Mas'ud Farzād, Shin Partow, and Bozorg Alavi, played a major role in the wave of translations from European literature. This group, also known as *Rab'eh* (Four), was officially formed in 1934 and translated a number of masterpieces of modern Western literature. The activities of this group are commonly seen as acting against a similar community with traditionalist inclinations called *Sab'eh* (Seven).

poem. Moqaddam uses freestyle rhyme to create a democratic collection of poetry in which various characters with distinguishable voices narrate their story in personalized tones. For instance, in the following stanza, the semi-alternate recurrence of rhymes at the end and in the middle of the hemistichs represents the melodic voice of the bird in a playful tone:

من مرغ شباویزم
روز پنهانم و از روشنیش پرهیزم
آشیانم کس ندیده هرگز
تاریک چو شد بیرون پرم و خوانم[9]

I am the bird of the night (Scops Owl)
I am hidden during the day and I avoid its brightness
No one has ever seen my nest
When it becomes dark, I will fly out and sing.

Derek Attridge proposes three interrelated analysing methods to measure rhyme scheme in free verse poetry. The first is 'phrasing analysis', a term which refers to the significance of phrasing in the formation of syntax, meaning and dynamic movement within the poem. Attridge writes, 'a poem's phrasing is an important part of its varying sense of pace and onward impetus, and of its different degrees and types of pause and closure.'[10] The second is 'rhythmic analysis', which examines the rhythmic quality of the components of non-metrical verse, particularly its syllables. This analysis focuses on understanding the rhythmic patterns and variations within the poem. The third method is 'metrical analysis,' which investigates how the verse, stanza, or the poem as a whole approximates a structured order.[11] In the case of Moqaddam's poetry, which incorporates both metrical and non-metrical verses, this chapter aims to study the poems using phrasing and rhythmic analysis methods. Furthermore, the chapter will explore Moqaddam's experiments with pseudo-prosodic rhythms through metrical analysis in subsequent paragraphs.

Moqaddam joins metrical and non-metrical stanzas to create poems that exhibit diverse rhythms, emphasizing various tones and moods within a single work. Moreover, on some occasions, he composes stanzas which consist of blended rhythmic systems. That is, these stanzas may contain combined metrical and non-metrical hemistichs. Wherever the overtone of the stanza requires, the poet adjusts the syntax with the meaning by

---

[9] Mohammad Moqaddam, *Rāz-e Nimshab; Rāhi Chand Birun az Pardeh* (Tehran: [n. pub.], 1934), p. 10.
[10] Derek Attridge, *Poetic Rhythm: An Introduction* (Cambridge: Cambridge University Press, 1995), p. 182.
[11] Roi Tartakovsky, 'Free, Verse, Rhythm: An Introduction', *Style*, 1 (2015), 1–7 (p. 5).

changing the disposition of phrases and rhythmic arrangement. In the following example, the narrator merges the conventional prosodic metre of the first two lines into a blended metre to simulate the movement of the bird among the trees:

در باغ های تنها
در دره های پر بیم
بر شاخ درختان تک رو
افراز درختان بلند پر برگ می پّرم و میخوانم[12]

In lonely gardens
In fearful valleys
On the branches of single trees
On top of the tall, leafy trees I will fly and sing.

In this example, the combination of the first two hemistichs forms a conventional prosodic metre named *mozāre' mosamman-e akhrab* (--∪-/∪--I --∪-/∪--). However, despite this traditional rhythmic system, the metrical arrangement does not repeat in all the hemistichs of the stanza. Indeed, the third hemistich starts with a similar metrical foot to the first two; however, its second and third foot are turned to (∪--). The final line deviates from the established pattern by starting with the same three feet as the third hemistich, but then transitions into a completely different and arbitrary metrical pattern (--∪/∪--/∪-- I --∪∪/---). One can consider the last hemistich as non-metrical since the pattern, although loosely resembling *mostaf'elo fa'ulon* which is close to a common rhythm found in nursery rhymes, does not approximate any of the distinguishable metrical patterns in Persian poetry.

Another remarkable experiment Moqaddam conducts with the traditional prosodic system is his inconsistent use of final metrical feet in the uneven verses of a stanza. In the following example, the first two hemistichs start with (--∪/--∪/∪--)[13], which is a rather odd variation of the *hazaj* metre. The last (fourth) foot in the first and the second hemistich, however, is scanned (--) and (∪--), respectively. The third hemistich is shorter and responds to the first three feet in the previous hemistichs. The last hemistich, also, is scanned as (--∪/∪-/∪--), which approximates the metrical arrangement in the third hemistich with a slight variation in the second foot:

چون نیمه‌ی شب گشت یکی پروانه
از دور بیامد برم و روشنیم خواست

---

[12] Moqaddam, *Rāz-e Nimshab*, p. 4.
[13] The first hemistich can also be scanned as (--∪/∪--/∪---/-).

از روشنیم بال و پرش سوخت
سوزی ز درون من بر آورد.¹⁴

> When it was midnight, a butterfly
> approached me from a distance and asked for my light.
> Because of my light, the butterfly wing burned
> And it made me depressed (I burned deep inside).

The skilful use of combining metrical and non-metrical, or even prosaic, lines in a poem allows the poet to diminish the dominance of a restricted prosodic metre and explore diverse aspects of poetic expression. In traditional poetics, the prosodic metre is considered one of the intrinsic elements which differentiates between poetry and prose. Thus, generating non-metrical lines in a poem questions the traditional significance of prosody. Almost all pioneer poets of the time, particularly Moqaddam, Nimā, and Kiā, saw traditional prosody as a representation of elitist and hierarchical, classical aesthetics. Thus, they attempted to invent new rhythmic systems in which the hegemony of classical prosodic metres was broken. These poets tried to reform the traditional conception of metre either by relaxing the quantity of feet in the hemistich or by mixing metrical and non-metrical rhythms. In fact, Moqaddam tried to replace the notion of rhythm with the prosodic metre as a vital component of poetry. Moqaddam simplified the notion of rhythm to one which is defined by regularity, repetition, and expectations. To explain this viewpoint on rhythmic systems, Roi Tartakovsky states that 'when the recurrence is palpable and recognisable enough, we would probably place the line within metricity, and therefore certainly within rhythmicity'.[15]

Moqaddam's exploration extended to inventing metrical patterns that deviated from the traditional prosodic standards. Despite their departure from strict adherence, one can still identify recurring prosodic feet within these lines. According to Attridge, this particular form of free verse calls for an analysis that focuses on its metrical aspects:

> Metrical analysis can reveal the way in which some free verse poems maintain a relation to metrical verse, approaching and deviating from regular metrical patterns. In passages where a metrical pattern is fully realised, the reader perceives beats, and variations such as demotion and promotion are possible. In other passages, there is only a slight feeling of metrical regularity.[16]

---

[14] Moqaddam, *Rāz-e Nimshab*, p. 14.
[15] Tartakovsky, p. 1.
[16] Attridge, p. 181.

Such lines in Moqaddam's poetry do not conform to specific metrical feet, nor are they completely devoid of rhythm like regular prose. Indeed, one can find rhythmicity in verses, but it is not possible to fit them in standard prosodic metres. Khānlari says the rhythm of Moqaddam's poetry is, at most, a 'rhythm-like' beat which, unlike conventional metres, is not based on the quality and quantity of syllables or feet in each verse.[17] One could argue that these poems, the tone of which may remind the reader of pre-Islamic poetic orisons, can be termed as 'rhythmic prose':

اکنون نیمی ز شب تیره گذشته
نیمی ز تنم سوخته
مانده به جای نیم دگرش
یا سوخته گردد یا نه.[18]

Now half of the dark night has passed
Half of my body has burned
Half of it remains
It may burn or not.

Having analysed Moqaddam's techniques in arranging new rhyme and rhythm patterns, one cannot detect any specific musical system in his poetry. Moqaddam says he had no specific model in mind when breaking his lines, so he cut the line where he 'felt it had reached a kind of rhythm'.[19] By declining to follow any kind of musical metre, Moqaddam, like other pioneers of the time, highlights the significance of a natural tone of speech in a poem.

It seems that Moqaddam was the first Persian poet who sought to achieve a natural tone of speech in the realm of prose poetry instead of conventional prosodic poetry. In this way, Moqaddam uses techniques which could be considered language errors in traditional literary discourse. He frees his language from the standard form of syntax in Persian to highlight the natural rhythm of the prose. In the following example, he lets the speech expand in the stanza through enjambment. Indeed, stanzas in this poem are composed of several unfinished hemistichs, in terms of syntax. Then, he allows the meaning to run over from one hemistich to another without completion. This technique enables the poet to harmonize the length of the hemistich with the natural tone of speech instead of confining it in the restricted units of traditional versification. Besides, the rhythm of the stanza is partly a

---

[17] Parviz Nātel Khānlari, *Haftād Sokhan*, 4 vols (Tehran: Tus, 1998), 1, pp. 273–4.
[18] Moqaddam, *Rāz-e Nimshab*, p. 13.
[19] Shams Langrudi, *Tārikh-e Tahlili-e She'r-e Now*, 1, p. 189.

result of overloading the sentence with complemental, prepositional phrases and relative clauses:

برای دوری از مردم از کارهایشان از اندیشه‌هایشان
از آرزوهای کوچکشان از دردهای پستشان
برای ندیدن ریختشان نشنیدن سخنشان بو نکردن بویشان
برای آزادانه تماشا کردن نیست شدنشان
در ویرانه دژ الموت که دست کس بدان نرسیدی
که تنها آله بلند پرواز گردش پریدی
و مار در ویرانه اش سوراخ داشتی
در همان دژی که روزگاری کلید زندگی و مرگ جهانی آنجا بودی
حسن آرام گرفته بود.[20]

> To keep himself away from people their work their thoughts
> From their little dreams from their cheap pains
> To avoid seeing their face hearing their words sensing their smell
> To freely watch them vanish
> In the ruins of Alamut Fortress which no one could reach
> Which only the high-flying eagle could fly around
> And snakes had holes in its ruin
> In the same fortress where once the key to the life and death of a world was placed
> Hasan had settled down.

Moqaddam effectively employs pauses within phrasal groups and clauses, thereby breaking each hemistich into two or three segments. This technique can be seen as a form of 'caesura', which is a pause between two phrases in a line of verse. Roger Mitchell, who analyses caesura in the poetry of Walt Whitman as a rhythmical element, writes:

> He uses the caesura to break the line into groups of various grammatical types. Though the grammatical nature of the groups varies, the principle by which the line is broken by the caesura is a single one. Whitman breaks the line for rhetorical emphasis. The resulting groups, as we will see, also have meaning rhythmically or prosodically.[21]

Similarly, Moqaddam tries to make a pattern out of pauses by placing them in specific parts of the sentence. Indeed, he activates the musical quality of prosaic lines by fracturing them into smaller chunks containing rhythmic similarities. The caesura in some poems breaks the lines unevenly to characterize different voices. In *Ātash-e Nimshab* (Midnight Fire), the

---

[20] Mohammad Moqaddam, *Bāzgasht be Alamut* (Tehran: [n. pub.], 1935), p. 11.
[21] Roger Mitchell, 'A Prosody for Whitman', *PMLA*, 6 (1969), 1606–12 (p. 1607).

EXPERIMENTALISM IN PERSIAN POETRY BETWEEN THE 1930S AND 1950S

composure of the narrator has been illustrated through longer hemistichs with fewer breaks, while recurring breaks indicate the enthusiastic tone of the fire angel and fairies in other parts:

آتش بلند می‌شود پاره های آن بالا می‌جهند
چکیدن سرشگ آتش و ناله‌ی آن شنیده می‌شود
این اشک فرشته‌ی آذر است
که از شادی و رنج بیرون می‌آید
[...]
فرشته آذر می‌خواند
از نو از نو
روشنیم تازه و
گرمیم سوزان
از نو
پریان با هم
از نو از نو.²²

The fire rises its pieces jump up
one can hear the fire dripping and moaning
These are the tears of the angel of Azar
which come from joy and suffering
[...]
The angel of Azar sings
Anew Anew
We have lightened afresh and
we are hot burning
Anew
Fairies together
Anew Anew.

The balanced literary style, which to some extent contains both the naturalness of expository language and the prosaic energy of fictional prose, is another idiosyncratic element of Moqaddam's poetry. Moqaddam's new language did not repeat the limited range of overused, poetical words and expressions and was not limited to merely inserting colloquial elements into the poem. Moqaddam's poetry is constantly shifting between literary and non-literary registers of Persian. This kind of combined language has broader boundaries than conventional literary language. It allows the poet to enter different voices into the poem and let them talk in their own natural tone. The multiplicity of voice and heterogeneity among components of the literary language, in turn, is a drive towards a more democratic poetic structure. The new language uses the whole Persian lexicon (not just the

---

²²Moqaddam, *Rāz-e Nimshab*, pp. 54–5.

conventional literary one) to award to all voices in the poem an equal opportunity to be heard and understood:

آهسته حسن نزدیک شد
پشت خود را به درختی داد
و خاموش ماتش برد
پس از لختی بنشست و خم شد تا چهره خود در آب شوید
چشمان خودش در آب او را گرفتند
و چون در چشمان خود در آب مینگریست
سرود پریان را شنید
وان سان سرودشان سبک و شیرین بود
که حسن نزدیک بود بلغزد و در آب افتد [...]
پری روی نیلوپر
خدای دژ الموت رو بنگرید
هوای کوه نمی‌خاد
خوراک و نوشاک خورده
بویی از دختر برده
دیگه تنهایی نمی‌خاد
پریان با هم
خدای دژ رو بنگر
شیفته شده به دختر
همچی که شد پس بهتر
و چون بدینجا رسید
حسن دید که چشمانش آذرین گشته [...] ²³

Hasan advanced slowly
He leaned his back on a tree
He stared silently
After a while, he sat down and bent to wash his face with the water
His own eyes caught him in the water
And as he was gazing at his eyes mirrored in the water
He heard the fairies singing
Their song was so light and sweet
That Hasan was about to slip and fall into the water [...]
Fairy on the lotus:
    Look at the god of Alamut Fortress
    He does not desire the mountain fresh air
    He has eaten and drunk
    He has sensed the girl
    He no longer wants to be alone

---

²³ Moqaddam, *Bāzgasht be Alamut*, pp. 52–6.

Fairies together:
    Look at the god of the fortress
    Infatuated with the girl
    Whatever happened, so better
And when it got to this point
Hasan noticed that his eyes were ignited [...]

In the above section, the voice of the narrator holds the same rank as the other voices and does not affect the language of the fairies. In contrast, the narrator of traditional poetry turns the suppressed, hidden language of different classes to the public transcript proportioning them to be presented in a highly valued poetic template, which automatically neutralizes its force and softens its edge. However, in this poem, the narrator has no dominant influence on the way that other characters speak. Fairies can represent their own group using the language of their choice. Thus, their words, unlike the narrator's, are colloquial and rhythmical. Using the whole Persian lexicon, Moqaddam provides all objects and characters (irrespective of their rank in the hierarchy of cultural values) with a distinctive language by which they can appear in the poem.

Moqaddam's unconventional ideas about poetics were not limited to his innovative rhyme, rhythm and language. Shafi'i Kadkani criticizes Moqaddam's attitude towards classical rhetoric and claims that there are no successful examples of figures of speech or rhetorical devices in his work. He goes on further to state that there is not even a single metaphor or simile in the whole poetry collection of *Rāz-e Nimshab*.[24] A major problem with Shafi'i's criticism is that he uses traditional definitions of rhetorical figures to analyse a radically experimental poem. A more suitable approach for achieving this objective would involve developing a new system that combines the criteria for evaluating non-Persian rhetorical devices with classical Persian ones. Simultaneously, it would be necessary to expand both systems by considering the qualities of non-literary written and spoken Persian.

One can argue that Moqaddam's poetry is based on converting the dead metaphors and public symbols of Persian literature into fresh, private symbols. These symbols mostly represent the figure of the pioneer poet who fights with the advocates of inherited culture and particularly the traditionalist literati. In the first collection, *Rāz-e Nimshab*, he uses the dead metaphors of traditional poetry – including the candle, the butterfly, the leopard, and the cypress – and turns them into symbols for the marginal experimentalist poet himself. Doing so, he explores widely for a characteristic of objects which can be associated with the conception of experimental poetry to use as the vehicle for the new metaphor. In the opening stanza of the collection, the

---

[24] Mohammad-Rezā Shafi'i Kadkani, *Bā Cherāq va Āyeneh* (Tehran: Sokhan, 2011), p. 582.

poet pictures a firefly in the darkness of the night. Both of these elements are public symbols. Darkness represents unawareness in most cultures, and the light of the firefly, as an inverse of darkness, signifies awareness:

در تاریکی شب
گفته‌های پراکنده من
همچون پروانه شب تاب
درخشند و پرند²⁵

In the darkness of the night
My scattered sayings
Like a firefly
Shine and fly

The firefly is a light-giver who represents an entity of enlightenment in the depth of darkness. However, by creating a direct context for the image, the poet turns this metaphor into a private symbol representing himself (the experimentalist poet) and his poetry as a provider of light at poetic and social levels. The words are scattered because his poetry is experimental, but they shine and fly to provide role models. This is the light (the new context) which transforms the meaning of the dead metaphors of the collection and symbolically brings them to a new life. In the last stanza of the collection, where the poet promises to return later to complete the journey and to reveal the mystery, he alludes to his next experimental attempts through the same private symbols:

تاریکی شب گفت مرا
این تابش تو جهنده بود و کوتاه
راز تو هنوز راز مانده
گفتمش آری بازمیگردم²⁶

The darkness of the night told me
This radiation of yours was transient and short-lived
Your secret is still a secret
I told him yes I would be back

The same stanza is repeated on the first page of the second collection, *Bāng-e Khorus*. This is followed by another stanza, saying that the author has come back in the brightness of the morning to awaken audiences and reveal his mystery to them. In this long episodic work, the poet presents himself symbolically as the rooster, which traditionally acts as an awakener. In his

---

[25] Moqaddam, *Rāz-e Nimshab*, p. 1.
[26] Moqaddam, *Rāz-e Nimshab*, p. 109.

introduction to *Yeki Bud Yeki Nabud* (Once Upon a Time, 1921), Sayyed Mohammad-Ali Jamālzādeh (1892–1997), a leading, modern Persian writer, gives this metaphor a new political sense to show the significant role of literary modernity in awakening people and informing them about the upheavals of their society.[27] Jamālzādeh states that writers and poets must explain the natural unity of political and literary despotism to their audiences.[28] In Moqaddam's work, probably inspired by Jamālzādeh, this metaphor has turned into a symbol representing a pioneering artist who is not directly involved with sociopolitical conflicts but still proposes emancipatory philosophical thoughts.

In *Bāng-e Khorus*, Moqaddam gives the symbolical character of the rooster the authority to question its identity. Similar to a pioneering artist living in a dictatorship and struggling with the social function and the political engagement of his work, the rooster is astonished by events in his surroundings over which he has no control. He finds the opportunity to break the rules and sings freely day and night to awaken people. However, the gardener and his wife (who represent dogmatic people) try to eliminate the rooster. In the eyes of the gardener's family, the singing of the rooster at sunset is unconventional, and thus they fear its consequences. In contrast, the gardener's son (potentially a representative of the younger generation of modern poets) is the only one who understands the rooster's concerns and tries to explain its emancipatory message:

خورشید پایین تر رفت دیگر پیدا نبود
ابرها کنار آسمان سرخ شدند
خروس پشت پنجره روی تخته ای
از این ور به آن ور میرفت
آرام نداشت
اندیشه ای سنگین در سرش بود
سرخی آسمان تاج سرخش را سرختر کرده
و پوشش سپیدش را آذرگون ساخته بود
ناگهان استاد
و نالهئی از ته دل برآورد
دو دو لو دو و و
زن باغبان با شوهر و بچهاش نشسته بودند
زن رو به شوهر خود کرد و گفت
ناله خروس را شنیدی
امشب چه شبی است بیگاه میخواند
که خواهد مرد
باید سرش را برید[29]

---

[27] Mohammad-Ali Jamālzādeh, *Yeki Bud Yeki Nabud* (Tehran: Parvin, 1941), p. 17.
[28] Jamālzādeh, p. 4.
[29] Mohammad Moqaddam, *Bāng-e Khorus* (Tehran: [n. pub.], 1935), pp. 23–4.

> The sun went down and disappeared
> The clouds turned red in the horizon
> The rooster behind the window on a board
> Was walking from side to side
> He was anxious
> His head was heavy with a thought
> The red of the sky had made his crown redder
> And his white feathers fire-like
> He suddenly stopped
> And cried from the bottom of his heart
> Du du lu du ...
> The gardener's wife was sitting with her husband and son
> The woman turned to her husband and said
> Did you hear the rooster's cry
> What a night his singing is untimely
> Who will die?
> His head must be cut off.[30]

The rooster, traditionally a symbol of the heralding of a new day and the triumph of light over darkness, takes on a different role in this extended poem. Instead of confidently proclaiming the arrival of dawn, the rooster grapples with uncertainty and internal struggles. It loses its metaphorical identity and becomes a reflection of confusion, torn by conflicting thoughts and doubts about the right moment to announce the new day. One can argue that this poem is Moqaddam's personal narrative, wondering if this is the right time for taking such a big step in modernizing Persian poetry, as with Nimā's belief that Moqaddam's experiments were 'too advanced for public understanding and sentiments'.[31]

In the final collection of poems, the poet depicts himself through a symbolic narrative involving Hasan-e Sabbāh, a renowned figure from history known for his rebellious missionary activities and the formation of the Assassins. Hasan-e Sabbāh represents an enduring symbol of oppositional leadership, veiled in mystery and unattainability. Within the poem, Hasan, akin to a pioneering poet, experiences rejection from the common people and those who influence public opinion. Hasan tries to break the conventions of his traditional society and teach *divānegi* (craziness) and *āzādegi* (liberality) to the youth:

---

[30] An old superstitious belief among Iranians considers the untimely crowing of a rooster unlucky and prescribes sacrificing the rooster as the only way to protect the household from the impending misfortune.

[31] Nimā Yushij, 'Arzesh-e Ehsāsāt dar Zendgi-e Honarpishegān', in *Darbāreh-ye She'r va Shā'eri*, ed. by Sirus Tāhbāz (Tehran: Negāh, 2006), p. 87.

اینجا استادان شاگردان را از نامه‌های نوشته
و گفته‌های ساخته و آماده میاموزند
شاگردان یاد میگیرند و پس میدهند
بیرون از نامه و دهان استادان چیزی نیست
و چیزی نمیخواهند[...]
نامه‌های دبستان را دور اندازید
چیزهای بزرگتر شما را آموزم
اینجا شما را خرد و مردمی و چیزهای ساختگی دیگر آموزند
من شما را دیوانگی آموزم آزادگی آموزم[32]

Here masters educate their students with written accounts
And structured prepared sayings
Students learn and recite back
There is nothing outside the books and mouths of their masters
And they do not desire anything [...]
Abandon schoolbooks
I will teach you more significant things
Here they teach you rationality and humanity and other artificial subjects
I teach you craziness I teach you liberality.

The craziness associated with liberality represents divergent thinking, which breaks the borders set by inherited culture and is a cause of creativity and progress in society in all directions. This divergent thinking in Moqaddam's world, of course, is embodied in experimental poetry which, because of its unconventionality, sounds somehow nonsense to its readers, yet liberates their minds to make them more open to changing the fundamentals of traditional literature. Masters and students represent conservative men of letters and readers, respectively. In this symbolic system, students understand art through the 'written accounts, and structured prepared sayings' of their teachers, which represent the traditional scholarly books and existing monuments of classical literature. However, Hasan wants to guide students towards innovative thinking. He places craziness against 'rationality' and 'humanity' to emphasize the role of anarchy and deconstructive approaches in experimentalism.

Therefore, in response to Shafi'i's argument concerning the absence of rhetorical devices in Moqaddam's poetry, one can argue that Moqaddam's entire oeuvre is based on a new rhetorical system. In his three collections, Moqaddam turns the dead metaphors and established symbols of Persian poetry into symbols representing elements of his era's literary revolution. Shafi'i Kadkani also argues that Moqaddam's poems did not influence the

---

[32] Moqaddam, *Bāzgasht be Alamut*, p. 34.

literary mood of the era. He claims that there is no trace of any critical essays or dialogues about these three collections of poetry during the 1930s and 1940s and concludes that this absence demonstrates the indifference of literary society to these experiments.[33]

The main problem with Shafi'i's perspective, in this case, is that he has wrong assumptions about the expected reception of experimentalism in society. Experimental works such as these three collections do not confront tradition in order to propose a new aesthetic regime or literary style to the public. They rather aspire to broaden the boundaries of the genre and pave the path of modernization for avant-garde poets and high modernists. Moqaddam's greatest influence, therefore, is to be found in the poetry of the following generation. With the foundations laid, the following generation and some of the poets of the same generation were able to construct a new building in the space that Moqaddam, as an experimentalist, had created by demolishing the old structures. Thus, the innovations that one can spot in Moqaddam's works are experiments with the potential of Persian poetry. These experiments came to fruition in the works of the next generation of poets, particularly Ahmad Shāmlu and the followers of his prose poetry, also known as *She'r-e Sepid* (White Poetry), or the poetry of avant-garde movements such as *She'r-e Digar* (Other Poetry), and *Mowj-e Now* (New Wave) in the 1960s.

Zabih Behruz: A wanderer poet in the city of drama[34]

Another writer who experimented with poetic and rhetorical aspects of Persian poetry in his plays and poems was Zabih Behruz. Although Behruz is best known for his plays and some satirical poems in classical templates, he conducted radical experiments with poetic expression in his plays. However, these experimental drama-poems were never proposed and examined as poetry by the author or literary critics. Choosing drama as a space of experimentation with the poetic aesthetic system was probably due to the pressure that the literary community exerted on experimentalist and avant-garde poets. In addition, drama, as a genre, already contained the dramatic elements which most of the Iranian pioneer poets were trying to develop in their poems. Finally, probably to protect his academic status, Behruz

---

[33] Shafi'i Kadkani, *Bā Cherāq va Āyeneh*, p. 586.
[34] Although most of Behruz's experimental drama-poems were published before Moqaddam's between 1927 and 1934, due to the significance of Moqaddam's experiments in forming the conception of experimentalism in Persian poetry, I decided to analyse Behruz's oeuvre after his.

preferred to be known as a respected linguist and playwright rather than an unconventional poet. This was partly because his poetic innovations were so radical that he might have been criticized by the majority of the literary scholars of his time if he had wanted to propose them in the genre of poetry.

Zabih Behruz was born in 1890 in a well-known family who traced their ancestry to the Safavids and were also related to the Qajars. His father, Abolfazl Tabib Sāvoji, was a famous writer who served in Naser al-Din Shāh's court. At the age of twenty, Behruz left Iran for Egypt, where he lived for ten years. Then, he moved to England and worked at the University of Cambridge with Professor Edward Browne. However, because of a dispute with Browne, he went to Germany for about a year before returning to Iran in 1924. In Tehran, he worked in the Ministry of Finance before he started teaching mathematics at the Air Force School of the Army University in Ahvaz. He wrote most of his literary and research works during the time that he was teaching at this university. He retired in 1965 and shortly after became a permanent member of *Farhangestan-e Zabān-e Fārsi* (the Academy of the Persian Language),[35] before he passed away in 1972. Behruz's writings, whether creative or academic, have been admired by both traditionalists and modernists.[36] This popularity among academics and artists is likely due to his experiences working in some of the most prestigious academic centres of the time, as well as his vast knowledge in a variety of cultural and scientific branches.

Behruz's publications can be categorized into three different types: language, pedagogy and literature. His research works on Middle Persian and New Persian are those by which he gained his fame as a prominent linguist. He and Mohammad Moqaddam were among the main founders of the *Irānvich* Forum and *Irānkudeh* journal. He was also a leading figure of the *Sereh-Nevisi* (Language purification) movement. His essays on the necessity of reforming the Persian language and purifying it of foreign words are some of the most critical works in favour of this movement. In addition, he published several pedagogical books for children, mainly on mathematics and literature.

In addition to all these activities, Behruz is best known for his poetry and plays. The most famous poetry book by Behruz is a long satirical poem entitled *Me'rāj-Nāmeh-ye Ebn-e Deylāq* or *Gand-e Bādāvard* (Ebn-e Deylāq's Book of Ascension or Wind-blown Stench).[37] Similar to the

---

[35] A governmental institution where a group of scholars were supposed to replace alien words with more natural and authentic ones.
[36] According to Vahid Ayubi, Jalāl al-Din Homā'i, a well-known traditionalist scholar, admires both Behruz's prose and poetry, although he was a serious opponent of literary change. See Vahid Ayubi, *Zabih Behruz: Zendegi va Gozideh-ye Āsār* (Tehran: Nik, 2007), p. 7.
[37] There is no accurate date of publication available for this work, but due to its similarity to other anti-Islamic works of the time, it is unlikely to have been composed earlier than the late 1940s to early 1950s.

satirical poetry of the constitutional era, this long *masnavi* is in colloquial language and is composed in a conventional prosodic metre. Thematically, the poem was in line with other anti-superstition and anti-Islam satirical works of the period such as Jamālzādeh's story, *Sahrā-ye Mahshar* (Desert of Resurrection, 1944), and Hedāyat's play, *Afsāneh-ye Āfarinesh* (Creation Myth, 1946). Another satirical poem by Behruz, *Mer'āt al-Sarā'er* (Mirror of Secrets), uses his experience of working at Cambridge and in Germany to ridicule European orientalists for their biased and superficial treatment of subjects. This work is written in prose and verse as a parody of old *tazkarehs* (biographies). He also composed a short collection of prose and poetry called *Gandestān* (Stenchland), which is a parody of Sa'di's *Golestān* (The Rose Garden). Behruz's last prosodic poem is *Gand-nāmeh* (Stenchbook), a satirical poem in the same prosodic metre as Ferdowsi's *Shāhnāmeh*.[38] Paul Sprachman argues that these satirical works illustrate Behruz's 'mastery of parodic technique, his extensive knowledge of both orthodox and folk Islam, and his splenetic Iranophilia, all of which coalesced to produce a major Persian parody'.[39]

As mentioned above, these works are composed of standard templates using conventional metres and traditional rhetoric. However, in his plays, Behruz creates poetic pieces with open forms which can be examined as some of the first experiments with free verse in Persian literature. Using Attridge's tools for analysing the qualities of free verse, one can explain poetic experiments in Behruz's dramas through phrasing, metric, and rhythmic analyses.

Shab-e Ferdowsi (Ferdowsi's Night, written in 1933 and published in 1967)[40] is a poetic play imitating the themes and tones of Ferdowsi's *Shāhnāmeh*. The main character of this play is Abolqāsem Ferdowsi (tenth and eleventh centuries) the author of *Shāhnāmeh* (The Book of Kings). The play begins with Ferdowsi expressing his sadness to Farangis, his wife, about the negligence of people in celebrating *Mehregān*, the ancient Persian Festival of Autumn. However, once he realizes that the people of the town are preparing to celebrate *Mehregān*, he cheerfully starts to compose the story of Bizhan and Manizheh. In this play, dialogues have been taken from both *Shāhnāmeh* itself and rhythmic prose lines which imitate the language and tone of the original verses:

---

[38] The composition dates of these works are not available. However, as a part of his *Gand-e Bādāvard* was published in a journal named *Ārmān* in 1931, one may estimate that they were composed no later than the late 1940s.

[39] Paul Sprachman, 'Behruz, Dabih', in *Encyclopaedia Iranica* https://iranicaonline.org/articles/behruz-dabih-1889-1971-persian-satirist-son-of-the-physician-and-calligrapher-abul-fazl-savaji [accessed 28 March 2019] (para. 5 of 7).

[40] This play was performed for the first time during the Ferdowsi millennial celebration in 1934.

کو آنهمه شهر و دهستان‌های آبادان و جوی و کشت و بستانش؟
کو شوش و جندی شاپور و دانشمندان و پزشکان و بیمارستان و تیمارستانش؟
ویران ... ویران ...
« نه دهقان نه لشکر نه تخت و کلاه نه آبادی و شهر و گنج و سپاه [...] »
این ویرانه آذرآبادگانست؟!
کو دهقان جنگی خرمدین و شهرستانهای آبادش؟!
گو آن آتشگاه سوزانش؟!
ویران ... خاموش ...
«دگرگون شده چرخ گردون بچهر ز آزادگان پاک ببریده مهر»[41]

> Where are all the cities and prosperous villages and their brooks, farms and gardens?
> Where are Shush and Jondishāpur, and their scientists and physicians and their hospitals and psychiatric care homes?
> Destroyed ... Destroyed ...
> 'Neither the landowner, nor the soldiers, nor the throne, nor the crown, nor the village, nor the city, nor the treasure, nor the army [...]'
> Is this ruin Azarābādegān (Azarbaijan)?!
> Where are its Khorramdin warrior landowners (or native Iranian), and its thriving cities?!
> What about that glowing fire?!
> Destroyed ... extinguished ...
> 'The face of the wheel of the firmament (fortune) has altered; it has completely withheld his love from the free people.'

In this example, the poet has reformulated the tone of *Shāhnāmeh* in prose poems. Phrasing plays a significant role in echoing the beat of an epic poem in prose lines. The caesura-like pauses within each line, line breaks, and repetition are formal devices that the poet uses for the phrasing of each piece. In addition, the lament-like overtone of lines leads the poet to create longer lines at a slower pace. Thus, the rhythm derived from the phrasing contributes to and reflects the syntax and meaning.

In addition to phrasing, rhythm in most of the poetic pieces of this play is formed by imitating the tone of the original verses. The play consists of dialogues formed by several prose lines supported by single verse lines from Ferdowsi's *Shāhnāmeh* at the end of each piece. Archaic words used in the prose lines harmonize the language and tone of the poetic dialogues with those of the original verse. In addition, the insertion of occasional rhymes in certain lines helps the poet to create a beat that is more closely aligned with the verse. Despite these attempts, *Shab-e Ferdowsi* fails to shape an independent poetic form, and Behruz's experiments remain limited to different angles of rhythmic prose.

---

[41] Zabih Behruz, *Shab-e Ferdowsi* (Tehran: Sāzmān-e Namāyesh-e Irān, 1967), p. 23.

Dar Rāh-e Mehr (In the Path of Love, 1934) differs from *Shab-e Ferdowsi* in one respect. *Shab-e Ferdowsi* contains prosodic verses from *Shāhnāmeh* or replicates its style, whereas the poetic lines of *Dar Rāh-e Mehr* are entirely in prose. The language and phrasing of the poetic pieces in *Dar Rāh-e Mehr* are affected by the theme of the play. *Dar Rāh-e Mehr* is a story about one of the Persian classical masters, Khājeh Shams al-Din Mohammad Hāfez (1315–1390), most famous for his love and mystical *ghazals*. The theme of the play is centred on the dialogues of Hāfez with symbolic personas of his own poems, such as *mohtaseb* (public inspector) and *rend* (vagrant), as well as his prayer-like monologues. The author uses the style and language of old mystical prayers, such as those in *Monājāt-Nāmeh* (Book of Hymns) by Khājeh Abdollāh Ansāri (1006–1088), which contains a considerable number of archaic and literary words. Also, the majority of the play's long lines are formed of several small sentences, divided by pauses. To approximate to the beat of old prayers, the poet has highlighted most of the internal breaks within the lines by *saj'* (prose rhymes):

خواسته جهان به چشم هیچ است و نام و ننگ پیشم پندار.
روزی از خروشی می‌خروشیدم و به این و آن می‌آگستم،
اکنون زیر تیغ بران پای کوبان می‌شتابم، جان می‌دهم و دم نمی‌زنم،
غمی جز غم دیگران ندارم و شادی مگر برای جهانیان نخواهم.
چیزی از تو درخواست نمی‌کنم ...
تو نخواسته داده‌ای و نیوزیده بخشیده
آنکه ندارد نکوشید و به دادهات پی نبرده.[42]
من؟! هرگز!
دربند گمان و نادانی من از هر دم باری صد میمیرم و
زندگی از سر میگیرم؛ کی از جان دادن ترسم.[43]

The attractions of the world are nothing to me and I consider both fame and shame insignificant thoughts
In the past, I was roaring in response to someone else's roar and grappling with this and that,
Now I am rushing under sharp razors dancing, I give up soul without uttering a word
I have no sorrow, but the sorrow of people and I would not wish happiness except for the whole world.
I would not ask you for anything ...
You have provided without my request and you have given without my begging
Those who do not have did not try and did not appreciate your gifts
I?! Never!

---

[42] Zabih Behruz, *Dar Rāh-e Mehr* (Tehran: Irānkudeh, 1944), p. 14.
[43] Behruz, *Dar Rāh-e Mehr*, p. 21.

In the shackles of doubt and ignorance, I die a hundred times every moment
And then I recommence life; I am not afraid of death.

The combination of internal pauses, line breaks, and the classical compositional technique of *saj'* shapes the rhythmic system in each piece. Joined with the rhythmic energy of the genre of Persian prayer, this phrasing style approximates an open poetic form in each section. Although these free verse pieces have a similar tone, one cannot see this play as an independent poem. Indeed, the poetic pieces of this work are just the components of a bigger form and cannot be considered a whole if one analyses them outside the play's structure. However, Behruz has another play, written about a decade before *Shab-e Ferdowsi* and *Dar Rāh-e Mehr*, in which he creates an entirely experimental poetic play which reads like a long poem.

Shāh-e Irān va Bānu-ye Arman (The Iranian King and the Lady of Armenia, 1927) is a poetic play/screenplay written entirely in free verse style. It contains a variety of prosodic, rhythmic, and prose lines. It also shares several remarkable rhetorical points with the experimental poetry of the time. However, the formal poetic properties of this work have not been welcomed by scholars of theatre studies. Ya'qub Āzhand states that the poetic dimensions of this work have a negative impact on the theatrical side of it, arguing that the poetic form of the text has transformed it into an unnatural text which does not follow 'the logic of drama'.[44] Jamshid Malekpur mentions that the language of *Shāh-e Irān va Bānu-ye Arman* is closer to that of modern free verse poetry than to the conventional language of plays written in that period.[45]

Despite these critical points, Malekpur states that *Shāh-e Irān va Bānu-ye Arman* is a successful adaptation of Nezāmi's *Khosrow va Shirin*, in that Behruz's rendition of the love triangle of Farhad, Shirin and Khosrow has been done much better than other adaptations of the story.[46] In his introduction to this play, Behruz writes that this work was initially written as a screenplay in English in 1920. However, to accentuate dramatic adaptations of classical Persian tales in modern genres such as cinema, he decided to publish the Persian version first.[47] Thus, he translated and released the Persian version of this play in 1927. Although writing a poetic screenplay based on traditional Persian literature is in itself innovative, one can argue that the screenplay template is a cover for the radical experiments in Persian poetics in which the author engages.

---

[44] Ayubi, p. 10.
[45] Jamshid Malekpur, *Adabiyāt-e Namāyeshi dar Irān* (Tehran: Tus, 2006), p. 217.
[46] Malekpur, p. 217.
[47] Zabih Behruz, *Shāh-e Irān va Bānu-ye Arman* (Tehran: Fārus, 1928), pp. a–b.

The template of *Shāh-e Irān va Bānu-ye Arman* allows the author to create a poem which might not have been accepted by the mainstream literary intelligentsia at the time of creation. Behruz thus seems to have tried to save himself from harsh criticism by presenting it in a genre which had not yet been institutionalized in Iran. In other words, literary critics were less likely to analyse the poetic experimentation of this work as it was not presented as a poetry collection. The fact that this work was written as a screenplay also allowed the author to use different literary and non-literary elements of the Persian language. This, in turn, helped him to expand the field by employing registers of Persian which were uncommon in contemporary literature.

One can argue that the major poetic innovations of this work are in line with the attempts of other pioneer poets of the time to break from their immediate literary tradition. Breaking away from traditional poetic metres was a tendency that Behruz shared with Nimā, Moqaddam, and Kiā. Tondar Kiā refers to *Shāh-e Irān va Bānu-ye Arman* as one of the first attempts in Persian literature to compose a poem with uneven verses.[48] In fact, years before the initial experiments with uneven verses by Tondar Kiā and Nimā Yushij between 1937 and 1939, Behruz had already embarked on the journey of challenging the dominance of traditional prosody and transforming Persian poetry. Through a combination of rhythmic and non-rhythmic prose lines, he crafted melodic pieces that defied conventional norms. This innovative approach, evident as early as 1927, marked Behruz as a pioneer in his endeavour to reshape Persian poetry.

In the following example, Behruz constructs a free verse stanza where the hemistichs possess a certain prosodic quality, albeit one that cannot be classified within any of the traditional metrical patterns:

اسپهبد ــ (به دختر مینگرد) آری شاها به از این صد چند و هزاران چندان.
شاه ــ کبود آن؟
اسپهبد ــ بانوی ایرانی ارمن: شیرین.
شاه ــ شیرین! هرگز نبود چون این!
اسپهبد ــ چونان نی ــ گر بینی شاها دانی ــ لیکن نا دیده چه بگویم ــ قدش مویش رویش خویش در گیتی نتوان گفتن به کسی ماند.
شاه ــ این سان! ؟[49]

The General – (Looks at the girl) Yes, my king, she is hundreds and thousands of times better than this one.

---

[48] Despite this acknowledgement, Tondar Kiā refers to *Shāh-e Irān va Bānu-ye Arman* as an unsuccessful attempt. He argues that Behruz could not reach a new rhythmic system, so he merely created uneven verses in the conventional template of *bahr-e tavil*. See Tondar Kiā, 'Che Avāmeli dar Tahavvol Mohtavā-ye She'r-e Farsi Ta'sir Dāshteh ast?", *Andishe va Honar*, Special issue (1962), p. 18.

[49] Behruz, *Shāh-e Irān va Bānu-ye Arman*, pp. 6–7.

The Shāh – Who is she?
The General – The Iranian lady of Armenia: Shirin.
The Shāh – Shirin! She is not like this [girl]!
The General – She is not_ if you see her, O my king, you would know _ but how can I describe her as long as you have not seen her _ One could not say that her height, her hair, her face, her attitude, is similar to anyone else in the universe.
The Shāh – To that extent!?

The beat of the fragment is also partly the result of rhyming '*chandān*', '*ān*', '*sān*', and '*Shirin*', '*in*' as well as '*ni*' and '*dāni*'. At the end of the fifth line, one can see that the recurrence of rhyming words in a fast beat approximates a distinctive prosodic-like rhythm. In the following example, the poet uses another open form of rhythm:

شاه ـ بشنو .... از من .... بانوی ارمن نادیده آنسان دل برده کز وی باز ستاندن نتوانم _ از مهرش با فکرش در پنهان میگریم در پیدا میسوزم و میسازم _ اکنون چاره ی درد م کن یا ما را بر وی می بر _ یا و یرا سوی ما میخوان⁵⁰

The Shāh – Listen .... to me .... The lady of Armenia has taken my heart even without being seen, in a way that I cannot take my heart back _ I cry because of my love for her, thinking about her secretly and burn openly _ Now find a remedy for my pain. Either take me to her _ or ask her to come to me.

The blended rhythm built in the previous examples can be studied through phrasal and metrical analyses. These lines are fragmented into hemistichs by placing dashes, which may function as a caesura, among different clauses. In addition, these clauses are made either in an uncommon variation of *bahr-e tavil* (repetition of the prosodic foot *mafʿulon*) or in a rhythmic prose.⁵¹ The poet tries to protect the rhythm from becoming a traditional *bahr-e tavil* by mixing prosaic phrases with prosodic hemistichs in the stanza. In the scansion of the following lines, one can see that, similar to traditional *bahr-e tavil*, the lengths of verses are variable. However, the lines are not built upon a consistent metrical pattern. In several cases, the poet changes the foot *faʿulon* (˘ ˘ ˉ) to *mafāʾel*

---

⁵⁰ Behruz, *Shāh-e Irān va Bānu-ye Arman*, p. 9.
⁵¹ *Bahr-e tavil* is a type of Persian verse generally consisting of the repetition of a whole foot (*rokn*) of the metre *hazaj* (˘ˉˉ) or of a whole foot of the metre *ramal* (ˉ˘ˉˉ) or of permissible variations of the two. See Mohammad Dabirsiyāqi, 'Bahr-e tawil', in *Encyclopaedia Iranica* https://iranicaonline.org/articles/bahr-e-tawil-type-of-persian-verse [accessed 11 May 2019] (para. 1 of 6).

(ᴗ--) and *maf'ulo* (--ᴗ) to distinguish his innovative open poetic form from the conventional templates with uneven verses:

فرهاد _ اکنون پیشت خرم و خوشدل _ لیکن چندی بندی و بیدل _ تا طوسم بردند و تن آزردند و رها کردند.
شیرین _ گفتندم کشتندت[52]

Farhad – Now I am with you, happy and gleeful _ but in shackles and anxious for a while _ they took me to Tus and tortured my body and then released me.
Shirin – I thought they had killed you.

The first two hemistichs are scanned as (---/--ᴗ/ᴗ--). However, this pattern does not remain consistent in other lines of the fragment. In the third hemistich, the pattern has been enlarged by adding two more irregular feet (---/--ᴗ/ᴗ--/-ᴗᴗ/---). Finally, the scansion of the last line shows the pattern (---/---). Mehdi Akhavān Sāles states that Nimā in his proposed rhythmic system tried to utilize the qualities of both *mostazād* and *bahr-e tavil* in shortening and lengthening lines. However, his short lines do not always consist of the first and the last feet of the longer lines as is the case in *mostazād*. Besides, the last feet of his long lines in *bahr-e tavil* are always consistent while Nimā consciously alters the last feet of each line to maintain their 'independence' and distinguish his new, open poetic form from the mentioned traditional templates.[53] One can argue that Behruz has used the same technique to distinguish his rhythmic system from that of classical prosody about a decade earlier than Nimā. Therefore, *Shāh-e Irān va Bānu-ye Arman* might be one of Nimā's sources in creating his *Nimāic* poetic form.

However, the major problem with this conclusion is that although Behruz (like Nimā) challenged the aesthetic regime of traditional prosody and poetic forms, he did not set out to create a full-scale poem in a conventional, organic form. He combined different elements of drama and the classical form of narrative poetry (*masnavi*) to create a hybrid form of the poetic play. However, the borrowed form of drama remained external, and the poetic parts seemed fragmented. In other words, Nimā ended up writing poems with dramatic qualities while Behruz inserted poetic fragments into his drama. Nevertheless, the fact that this play was written years before the appearance of the first poems of Nimā's second phase (*Nimāic* style) and those of Tondar Kiā might draw scholars' attention to this experiment as a source of inspiration not only for Nimāic poets but also for other marginal poets of the later generations.

---

[52] Behruz, *Shāh-e Irān va Bānu-ye Arman*, p. 28.
[53] Mehdi Akhavān Sāles, *Bed'at-hā va Badāye'-e Nimā* (Tehran: Zemestān, 1995), p. 276.

Shin Partow: A bridge between Nimāic and experimental poetry

Another marginal poet who can be considered an advocate of experimentalism in the 1940s was Ali Shirāzpur Partow (1907–1997). Partow studied in France and was awarded a PhD in French history and literature. In 1931 he returned to Iran, where he contributed to the foundation of the *Armān* literary journal. In this journal, he worked with a group consisting of well-known academics, including Mohammad Taqi Bahār, Badi' al-Zamān Foruzānfar (1904–1970) and Abbās Eqbāl Āshtiāni (1896–1956), as well as pioneer modernist writers, including Sādeq Hedāyat and Bozorg Alavi.[54] He also served the government as the Iranian consul in Baghdad and ambassador to India.[55] Partow published several novels and stories which were admired by his contemporaries. In addition, he composed five innovative collections of poetry, namely *Samandar* (Salamander, 1946), *Dokhtar-e Daryā* (Girl from the Sea, 1946), *Zhinus* (1946), *Khusheh Parvin* (The Pleiades, 1946), and *Ghozhmeh* (Grape, 1950). He reprinted all his works in a collected volume in 1974 under the title of *Ghazāleh-ye Khorshid* (Gazelle of the Sun).

In a letter to Nimā Yushij dated 29 September 1946, Partow expresses his main objective in writing experimental poems as the 'simplifying and pushing the Persian language forward'. This suggests that his primary focus was on transforming the literary language itself rather than poetry as a whole.[56] It can be argued that Partow's emphasis on the literary language as the most innovative aspect of his poetry stems from his reliance on Nimā Yushij as the true leader of new poetry.

In his efforts to align himself with Nimā, Partow is careful to classify his non-Nimāic writings as literary prose, not poetry. There is a list of Partow's publications on the first page of *Dokhtar-e Daryā*, in which the phrase '*nasr-e āhangdār*' (rhythmic prose) is written in front of *Zhinus*, *Samandar*, and *Dokhtar-e Daryā*. In the same list of publications, he labelled *Khusheh Parvin* as '*She'r be sabk-e farangi*' (European-style poetry).[57] Partow emphatically acknowledges Nimā as the main and sole founder of new Persian poetry.[58] However, it should be noted that Partow's own innovations in poetic form may not align directly with the characteristics of the Nimāic style. Instead, it is more plausible that Partow drew inspiration from earlier

---

[54] Shams Langrudi, *Tārikh-e Tahlili-e She'r-e Now*, 1, p. 343.
[55] Partow did much of his research – and hosted Hedāyat when he wrote *Alaviyeh Khānom* and published *Buf-e Kur* (The Blind Owl) – when he was serving the government in India.
[56] Ali Shirāzpur Partow, *Do Nāmeh* (Tehran: Chāp-e Zarrin, 1950), p. 118.
[57] Ali Shirāzpur Partow, *Dokhtar-e Daryā* (Tehran: [n. pub.], 1946), p. 2.
[58] Partow, *Do Nāmeh*, p. 119.

experimental poets like Moqaddam and Behruz in his approach to bringing about poetic change.

Similar to the works of Moqaddam and Behruz, Partow's poetry also incorporates elements of both modern Persian prose and Western free verse. This amalgamation of styles allows Partow to explore and experiment with different poetic techniques, creating a unique and dynamic poetic expression. Partow's experiments, like those of his contemporaries, fall into three categories: (1) broadening the conventional literary language, (2) using fictional narrative techniques, and (3) developing free verse rhythmic systems.

Partow's works follow the revivalist trend promoted by a considerable number of language and literature scholars of the time. Advocates of this trend portrayed it as a way of reforming the traditional aspects of the dominant Iranian culture by reducing its Islamic-Arabic dimensions. In poetry, the purpose was to replace the rhythms of the traditional prosodic system, which had evolved from Arabic poetics, with a variety of innovative rhythmic systems. Sa'id Nafisi (1895–1966), a prominent literary scholar of the period, admires Partow's attempts in the 'new style' of composing 'poetic prose or free poetry' which seeks its roots in ancient Iranian poems. He sees Partow's efforts in reviving the forgotten poetics of ancient literature as being in line with those of Vladimir Mayakovsky (1893–1930) and Louis Aragon (1897–1982) in Russian and French literature, respectively.[59]

Partow's revivalist approach towards language gave the poet the opportunity to build a poetic language beyond the boundaries of the literary lexicon. To create an unconventional poetic language, Partow utilized all the grammatical potential of the Persian language rather than the limited, standard language. For instance, the word *'farāmushideh'* in the line *'khod rā farāmushideh'* (she has/had forgotten herself) is the past participle form of *'farāmushidan'* which in turn is a less common form of *'farāmush kardan'*. The new verb *'farāmushideh'* is grammatically correct yet possesses an odd inflexion and is almost never used in literary language.

Partow's attempts to use the full potential of the Persian language were not limited to creating unusual inflexions. Like the earlier experimentalists of this era, Partow tended to use archaic Persian words instead of their more regular Arabic counterparts. Furthermore, he created new words based on the models of old Persian inflexion and grammatical rules to broaden the Persian literary lexicon. These words, mostly nouns, sometimes look unnatural to Persian speakers. Indeed, in some of his poetry collections, Partow provides readers with a glossary of unfamiliar words. For instance, in *Dokhtar-e Daryā*, the word *'Muzigar'*, which is the name of one of the main characters, is taken from the French word 'musique' being altered to

---

[59] Shams Langrudi, *Tārikh-e Tahlili-e She'r-e Now*, 1, p. 342.

'*muzi*'. He also added the suffix '*gar*', indicating a sense of profession or occupation, to create a synonym for *navāzandeh* or *musiqidān* (performer or musician). *Navāzandeh* is Persian and *musiqidān* is an Arabic-Persian term extracted from Greek; however, the poet created a French-Persian word to replace them. This, in turn, shows that Partow's motivation for the creation of new words was not entirely related to the revivalist trend of language purification. It was more about experimenting with the language of poetry to give the poet an authority to go beyond the existing conventions and build an idiosyncratic poetic diction.

The second similarity between Partow's poetry and that of other experimental poets was the use of modern Persian prose as a source of inspiration. Like Moqaddam, Partow, who was best known as a fiction writer, borrowed his style of narration from the modern stories of the time. Nimā Yushij, in his letter to Partow, admires this dialogue between Partow's poetry and modern fiction and particularly his 'skilful use of story – writing techniques'. Indeed, the presence of fictional features in Partow's poetry is so bold that in some cases it makes these works indistinguishable from short stories.

One of these elements in Partow's works is the third-person omniscient point of view. Of course, the omniscient narrator is a constant presence in narrative poetry too; however, Partow's clear inclination towards fictional prose suggests examining this narrative form more openly. In Partow's poetry, all characters and even objects have their own personal voice, and the narrator is the one who ties all the events and images together. For instance, in the following stanza, the narrator is a third-person omniscient who tries to articulate the inner sentiments of the characters which might not be comprehensible from the dialogues alone. The omniscient narrator, the poet, jumps between the lines to express the hidden thoughts of the characters:

وقتی که من مردم، یکبار دیگر
آن سرود "هر دو به هم شادیم" را
از برایم بنواز
ولی موزیگر مست او بود
مست عشق آویسا بود
در اندامش میل بزرگی
چون یک بچه پلنگ دیوانه
که میخواهد خود را از بلندی پرتاب کند
او را میآزرد
و چون اندر کورهِ فروزانی میسوخت
آویسا هم از پرستشهای آتشین دلدارش
سرمست و نادان از هستی
خود را فراموشیده
تن زیبایش را به موزیگر داد ...

تمام هستی همه گیتی، این دم خامش بود
موزیگر و آویسا هم خاموش [60]

> When I die, once again,
> play the song 'We are both happy together'
> for me
> But the musician was intoxicated with her
> Intoxicated with Āvisā's love
> A great desire in his body,
> like a crazy leopard cub
> who wants to throw himself from a height,
> was bothering him
> And he was burning as if he were in a blazing furnace
> Āvisā also due to the fiery adorations of her lover,
> charmed and unconcerned about life
> and oblivious to herself
> gave her beautiful body to the musician …
> The whole existence of the entire universe was silent at that moment
> The musician and Āvisā were silent too.

According to Karimi-Hakkak, this kind of poetry is only distinguishable from prose by its 'use of space' and 'the presence or prevalence of poetic images'.[61] This poem does not display the metrics and regularity of rhyme of prosodic poetry. Therefore, its rhythm is formed based on phrasing a prosaic, narrative text. Additionally, the relatively fresh images of the 'crazy leopard cub' and 'silence of the world' poeticize the expository, prosaic tone of the poem.

According to Attridge, free verse in this sense is 'the introduction into the continuous flow of prose language, which has breaks determined entirely by syntax and sense, of another kind of break'. These breaks are shown on the page by means of a different typeface which indicates a slight pause in the flow of words.[62] Most of Partow's prose poems consist of short prose lines in which all the components of the sentence are in their logical order. However, the breaks in sentences in the form of enjambment indicate a sense of rhythm to the reader.

In some other poems Partow uses a few simple techniques to create a distinguishable rhythm. For instance, in the first part of *Zhinus*, the poet simply repeats certain words to create a beat. Besides, to make a stronger

---

[60] Partow, *Dokhtar-e Daryā*, pp. 40–1.
[61] Ahmad Karimi-Hakkak, 'Free-verse', in *Encyclopaedia Iranica* https://iranicaonline.org/articles/free-verse- [accessed 5 February 2019] (para. 3 of 4).
[62] Attridge, p. 5.

EXPERIMENTALISM IN PERSIAN POETRY BETWEEN THE 1930S AND 1950S

rhythm and give a specific character to it, the poet places commas, as the moment of pause, among fragments of sentences to indicate offbeats:

آمد باد، باد آمد، یک دسته ابر همره آورد
ابر پر تخم تیره، روی زمین تن انداخت
پر از ورون، نرمک نرمک، با میغ و مه، در هم آمیخت
وندر دل ابر و میغ، رگباری یکباره ترکید[63]

The wind came, came the wind; it brought a bunch of clouds
The dark cloud, full of seeds, spread its body over the ground
Full of lust, gently, mated with the mist and fog
And in the heart of the cloud and the fog, a downpour suddenly
burst out.

Another set of techniques he uses is associated with the phrasing aspect of the poetic form. Indeed, the phrasal movement in a free verse poem could simply happen by changing the sequence of words in the sentence. This not only gives rise to an external rhythm but also enhances the effectiveness of the speech. Creating reverse adjectival clauses is a kind of phrasal movement which regularly appears in conjunction with metrical movements in the works of Partow's contemporaries, particularly Nimā. In the following example, the adjectival phrase '*rangi vizheh*' has turned into '*vizheh rang*', which, though grammatically correct, is unnatural in standard Persian:

هر شاخه اژدهاوارش ویژه رنگی داشت
تنه اش رنگ مس بگداخته
برخی از شاخه ها دودی، چند تا کبود و تار
برخی دیگر به رنگ یشم ...
وین آرایش رنگینش در اسپیده دم، یا در آفتاب
یا در فرو رفتن آفتاب در لای میغ، یا در پرتو مهتاب
دگرگونه شده هر زمان رنگی میافت[64]

Each of its dragon-like branches had a unique colour
Its trunk the colour of molten copper
Some branches smoke-coloured, some bluish and dark
Others jade-coloured ...
And its colourful makeup at dawn, or under the sun
Or during the setting of the sun between the evening clouds or under
the rays of moonlight
changes colour every time.

---

[63] Ali Shirāzpur Partow, *Zhinus* (Tehran: [n. pub.], 1946), p. 9.
[64] Ali Shirāzpur Partow, *Samandar* (Tehran: [n. pub.], 1946), p. 5.

In some of his poems, it is also possible to analyse the free verse through metrical and rhythmical analysis. For instance, in the previous stanza, the line *'Taneh-ash rang-e mes-e bogdākhteh'* is scanned (⏑⏑--/⏑⏑--/-⏑-), which is a popular classical metre named *ramal-e mosadas-e makhbun-e mahzuf*. This line is followed by two prose lines with a distinguishable phrasal movement in which omitting the verb '*bud*' disturbs the logical order of the words and consequently indicates the form of the beat. Moreover, other lines of the stanza rely on the signalling of line ends by rhymes to generate an alternative rhythmic system.

One can question the significance of Partow in comparison with the other experimental poets of this era. Upon closer investigation of the poetry of Nimā, Moqaddam, and Behruz, the originality of Partow's experiments may indeed be called into question. However, Partow acted as a bridge between the two major fronts of literary modernization. He maintained his ties with *Nimāic* high modernists while collecting and working with specific elements borrowed from earlier experimental poets, including the insistence on expanding literary diction, using fictional prose techniques, and writing free verse. Furthermore, the wide reception of his works at the time of composition due to his fame as a writer, his literary relationships with influential men of letters and Nimā's endorsement of his poetry made him one of the leading experimental poets of this period. It is also possible to argue that these characteristics allowed Partow to effectively transmit the accomplishments of his fellow experimental poets to future generations, notably the younger Nimāic poets and the avant-garde poets who will be examined in the upcoming chapter.

6

Avant-garde poetry between the 1940s and 1950s

Persian experimental poets might not have directly confronted either the modernist or the traditionalist literary body of their time, but they played a major role as facilitators in the process of poetic change. They experimented in different ways to achieve new conceptions of poetic form, rhetorical device, rhythmic system and rhyme scheme, and diction. The results of these experiments, however, blossomed in the works of the high modernists and the avant-gardes, with the latter group calling for the destruction of all dominant, institutionalized literary traditions and the introduction of an entirely new aesthetic system for Persian poetry.

This chapter aims to analyse Persian avant-garde poetry as a cultural product which not only pursued the idea of aesthetic revolution but also resisted the sociopolitical and cultural hierarchies of the time. In so doing, I focus on the oeuvres of the most significant, yet neglected, avant-garde poets of the 1940s to 1950s, namely Tondar Kiā and Hushang Irāni. The aesthetic changes proposed in their works, as well as their particular method of engaging their poetry with sociopolitical issues, are the most important heritage that these poets have passed on to the next generation of avant-gardes. The following sections analyse the works of these two poets as historical avant-garde movements and ultimately attempt to shed light on the dimmed role of these poets in the process of poetic change.

Peter Bürger writes that theories of avant-garde art analyse avant-gardism on two levels. The first level is what he describes as the 'intention' of historical avant-garde movements, and the second is the structure of avant-garde works. The intention of avant-garde movements, in Bürger's theory, is defined as 'the destruction of art as an institution'.[1] In the case of modern

---

[1] Peter Bürger, *Theory of the Avant-Garde* (Manchester: Manchester University Press, 1984), p. 83.

Iranian Persian poetry, avant-gardes attacked institutionalized literature on two different fronts. The first was the traditional aesthetic regime, which restricted the artist to creating works based on the established principles of classical art. The second was the new-born modern and high modern movements, which rapidly occupied the literary mainstream scene and drove experimentalists and avant-gardes out of the picture.

At the level of structure, Bürger argues that avant-garde work should be scrutinized as a non-organic structure. He constructs the idea of non-organic composition in a relational and comparative manner, based on its contradiction with the notion of organic work. In an organic work of art, the parts are connected cooperatively in a way to generate a consolidated body. In contrast, a non-organic work consists of autonomous components.[2]

Both sides of the foregoing argument expose the emancipatory nature of avant-garde art. In all avant-garde works the attack on institutionalized art is rooted in, and reinforces, the artists' determination to break the barriers of cultural values designed by dominant groups. Avant-garde movements embarked upon discrediting the status of the canon in the hierarchical regime of values to make room for suppressed, marginal poets, poetic forms, and poetic discourses. Moreover, the autonomy of components permits all subjects, themes, and elements (both political and non-political), to exist equally in an individual work.[3] However, in an organic form, the expression of political and moral contents by the author is inherently subordinated to the organicity of the whole.[4] Indeed, different subjects in an organic form must contribute to the constitution of the poem as a whole, which in turn prohibits equality among subject matters.

Historically speaking, the concept of emancipation in avant-garde works has not always been the same. Renato Poggioli distinguishes two types of sociopolitical engagement in avant-garde arts. In the first type, the term 'avant-garde' only pertains to radical, leftist authors, particularly those living in Europe during the nineteenth century, who were willing to express their political viewpoints in their writings.[5] In the second type, the artist creates a cultural product which independently opposes the dominant institution of art and the established aesthetic regime.[6]

---

[2] Bürger, pp. 83–4.
[3] Bürger, p. 91.
[4] Bürger, p. 90.
[5] Renato Poggioli, *The Theory of the Avant-Garde* (Cambridge, MA: Belknap Press of Harvard University Press, 1968), p. 10.
[6] For a thorough discussion of the interplay between the Enlightenment notion of aesthetic autonomy and the emergence of novel forms of autonomy in the nineteenth century through the convergence of avant-garde art and vanguard politics, see Grant H. Kester, *The Sovereign Self: Aesthetic Autonomy from the Enlightenment to the Avant-Garde* (Durham: Duke University Press, 2023).

Arta Khakpour identifies the early avant-garde phase in Iranian literature of the 1940s and compares its viewpoint on sociopolitical engagement with the first model of avant-gardes in Poggioli's theory. He mentions the First Iranian Writers' Congress, held in Tehran in 1946, as a point of departure for the development of (largely leftist) politically committed literature in Iran, and writes:

> In fact, it too signalled the birth of an avant-garde, but not in the contemporary sense of aesthetic iconoclasm. This was instead an avant-garde of Poggioli's first type, the political avant-garde of the Paris Commune. Like their Parisian predecessors, the Iranian 'avant-garde' viewed literature as an instrument with which they could educate, highlight capitalist and monarchical oppression, and spread a radical political ideology.[7]

The early political avant-gardes included a group of *Nimāic* modernists who were determined to declare the political interests of leftist parties in their poems. As Ahmad Karimi-Hakkak articulates, poets such as Ehsān Tabari (1917–1989), Siyāvash Kasrā'i (1927–1996), and even Mehdi Akhavān Sāles (1929–1990), 'exemplify the need to transfer the textual energies of Nimā's modernist poems from their abstract and potential meanings to the specific socio-political statements they judged relevant to contemporary readers'.[8]

Another major group of *Nimāic* poets saw poetry neither as a medium for propagating political opinions nor as an utterly and solely aesthetic artistic production. They defined the sociality of their poetry based on Nimā's primary intention of adapting Persian poetry to the experience and the demands of modern human life. As Karimi-Hakkak states, these poets regarded the poetic text as an 'abstract social structure'. They believed that the form and functions of this structure were 'related to and reflective of the evolution of concrete social structure'. Nevertheless, even they did not comprehend the intrinsic antagonism of pioneering literature towards the traditional aesthetic regime as 'an aspect of social setup mediated through language'.[9]

One can argue that the second type of 'avant-gardism', which refers to the aesthetic and figurative sense of this term, is more appropriate for the marginal pioneer poets who started their work in the 1940s and 1950s, particularly Tondar Kiā, Hushang Irāni, and their followers. These poets

---

[7] Arta Khakpour, 'A Divorce of Avant-gardes: Surrealism and Socialism in Post-Reza SHāh Iran', *Middle Eastern Literatures*, 2 (2016), 119–34 (p. 121).
[8] Ahmad Karimi-Hakkak, *Recasting Persian Poetry: Scenarios of Poetic Modernity in Iran* (London: Oneworld, 2012), p. 284.
[9] Karimi-Hakkak, *Recasting Persian poetry*, p. 284.

preferred 'the isolated image and the abbreviated term avant-garde' which is established as the 'artistic avant-garde'.[10] However, it is important to note that their works should not be dismissed as apolitical. According to Poggioli, within avant-garde artistic poetry, the political element served primarily as a rhetorical device and was no longer exclusively utilized by those dedicated to revolutionary and subversive ideals.[11] In essence, the avant-garde artistic movement is characterized by its inherent opposition to prevailing values. As Richard Schechner highlights, the embrace of radical ideas, rhetoric, and actions as a means of challenging established norms not only formed the core of the historical avant-garde's political stance but also constituted an essential aspect of its bohemian lifestyle.[12]

This chapter begins with an analysis of avant-garde moods in Tondar Kiā's theory and practices, employing Poggioli's idea of avant-garde 'moments'. It also explores Kiā's dispute with both modernists and traditionalist literary communities of the 1940s. Using Benjamin's concept of the 'ragpicker', I will first scrutinize how Kiā collects different components of his works from the refuse of art history in order to resist the hierarchical, archival regime of cultural values. I will then discuss the non-organic nature of both poetic forms and the arrangement of segments in each of Kiā's books, and finally explicate the dialogue between Kiā and Western Dadaism to determine the intensity of the influence of Dada art on the multimedia spirit of Kiā's works.

In the second half of the chapter, I will analyse the avant-garde moods and moments in the published manifesto of Hushang Irāni and his associates in the first Persian avant-garde journal, *Khorus Jangi* (The Fighting Rooster). This section embarks upon a close reading of some of Irāni's most well-known poems, with emphasis on their avant-garde elements, such as non-organic forms and techniques associated with 'automatic writing'.

Tondar Kiā: Poet of cabarets

Aqā Abbās (often referred to as Shams al-Din), the son of Mirzā Hādi and grandson of Sheykh Fazlollāh Nuri, was born in the Sanglaj neighbourhood of Tehran in 1909.[13] His father was a magistrate, and his mother was the daughter of a noted cleric. Shams al-Din, who later

---

[10] Poggioli, p. 12.
[11] Poggioli, p. 12.
[12] Richard Schechner, *The Future of Ritual: Writings on Culture and Performance* (Abingdon Oxfordshire: Routledge, 1993), p. 7.
[13] Kiā's grandfather, Sheykh Fazlollāh Nuri (1843–1909), was a prominent cleric figure in the Iranian Constitutional Revolution of 1906. However, he turned against the Revolution and was executed for treason by Constitutionalists in 1909.

chose the pen name 'Tondar Kiā', finished his elementary education at Sharaf Mozaffari School. In 1928, notwithstanding his intention to attend military school, the objections of his parents saw him redirect his interests towards politics. Tondar Kiā graduated from *Maderse-ye Siyāsi* (School of Politics) in 1932,[14] when he also finished composing his first play, *Tisfun* (Ctesiphon). After receiving his BA, Kiā, along with several other students, won a national scholarship and was sent to France in September 1932. He spent the first year of the extension of his BA in Lyon, before commencing his studies as a postgraduate student in Paris, where he received his PhD in Law in 1939. Shortly after his graduation on 16 April, he returned to Tehran.[15]

Claiming to have founded a new literary movement to shatter the literary edifice of Persian literature, in 1939 Tondar Kiā presented his reflections on the matter under the title of *Nahib-e Jonbesh-e Adabi-e Shāhin* (The Waking Call of the Falcon Literary Movement). He published the first manifesto of the *Falcon* in the *Ettelā'āt* newspaper on 26 November 1939. Shortly afterwards, several well-known literary critics, both traditionalist and modernist, published articles which harshly criticized Kiā's early poems and manifesto.[16] A year passed and, despite being drafted into the army and facing various obstacles in receiving a publishing licence for his works, he finally managed to publish *Falcons* 1, 2, and 3 in one volume in 1940. A few years later, in 1943, *Falcons* 4 to 25 were published in a thirty-one-page pamphlet. In the winter of 1944, as Kiā himself states, 'an intellectual revolution' took place in his personal life which made him withdraw from studying and working until 1955. He states that at that stage he had come to the realization that no book in the entire world could be of use; only 'the grand book of life' was apt to teach him something.[17] After a period of non-activity on his part, *Falcons* 26 to 31 were published in 1956. Tondar Kiā had continued writing but, apart from a long, written interview with *Andisheh va Honar* and an anonymous article in the same journal between 1960 and 1962, he had no notable publishing activity. Even though he gradually completed the *Falcon* collection in the years 1964, 1970, and 1975, he consistently refrained from appearing in literary circles or giving interviews to the extent that he had almost no contact with any members of the literary community.

---

[14] This specialized high school later underwent an evolution, along with other schools, resulting in the establishment of the Faculty of Law and Political Science at the University of Tehran.
[15] Farshad Sonboldel, *Tondar Kiā; Gozaresh-e Nahib-e Jonbesh-e Adabi-e Shāhin* (Tehran: Gusheh, 2015), p. 11.
[16] Sa'id Nafisi, A. Khājeh Nuri, Lotf-Ali Suratgar, Zabihollāh Safā, and Moshfeq Hamedāni were among the very first critics of Kiā's works. Sonboldel, pp. 81–6.
[17] Tondar Kiā, *Nahib-e Jonbesh-e Adabi-e Shāhin* (Tehran: [n. pub.], 1975), p. 1357.

Regrettably, Kiā's ideas were met with little credibility or serious consideration from others during that time. Apart from Nāser Vosughi (1922–2010), the chief editor of *Andisheh va Honar*, no one provided him with the space to express his ideas. Among the literary figures of the following generation, it was only Bizhan Elāhi (1945–2010) who expressed any interest in him. Even his own relatives mocked him and would recite and laugh at his poetry in their reunions – a potential explanation for his severing contact with all his relatives, except his sister and one of his cousins, for the rest of his life.[18] Since he never married, there are limited sources from which we can learn about his life: the memories of Khojasteh Kiā, his cousin, his own foreword to *Tisfun*, his article on Sheykh Fazlollāh Nuri's life, the *Falcon* collection, and his interviews with *Andisheh va Honar*. After his death in 1987, his landlord threw away his writings and daily notes, making it impossible to learn about his final years, especially his life after the Iranian Revolution of 1979.

Moods and moments

In studying Tondar Kiā's career, one can identify several features of avant-gardism which are shared by most avant-garde movements of the twentieth century. Poggioli states that one should study 'the dialectic' of an avant-garde movement 'both internally and externally, its ideological and psychological motivations as well as its practical, sociological consequences'. In so doing, he classifies the shared aspects among avant-garde movements into four 'moments': activism, antagonism, nihilism, and agonism.

First of all, Poggioli explains that avant-garde activism refers to the primary incentive for creating avant-garde art products as a collective desire to reach the stage of success as a movement. He writes:

> A movement is constituted primarily to obtain a positive result, for a concrete end. The ultimate hope is naturally the success of the specific movement or, on a higher, broader level, the affirmation of the avant-garde spirit in all cultural fields.[19]

However, in the case of Tondar Kiā, the activistic moment is more of a solitary drive towards literary change. As a result of this solitude, Kiā's

---

[18] Zahra Kiā's donation to Grand College of a copy of *Tisfun* in 1936 and the contact details of Kiā's brother in an advertisement for his book in 1939 suggest that he kept in touch with this sister and his brother at least during the first years of his career.
[19] Poggioli, p. 25.

avant-garde activism might properly be perceived as an adventurous experiment arranged 'for no other end than its own self'. On the other hand, activism, by its nature, inspires a mood of agitation against mainstream art, tradition, public taste, and even dominant powers. This state of hostility and opposition in avant-garde art is what Poggioli determines as the second shared mood of avant-garde movements, and terms as antagonism, or the antagonistic moment.[20]

Tondar Kiā failed to garner the attention of fellow poets necessary to establish a cohesive movement. Still, alone, he attempted to promote his doctrines through manifestos, interviews, and essays. He called on young poets to peruse his experiments and to publish their works under the title of *Jonbesh-e Adabi-e Shāhin* (the Falcon Literary Movement). From his first manifesto published in November 1939, he frequently declared that his endeavour was to initiate a 'literary revolution'. He enthusiastically proclaimed the victory of his revolution in every volume of his works. Emphasizing the word 'revolution', Kiā endeavoured to accentuate his rebellious posture against established and institutionalized art, as well as the more recent *Nimāic* modernism. In other words, Kiā remained energetically active throughout his forty-year career in order to expand the avant-garde spirit of '*Falcons*' in every field of modern Persian literature. His enthusiastic opposition to the Persian literary tradition and its establishments was driven by his confrontation with both traditionalists and modernists, particularly Nimā Yushij, whom he considered his main rival.

Kiā's antagonism towards Nimā played an essential role in fashioning the relationship between the avant-gardes and the political and literary intellectuals of the 1940s. Kiā's posture as a marginal poet was, to some extent, a result of his neglecting the vital role of political intellectuals and activists in the power relations within the literary community. He also overlooked the role that this group played in shaping the taste of the intelligentsia through their journals and cultural events. In contrast, Nimā's positive relationship with political intellectuals, and, of course, his acceptance by the literary community, contributed to his recognition as the leader and mentor of young modernist poets. Kiā noticeably avoided exposing any social or political commitment in his writings and poems, even during historical turning points such as the 1953 Iranian coup. Yet, through their works and their attendance at events, *Nimāic* poets established an excellent relationship with the leftist community. As a result, *Nimāic* poetry conquered the most important podiums of modern literature at the time, that is, the literary pages of left-wing journals and the literary events held or powered by them.

---

[20] Poggioli, pp. 25–6.

In addition, because of the extreme hostility they showed towards traditional aesthetics and men of letters, Kiā, and consequently other avant-gardes of the time, missed the opportunity to be seen through moderate journals, which were run chiefly by academics. In contrast, this antagonism, particularly towards accepted literary principles, made Nimā's moderate innovations appear more rational and more palatable to the educated reader with an inclination towards traditional literature.

According to Poggioli, antagonism towards entrenched aesthetic systems may lead avant-gardes to the idea of destroying the barriers of tradition and 'whatever they perceive as an obstacle in the way of change'. He describes this mood as a transcendental antagonism and terms it avant-garde 'nihilism'.[21] In this nihilistic moment, the vanguards are in a state of constant tension between construction and destruction. This is exemplified by Nimā, who intended to reform classical poetics constructively, and Kiā, whose innovations can be characterized as destructive labour. The lack of intellectual resources needed for the construction of a new regime led Kiā to the idea of deconstructing the existing traditional monuments in an anarchistic manner. In contrast, Nimā and his disciples were concerned with recreating the entire regime of aesthetics based on a constructive revisionary approach towards the past.

Another phase shared among avant-garde artists is the 'agonistic moment'. In this instance, the artist does not perceive damage and failures, even his own. Poggioli points out that in this phase, the artist 'even welcomes and accepts this self-ruin as an obscure or unknown sacrifice to the success of future movements'.[22] In his agonistic moment, Kiā decided to sacrifice his dreams of being a bold poet of his time, or even a leading figure of the mainstream, in order to pave the way for the future generation of avant-garde poets. He radically pushed the boundaries of innovation in Persian poetry and chose to be unacceptable. Kiā demonstrated his awareness of being an unacceptable poet in his writings several times. Indeed, he consciously developed his posture as a ridiculed, unbearable artist who sacrificed his public face for the sake of his avant-garde ideas. He writes:

> O you who read my writing. I tell you not to laugh foolishly and do not criticise me in vain. Your laughter and criticism are ineffective. Because before you laughed at me, I laughed at myself, and before you criticised me, I criticised myself.[23]

According to John Ashbery, being unacceptable is an indispensable characteristic of early twentieth-century avant-garde art. On the one hand,

---

[21] Poggioli, p. 26.
[22] Poggioli, p. 26.
[23] Sonboldel, p. 19.

there are always traditional artists (and even moderate modernists) who wish to be acceptable to potential audiences. On the other hand, some avant-garde artists in this era claimed that works should only be acknowledged as successful practices when they faced resistance from society.[24] This idea is simultaneously agonistic and antagonistic. It is agonistic as it requires the artist to ignore his/her desire to be known; it is antagonistic because it manifests a clear hostility towards public taste. Ashbery states that once artists accept their acceptability, they can no longer exist in the absence of public acceptance. Conversely, the works of avant-gardes who have come to terms with their unacceptable status survive without public acceptance.[25] One may argue that ignoring public recognition, however, can be perceived as implied hostility towards the dominant principles of a society's cultural values.

Kiā: Ragpicker in modern Tehran

Kiā's attraction to so-called degenerate and vulgar art may be associated with his stance against the dominant regime of values in his society. In his creative and historical writings, Kiā ventures to feature the rejected features of various texts, visuals, and performances, regardless of the judgment of the general public. Indeed, Kiā attempts to create anti-hierarchical works in which multiple features with diverse levels of cultural and political values can exist on equal terms. Poggioli argues that this 'desire to inaugurate new orders' is characteristic of the avant-garde anarchistic culture and is termed 'alienation'.[26]

Walter Benjamin describes such an alien person as a ragpicker in a modern metropolis who wanders around public places occasionally, living in the margins and remaining unmarked in history. The ragpicker, in Benjamin's view, is a historian whose methodology is to reassemble cultural leftovers through a literary montage practice.[27] Frederik Le Roy explains the method of the cultural ragpicker as follows:

> The ragpicker who roamed the streets to gather waste material, embodies the writing of history as a performative practice premised on gathering snippets of historical waste material and reassembling them in collage-like

---

[24] John Ashbery, 'The Invisible Avant-Garde', in *Poetry in Theory: An Anthology 1900–2000*, ed. by Jon Cook (Oxford: Blackwell, 2004), p. 393.
[25] Ashbery, p. 396.
[26] Poggioli, p. 110.
[27] Walter Benjamin, *The Arcades Project*, trans. by Howard Eiland (Cambridge, MA: Harvard University Press, 2002), p. 460.

juxtapositions that have the potential to produce unseen and unforeseen 'dialectical images'.[28]

In a similar vein, Kiā creates pamphlets, mostly like miscellanies, in which he merges multiple pieces collected from various literary and unliterary sources. He carries out the organization of the random pieces with the precision of an archivist, in order to create a 'dialectical image' of his practice as a whole. These pieces can be in many forms, such as poems, stories, articles, interviews, photographs, photomontages, paintings, drawings, collages, and so on. Also, he enters works of other artists in his volumes, either as quotations or in distinct sections. For instance, the volume published in 1956 consists of literary prose passages, some short articles on Iranian history and Persian literary history, a manifesto, an extended essay on his grandfather's life, and six poems/*Falcons*. In later volumes (1964, 1970, and 1975), a considerable number of images, especially collages, photomontages, and concrete poems are added.

Like a collector who exhibits his culturally valuable collection, a ragpicker displays his organized, but un-organic, selection of cultural trash to a range of viewers. In so doing, the ragpicker attempts to repurpose what has been labelled as degenerate material and even foist it upon the public's awareness. Kiā, likewise, presents what has been deemed as culturally rubbish in place of highly valued, inspirational works of art. He designs collections made of literary texts rooted in vulgar street songs, as well as unrelated visual pieces, and exhibits them as a series of fine products.

Kiā, in both his prose and his poetry, makes use of Tehrani colloquial expressions and slang, and the effective rags and refuse of the Persian literary language. The use of colloquial language emerged in the works of constitutional and post-constitutional poets, such as Sayyed Ashraf al-Din Hoseyni (1870–1934), Iraj Mirzā (1874–1926), and Mirzādeh Eshqi (1893–1924), and others. Years before Kiā, these poets used a blend of the everyday language of their age and traditional literary language to convey significant cultural and political perspectives and experiences to a wide-ranging audience. However, Kiā has repurposed slang to focus on its formal and experimental capability. Indeed, Kiā uses colloquial language as an incongruous element to dismantle belletrist features of literariness and to generate antithetical, innovative forms.

One can argue that Kiā's primary means of accessing this anti-belletrist language is through Tehran's popular, commercial songs, particularly the *Lālehzāri* lyrics of the first Pahlavi period. Sāsān Fātemi categorizes post-eighteenth-century Iranian songs as 'musicians' songs' and 'street songs'.

---

[28] Frederik Le Roy, 'Ragpickers and Leftover Performances', *Performance Research*, 8 (2017), 127–33 (p. 128).

Musicians' songs are satirical or lyrical verses in the style of classical poetry, while street songs are mostly sociopolitically charged pieces composed in a looser style. Fātemi describes street songs as lyrics with one or more musical theme and no strict literary standards, being largely produced by members of the general population.[29] Mahmud Khoshnām categorizes these street or urban popular songs in four subgroups. The first type is 'national songs', such as *Hāji Firuz Umadeh* (Hāji Firuz has Arrived)', sung by street performers before the Persian New Year. The second is sentimental songs, including lullabies and love songs. The third type, which reached its peak in the 1940s, is *pishpardeh-khāni* (curtain-raisers), independent rhythmic monologues performed before or between two scenes of a play. The last type is *motrebi* and *ru-howzi* songs, which were performed by musicians and actors in private ceremonies and parties.[30]

At the time of Kiā's return to Iran, stage songs based on these urban songs were common in Tehran, particularly in the theatres and cabarets of Lālehzār Street. Popular songs performed by famous singers were also printed as small pamphlets and sold to the general public.[31] In addition, sometimes *pishpardeh-khāns* distributed their satirical songs among their audiences in playhouses.[32] These songs, printed or presented, were the primary source of inspiration regarding rhythm, theme, and language within Kiā's works. Such an influence, one could argue, was occasionally reduced to sheer imitation; however, in general they led the poet away from merely reproducing work towards new forms. Indeed, this category of Tehrani popular music was one of Kiā's uniquely original sources for developing his proposed avant-garde aesthetic system.

Similar appropriations of popular songs were not exclusive to Iran or limited to Tondar Kiā. In the United States, for example, Mina Loy (1882–1966), whose poetry exhibited a proclivity for futurist and American Dadaist modes of expression, incorporated elements from the popular artistic forms of American culture, particularly jazz. Inspired by jazz music, Loy attempts to create new rhythmic arrangements to reflect the cadence of modern everyday life in poetic forms. Kiā, too, employs the rhythm and language of street songs, especially those performed in the theatres and cabarets of Tehran, to establish what he assumed to be an entirely new

---

[29] Sāsān Fātemi, *Peydāyesh-e Musiqi-e Mardom Pasand dar Irān* (Tehran: Māhur, 2013), pp. 22–30.
[30] Mahmud Khoshnām, *Az Najvā-ye Sonnat ta Ghoghā-ye Pāp* (Tehran: Farhang-e Jāvid, 2018), pp. 515–29.
[31] Some of these pamphlets are published as a part of the *Gulistan* project under the title 'Tasnif-e Jadid (doktor) va Majmu'eh-ye Tasanif'(The New Song (Doctor) and a Collection of Songs)). *Tasnif-e Jadid (Doktor) va Majmu'eh-ye Tasanif* (Tehran: Matba'eh Eqbāl, 1952) https://golistan.org/pamphlet-1-new-songs-dokhtar-others/ [accessed 20 August 2020].
[32] I am indebted to my supervisor, Dr Saeed Talajooy, for this information.

musical system for Persian poetry. To describe the desired relationship between poetic rhythms and the poet's sensibilities, Loy states that 'Poetic rhythm ... is the chart of temperament'. Jon Cook, too, explains Loy's colourful rhythms and her innovative musical arrangements according to this statement, asserting that the poet needs freedom to experiment with the formal aspects of the poem in order to determine his/her sentiments through the rhythm. This freedom, which enables poetry 'to express a diversity of temperaments', can be attained, however, merely through revolt against tradition.[33] Kiā, in a similar vein, uses the musical variation of street songs to create freer rhythmic forms and to free his poetry from the restraints of the traditional prosodic system. In the following example, from the poem *Dans* (Dance, 1943), Kiā attempts to use the rhythmic variations of dance music to form the rhythmic of the poem:

سلام خانم شمایید؟!
میدانستم ببال میآیید!
اما ترا بگویم بکه، ای ترا به پیراهن نیمه لخت امشبت قسم بخود مگیر اینهمه
حیف نباشد از تو ز ن
از تو ملوس دمدمی ناز و ستیز با چو من با من مست یکدمه؟
بیا دستم بگیر بدست
کمرت را بده والس است: ... [34]

Hello ma'am, is that you?!
I knew you would come to the ball!
By whom should I swear? Oh, I swear to your half-naked shirt tonight, don't be so hoity-toity
O Lady, isn't it a pity
that you, capricious cute thing, are quarrelsome with me, a drunk?
Come hold my hand
Give me your waist; it is a waltz: ...

In this poem, the narrator engages in a dance with a lady, adapting the length of his lines to synchronize with the rhythm of the dance music. Besides, the rhythm of the lines is built upon both metrical and non-metrical systems. The fourth and fifth lines are created by the repetition of two prosodic feet, *mofta'elon* and *mafā'elon* (-∪∪-/∪-∪-), in an alternate order. However, the rest of the lines are rhythmic prose lines with couplet rhymes. Additionally, the rhyme arrangements, particularly in the third to fifth lines, place the stress on the beat and highlight the theme of dance, rather than merely flagging the end of the line.

---

[33] Jon Cook, *Poetry in Theory: An Anthology 1900–2000* (Oxford: Blackwell, 2004), p. 132.
[34] Tondar Kiā, *Nahib-e Jonbesh-e Adabi-e Shāhin* (Tehran: [n. pub.], 1943), p. 146.

In addition to the recurring theme of dance and rhythms associated with it, one can identify the footprints of street songs in Kiā's narrative forms. Kiā has several poems in which he adopts the techniques, tone, language, and, more importantly, the narrative forms of the sentimental *Lālehzāri* songs. Mahmud Khoshnām argues that there is a typical narrative pattern in street love songs, taken from the folk tradition in tales and poems, which is used to hold and link together all the components of the poem. He calls this pattern *jariyān-e estehāleh* (stream of metamorphosis) or *tarāneh-ye degardisi* (lyrics of transformation). He describes this as a process in which the memory of the beloved, before it can fade away, turns into a variety of elements and motifs.[35] For instance, in the following street song, the memory of kissing the beloved on a rainy night turns into the imagery of the blood that has dropped from her lips, a bouquet, petals in the air, a pigeon, a deer, and, finally, a fish in the sea:

دیشب که بارون اومد / یارم لب بون اومد

رفتم لبش ببوسم / نازک بود و خون اومد

خونش چکید تو باغچه / یه دسه گل در اومد

رفتم گلش بچینم / پرپر شد و ور اومد (هوا رفت)

رفتم پر پر بگیرم / کفتر شد و هوا رفت

رفتم کفتر بگیرم / آهو شد و صحرا رفت

رفتم آهو بگیرم / ماهی شد و دریا رفت

Last night, when it rained, my beloved stepped onto the edge of her house roof
I went to kiss her lips, but they were so delicate that they bled
Her blood dropped into the garden, and a bunch of flowers bloomed there
I went to pick those flowers, but they withered and hopped into the air
I tried to catch the withered flower petals, but they turned into a dove and flew
I went to grab the dove, it became a deer and fled into the desert
I went to get a deer, it turned into a fish and left for the sea.

One finds that in poems such as *Khāb Didam Mast Kardam!* (I Dreamt that I am Drunk!, 1943), Kiā employs a narrative structure that bears resemblance

---

[35] Khoshnām, p. 522.

to the stream of metamorphosis or stream of consciousness technique, albeit in a simplified manner:

سنگ صحرا چوب آی میروم میلولم چه خوب آهویم جنب و جوش کوه و دشت سیر و گشت
تشنه از این چشمه بیفت و بنوش شیرین بود به به چه آبی آسمان را بپّا لعابی است بمرگ شما که
چاکر مردم ایوای ریش درآوردم اما نه بابا بیخود ترسیدم پشم نبود و پر است آهای پریدم پرواز
ای کبوترها بهتر از عشق اگر بود چیزی دیگر در بساط خدا پس چرا چلچله‌ها میکند ولوله شاه
پروانه‌ها پاک و پاکیزه‌تر از هوا شوخ و شنگ و مست و حال میبرد گل بگل با دوبالی قشنگ
بیخیال خیال نکنید بنده خوابم یا خدانکرده مستم حیف که کوکم خیلی کیف است وگرنه میدیدید همه
من هستم مگر دیوانه‌ای بچه جان پروانه را چه بآسمان...[36]

> Stone, desert, wood, Hey! I go, I wriggle, that's good, I am a deer, motion, mountains and the plains, sightseeing, if you are thirsty lie down and drink from this spring, is that sweet? Nice! What water, watch the blue of the sky, what an enamel it is. I swear to your soul that I am at people's service, oh no, I grew a beard. Wait, no, it wasn't beard, it was a feather. Hey, I fly. O, pigeons, if there is anything better than love in the sight of God then why do barn swallows make too much noise? The king of butterflies, neat and cleaner than the air, waggish and playful, jumps from one flower to the other by his beautiful wings. Forget it! Don't think I am sleeping, or God forbid, I am drunk. That's a shame that I am so happy. Otherwise, they are all me. Kid! Are you crazy? What has a butterfly got to do with the sky?

In this poem, the poet, who is unconscious, metamorphosizes into a deer, a pigeon, and various other objects. This trend of transformation continues until the very end of the poem, when the narrator wakes up and finds himself in the middle of his own funeral service. Then, remembering what he imagined during his unconsciousness, he asks people to bury his body, or, in his words, 'his unwanted self'.

Besides repurposing the principal techniques and themes of street songs, Kiā transforms his poetry into a vibrant stage where a diverse array of voices can find a platform to be heard. Advancing the idea of the constitutional poets, Kiā demolishes the boundaries between fine and street literature, and rebels against the dominant voice of the elite. He attacks the hierarchical system of valuation by releasing the suppressed voices of street artists. The vernacular voices eliminate the dominant accent of the intelligentsia from his poetry in an anarchistic manner.

Unlike classical poetry, which is designed on a predetermined, orderly arrangement of subject matters and formal properties, Kiā, as an avant-garde

---

[36] Kiā, *Nahib-e Jonbesh-e Adabi-e Shāhin* (1943), p. 139.

poet, creates disruptive equality in his works. Jacques Rancière believes that 'everyone thinks. Everyone shares equal powers of speech and thought'.[37] Peter Hallward explains the Rancièrian sense of equality as exploring 'the various resources of displacement, indistinction, de-differentiation or de-qualification that are available in any given field'.[38] Kiā, also, shows a high tendency to create a podium for unclassifiable or out-of-class street performers and provides them with an equal opportunity to speak, even if their speech does not contain a highly valued subject or an elegant structure.

Kiā consistently highlights his conflict with the elitist narrative of the men of letters (adibān) from within the Persian literary heritage. In the opening of a manuscript of the first volume of his works, he writes: 'Lo! The National Consultative Assembly! I hereby hand in to you this literary truth so that you may preserve it from the evil of the men of letters!'[39] In so doing, he determines the boundary between the avant-garde and the conservative, regressionist, and resentful literary men of his time. Kiā sees the mannerist men of letters as passive consumers of cultural heritage, blindly reassembling the accepted components of sublime classical literature. Hence, he actively seeks scattered parts of both literary history and contemporary art which might potentially lead to original creations in the future. As Le Roy writes:

> The ragpicker actively pursues waste, creating the potential to transform sudden acts of historical remembrance into a politics of memory. For Benjamin the ragpicker points towards the capacity to unlock the revolutionary potential stored in forgotten or wasted historical events.[40]

Kiā accuses mainstream historical narratives of being misleading and of propagating a particular literary trend. Thus, he attempts to pass his own idiosyncratic, unacceptable version of the history of Persian literature to the next generation, both through his writings and through events such as his long interview with the *Andisheh va Honar* magazine published in separate complementary issues from 1960 to 1962. However, the public promptly repudiated his narrative because his attitude towards literary history was in stark contrast with the central narrative of the time and, more importantly, that of academia. Kiā sought to devalue some of the most accepted traditions in the history of classical and modern Persian poetry, while prizing what was – and still is – broadly considered degenerate art.

---

[37] Peter Hallward, 'Staging Equality', *New Left Review*, 37 (2006), 109–29 (p. 110).
[38] Hallward, p. 111.
[39] A manuscript of '*Nahib-e Jonbesh-e Adabi-e Shāhin*' preserved in the Parliamentary Library of Iran. Tehran, The Parliamentary Library of Iran, *Nahib-e Jonbesh-e Adabi-e Shāhin*, MS 9548.
[40] Le Roy, p. 129.

One can explain this antagonistic attitude through the Bloomian theory of 'the anxiety of influence'. Kiā intentionally attacks constitutional poets who are famous for their innovative poems and revolutionary content – poets whose works are undoubtedly the primary sources for modernization in Persian poetry. Yet Kiā denies the originality and trustworthiness of the mainstream narratives of constitutional literature. In his lengthy interview with *Andisheh va Honar*, he attempts to show how changing the focal point in the history of modern Persian poetry can release the revolutionary potential of marginalized trends. Although he was clearly influenced by the stylistic colloquialism of constitutional poets, he always tried to deviate from their ways. Indeed, he shows a corrective approach towards the heritage of constitutional poets in his theoretical writings which can be explained by the Bloomian notion of '*clinamen* or poetic misprision'. This term refers to 'an instance of creative revisionism' in which the new poet is adamant about diverging from the path of his poetic father. *Clinamen* is the proper form of misreading and misinterpreting the works of prior poets.[41] Bloom states that 'a poet swerves away from his precursor, by so reading his precursor's poem as to execute a *clinamen* in relation to it'.[42] In his reading of the history of Persian poetry, Kiā attempts to demonstrate that the poetry of the classical masters was flawless prior to the rise of constitutional poetry. However, Persian poetry should have swerved fundamentally since the very beginning of the twentieth century in a way that the initial ideals of constitutional poetry suggested. He does not support the experiments of his immediate precursors, constitutional poets, as he believes that their experimental works have been compromised by the principles of the journals and political groups of the time, as the new literary establishments.[43]

Likewise, the ragpicker, as Le Roy writes, 'first, stands for the undoing of established historiography and the institutions that support it'.[44] This is where Bürger's avant-garde as an anti-institution and Benjamin's ragpicker as the historian of margins meet. A significant portion of Kiā's literary works is dedicated to the reimagining and rewriting of Persian literary history. He ventures, sometimes in an excessive way, to devalue institutions such as constitutional and post-constitutional mainstream poetry, which are considered culturally valuable in the hierarchy of Persian literature. In fact, Kiā, in his interview with *Andisheh va Honar* and the theoretical sections in the last volume of his works, offers a critique of the violence of Persian literature's archival system against unconventional cultural products and

---

[41] Harold Bloom, *The Anxiety of Influence: A Theory of Poetry* (New York: Oxford University Press, 1997), p. 30.
[42] Bloom, p. 14.
[43] Kiā, *Nahib-e Jonbesh-e Adabi-e Shāhin* (1943), pp. 861–6.
[44] Le Roy, p. 130.

their creators. The violence implicated through the exclusion of radical, experiential poetry from the main narrative of Persian literature underlies the foundation and the maintenance of the archive. Thus, Kiā's rewriting of the history of Persian literature and devaluing of the works of his precursors in a project that involved using repudiated materials is a symbolic practice that attacks the central, accepted narratives, while challenging the operation of these narratives in the future.

Non-organicity

In line with his attempts to unsettle Persian literature's archival regime, Kiā attacks the idea of organic unity, which is another factor that the elitist modernists used to distinguish between fine and poor art. To explain the notion of organic unity, David Granger refers to notes by Samuel Taylor Coleridge (1772–1834) as 'the most influential and categorical comments' in shaping modernists' understanding of this term. Coleridge contends that the 'legitimate poem' is the one in which the components 'mutually support and explain each other; all in their proportion harmonising with, and supporting the [larger whole]'.[45] In contrast, Bürger states that in avant-garde art, it is not the harmony and interdependence of the different parts of the work which create the whole but 'it is the contradictory relationship of heterogeneous elements'.[46] One can argue that Kiā rebels against the concept of organic unity on two levels: (1) non-organic poetic forms, and (2) the structure of books as collections of miscellaneous art works.

In terms of form, Kiā attempts to combine different rhythms, tones, and voices to showcase the disintegration of narratives in the poem. However, he first needed a new hybrid (prosodic and prosaic) rhythmic system in which he could freely change the rhythm and tone. Describing this neoteric system, he writes:

> *Falcon* is neither prose, nor verse, nor prose-poem, but it is all these three together at once. So, what is *Falcon*? *Falcon* is rhythmical, and the *Falcon*-writer has a rhythmical saying that starts off from the most rigid kinds of poetry and moves along prose-poems and finally arrives at the swiftest prose and thus forms the discourse in agreement with signification; the discourse of the living tongue.[47]

---

[45] David Granger, 'Expression, Imagination, and Organic Unity: John Dewey's Aesthetics and Romanticism', *The Journal of Aesthetic Education*, 2 (2003), 46–60 (pp. 54–5).
[46] Bürger, p. 82.
[47] Tondar Kiā, *Nahib-e Jonbesh-e Adabi-e Shāhin* (Tehran: [n. pub.], 1940), p. 10.

Kiā's suggested rhythmic systems aim to deconstruct the monotony of the standard poetic forms of Persian poetry, in which the prosodic arrangement remains fixed throughout the poem. This, in turn, restricts the ways in which the poet can adapt the rhythm to the tone of different voices and the different settings in the poem.

Kiā uses tonal fluctuations to create polyphonic forms in a disruptive manner. One might argue that the polyphonic forms in Kiā's poetry aim to disturb the unity of the text by allowing these voices to interrupt each other. Thus, although one encounters various voices in Kiā's poems, the Bakhtinian notion of polyphony is not precisely applicable to the polyphonic mood in Kiā's poetry. The Bakhtinian term refers to works in which one encounters several distinct voices or points of view which interact on relatively equal terms. However, in Kiā's poems, there is almost no interaction or dialogue, yet voices tend to push each other out of the scene and disrupt each other's narratives. This irreconcilable inner struggle also differentiates Kiā's chaotic non-organicism from the Coleridgean concept of the reconciliation of opposites. In this conception of poetic form, two opposite but interrelated elements with equal forces create a unity resulting in a third force. In contrast, in Kiā's non-organic form, various elements attack each other to disrupt the interrelation among elements and consequently the unity of the form.

In other words, voices in Kiā's poems appear in a simultaneous and disorderly manner with no organization or unity. Every voice constantly fights for its share of the scene, which is occupied by the dominant voice of the poet/narrator. From the deconstructionists' point of view, as Granger states, 'organicisms' tend to side-line some elements of the text in order to maintain its 'integrity and wholeness'.[48] Protesting against the restrictive nature of organic unity, Kiā seeks the emancipation of aesthetically devalued parts of Persian poetry: vulgar and unrefined voices.

The second level of Kiā's antagonism towards organic unity can be observed in the way that he juxtaposes literary and unliterary segments in his collections. Kiā's publication of his works in such miscellaneous collections was an unconventional way to present literature, but it was also an assault on the traditional gestures of Persian poets. Indeed, Kiā replaces the image of the sophisticated poet, who believes in the sacredness of the poetic practice, with that of the irrational and rebellious avant-garde artist, who experiments with assorted genres. This gesture, as Prita Meier explains, is a shared trait among most avant-gardes of the twentieth century:

> Artists utilised artistic techniques, including montage, performance, found-object assemblage, pictorial abstraction, and the appropriation of

---

[48] Granger, pp. 54–5.

vernacular (including non-Western) and mass media forms, to shock the viewer and reject perceived traditions in both art and life.[49]

Kiā's books are fundamentally conglomerates of texts and visual arts, most of which are irrelevant to both the texts that they follow and the other images in the collection. In this way, Kiā initially attacks the imperative of organicity, homogeneity of components, and retaining structural consistency. On the other hand, he generates a new posture for the Persian poet in which the poet is allowed to experiment with the borders of different genres, regardless of their distinctions.

A dialogue with Dadaism

When it comes to the multimedia experiments of the Iranian avant-gardes, much of the current literature deals with the question of the authentic or imitative nature of their works. Some authors have attempted to prove that the idea of creating multimedia cultural products is at best an imitation of Western avant-garde movements. Others emphasize the intercultural nature of avant-garde art and investigate the works of Iranian avant-gardes as local interpretations of universal, post-Second World War art movements.

One of the most repeated of these multimedia exercises is the combination of text and image. The union of visual arts and literature is a legacy of both nineteenth-century cultural movements like Romanticism and Symbolism and early twentieth-century movements such as Futurism, Expressionism, and particularly Dadaism.[50] David Hopkins notes that disciplinary and formal purity were vehemently rejected by the majority of Dada and Surrealism practitioners. Within their creative endeavours, artistic disciplines frequently intersected, with text, visual elements, and performance blending together in a state of unrestrained experimentation. Likewise, the pursuit of formal beauty appeared inconsequential to these artists, considering the tumultuous world they inhabited.[51]

Likewise, Kiā's collections are mixtures of photomontages, collages, and drawings, as well as visual and sound poetry. These incompatible compositions aim to desacralize the conventional aesthetics of classical art

---

[49] Prita Meier, 'Authenticity and Its Modernist Discontents: The Colonial Encounter and African and Middle Eastern Art History', *Arab Studies Journal*, 1 (2010), 12–45 (p. 22).
[50] David Hopkins, *Dada and Surrealism* (New York: Oxford University Press, 2004), p. 7.
[51] Hopkins, p. 62.

and its formal narrative of beauty.⁵² They also oppose the idea of the purity and sacredness of Persian poetry, which makes it incompatible with other artistic genres, especially those emerging in the modern era and those being consumed by ordinary people. In other words, by granting equal values to the constituent parts of the collection, Kiā aspires to degrade sublime Persian poetry to the level of so-called degenerate art forms.

Kiā joins a series of texts in varying forms (poems, prose, essays, and jokes) to visual items and calls this combinational poetic form '*chizak*' (a small thing). On some occasions, there is no clear distinction between the visual and the literary parts of *chizaks*. That is, the visual parts either contain a text or act interdependently to the text that they follow. Indeed, one could view these pieces as visual poems. For instance, in *Chizak-e Sā'at* (The Clock, Figure 6.1) words are written in the backdrop of a drawing.

Some have associated this practice with 'concrete poetry', which reached its apex in Dadaist and Surrealist collections. Visual *chizaks*, like concrete poems, are fundamentally typographical practices which aim to make poetic pictures or even visual jokes. Nevertheless Kiā, in *Chizak-e Sā'at*, does not follow the principal procedure of concrete poetry which is to shape the words in a way that represents the described object. As Martin Gray states, 'concrete verse is usually immediate and total in its effect, and because of this, its exponents have claimed it transcends ordinary, sequential language, allowing words (if words are used) their full potentiality of meaning'.⁵³ For instance, in Guillaume Apollinaire's *Il pleut* (It's Raining, 1918), the words appear as drops of rain falling to the bottom of the page. Here, the text is 'concrete' and directly reflects the physical aspects of the object. In *Chizak-e Sā'at* the words are written with no gaps between them to reflect the progression of time. Although Kiā's poem gives body and space to the words, it is 'abstract' as it reflects the concept of ageing, which is metonymically associated with the clock as a concrete object.

Moreover, in *Chizak-e Sā'at*, although words are written in the backdrop of an image, the focal point is not their appearance on the page. Instead, the main goal is to create a rhythm based on the sequence of sounds and consequently to turn the text into a potentially performative one. Kiā states that his poems are composed for 'ears' rather than 'eyes'; that is, one should 'read *Falcons* energetically (*jāndār*) and not merely watch them soundlessly on the page'.⁵⁴ This is similar to Mina Loy's statement in which she says that the reading of an avant-garde poem does not always happen through eyes,

---

⁵²In addition, he mocks styles and schools by creating meaningless terms for his visual works like 'Neo-abstraction-nism-mism', which uses a colloquial Persian wordplay to mock 'Neo Abstractionism', a style of the late-modernist or early-postmodern visual arts.
⁵³Martin Gary, *A Dictionary of Literary Terms* (Essex: York Press, 1999), pp. 68–9.
⁵⁴Kiā, *Nahib-e Jonbesh-e Adabi-e Shāhin* (1940), p. 124.

FIGURE 6.1 *Chizak-e Sā'at (The Clock)*. *Image in the public domain.*

but by ears too.[55] In this work, the sound '*dam-dim*' signifies the sound of a clock. This sound turns into the inflexion of the verb 'to go' (*raftan*), which in turn implies the ticking sound of a clock. Even when the sounds transform into significant words, the poet still makes use of the vocal aspects of the language instead of its significations.

One might argue that composing a poem based on the sound of words and rejecting the semiotic capacities of language in conveying the meaning of the poem is a feature of 'phonetic poetry'. Describing Hugo Ball's practice of phonetic poetry, David Hopkins states that the poet of this type returns to the basic layers of language most likely to place stress on the autonomy and self-sufficiency of language. He believes that this type of poetry, rather than being wholly absurd or abstract, can often communicate 'a mystical desire to find new names or words for things'.[56] Kiā's poetry comes very close to

---

[55] Cook, p. 132.
[56] Hopkins, p. 64.

phonetic poetry, conveying its meaning through vocal aspects of language. For instance, in *Chizak-e Sā'at*, the poet creates new signifiers for concepts of time and death and supports this by defamiliarizing the conventional onomatopoeia for the ticking clock. In fact, he attempts to draw the readers' attention to the unusual implication of sounds/signifiers by using '*dam-dim*' instead of '*tik-tāk*'. In the following example, the poet tries to reflect the sense of frustration through a minimum amount of significant words, phrases and sentences:

های هیهای هان، هو هو، توفان هو هو هیاهو هو که چه اهتزاز و چه غوغائی دارد وزیدن، بوز بوز؛ پریدن، پیر پیر که راستی زیباست پریدن، همه را زیر خود و خود بفراز همه دیدن هو هو، هیاهو و زهی زهی پرواز! هی هی بفراز! بزن بزن پر و بالی چابک و نیک، تیک تیک، تیک تاک مرحباک که چه چالاکی تو به به، دل ای دل ای چه چها و چه خوش است پرنده برقص علی الله: دیّلالاً، دیّلالاً، دیّلالالاه، واه واه خسته شدم! چه شدي؟! چه؟!! خسته؟!! واویلاه![57]

Hay Hihay Han, Hu Hu, storm Hu Hu Haiahu (clamour) Hu has what vibration and what a rage, blow blow, flying, fly fly as flying is truly wonderful, seeing everyone below yourself and yourself above all Hu Hu, Hiahu Hu and Huzzah Huzzah flying! Hey Hey (constantly) ascend! Flap flap and flap nice and fast, tik tik, tik tak bravo! You are so fast, well, oh my heart, oh my heart, chirrup, how happy is the bird, dance cArefree: Dilala, Dilala, Dilalalah, pshaw pshaw I got tired! What's wrong?! What?! Tired? Oh, my God!

In this example, the agitation of the narrator is reflected through the basic layers of the language, mainly syllables and words which phonetically imitate the sound of the described objects or situations. The sequence of onomatopoeias for the wind ('*Hu Hu*') and the ticking of a clock ('*tik tāk*') reflects a sense of inner turmoil. The poet also creates the image of a bird fluttering frantically through sounds instead of rhetorical devices. In other words, he conveys the sound of a fluttering bird by repeating syllables and words such as '*par*', '*bezan*', '*del*', and so on. Later in this paragraph, the poet uses an unclear Arabic-like word '*Dilālā*', which suggests the voice of the narrator cheering and dancing. Finally the onomatope '*vāh*' (pshaw) indicates tiredness.

In addition to his experiences in phonetic poetry, Kiā has suggested another way of extending the vocal realm of poetry. One can see the idea of creating spoken poems called '*Shāhin-e Guyā*' (Talking Falcon) as another attempt to combine the worlds of poetry, performance, and music. He suggests that his poems (and others' poems of this sort) can be performed and

---

[57] Kiā, *Nahib-e Jonbesh-e Adabi-e Shāhin* (1940), p. 17.

combined with music.⁵⁸ Emphasizing the multimedia nature of his poetry, he announced that he would record some *Shāhin-e Guyā* by phonograph, instead of printing them on paper.⁵⁹ Although this idea is mentioned in a few sentences and was never actually implemented, one can view it as a call to experiment with a form of performance poetry in the Persian language.

Kiā mentions 'dancing and musical upbringing' as inspirational experiences he gained during his stay in France. It is possible that he is referring to the dance performances and poetry readings of the French avant-gardes of the 1930s. These performances first appeared in Cabaret Voltaire in Zurich in 1916, and then in other places by Dadaist artists. Hugo Ball, the founder of the cabaret, also composed performative poems in association with other Dada artists. His most well-known performative poem was *Karawane*, performed in 1917, which portrayed the trumpeting and slow movements of a caravan of elephants. This performance was in line with the idea of 'simultaneous poems' in which different performers read their texts aloud or chant concurrently.

Although Kiā could not perform a multi-vocal poem, he tried to incorporate different voices from different personas and a considerable volume of noises in his works. For instance, in the poem below, he uses exclamations and noises to simulate the atmosphere of avant-garde collective performances:

- تقویمی جانم!

خواهشی ای ماه!

کاغذی بردار!

بنویس!

امروز: بسلخیم!

امشب: قمر در عقرب!

ساعت: سیزده و سیزده دقیقه کم!

قاه قاه!

خدا نگهدار!

هیس!

هشدار! بچرخ تا بچرخیم:

هیس! هش! اتیک! اتاک! شب! توغ! اروز! اشب شد باز روز آمد! تغ، آنهفته! تغ تغ تغ، ماه! تغّی چند و چند ماهی تغ، این یکسال! تغ تغ تغ، پار و پیرار و هر ساله مانند همه ساله شب و روز و هفته و ماه و سال پیاپی گرّ وگرّ میگریزند و هی تغ تغ حال گذشته میگردد و آینده حال! تغ، پرید جوانی! وای! تغ، مرد زندگانی! های های!⁶⁰

---

⁵⁸ Kiā, *Nahib-e Jonbesh-e Adabi-e Shāhin* (1940), p. 22.
⁵⁹ Tondar Kiā. 'Che Avāmeli dar Tahavvol Suri-e She'r-e Farsi Ta'sir Dāshteh ast?', *Andishe va Honar*, Special issue (1961), 271.
⁶⁰ Kiā, *Nahib-e Jonbesh-e Adabi-e Shāhin* (1940), p. 56.

- My dear calendar!
O precious! I have a favour to ask!
Take the paper!
Write!
Today: We are at the end of the month!
Tonight: The Moon in Scorpio!

Clock: Thirteen minutes to thirteen!
HA HA!
Goodbye!
Shush!
Beware! Turn around, so we turn:
Shush! Whish! Tik! Tak! Knock! Night! Pok! Day! The night left; the day came again! Knock! That week! Knock, knock, month! A few knocks and a few months knock, this year! Knock, Knock, Knock, last year and the year before that and each year just like every year night and day and week and month and year, one after another, run rapidly and again Knock, Knock, the present becomes past, and the future becomes present! Knock youth escaped! Oops! Knock, life is dead! Hey Hey!

In another part of the same poem, Kiā attacks the solidified monotonic structure of traditional poetry, allowing different characters, objects, and concepts to have distinctive voices. The poet attempts to utilize the facilities of performative arts to change the position of the traditional poet as an absolute voice:

- چشمت را ببند و واکن   خوب تماشا کن

شهر شهر دیگریست:

خاکی بلند میشود، اتومبیلی تند میرود و تویش

کچلی کوسه باد پول گرفته است:

«من قاضی الحاجاتم!»

«حلال مشکلاتم!   بلای جیب لاتم!»

«پس خاک بر سر لات!»

[...]

- چشمت را ببند و واکن   خوب تماشا کن

شهر شهر دیگریست:

مجسمه‌ایست ایستاده که دو گوشت کوب بدو دستش داده‌اند! گویا

پهلوان است، شاید قهرمان هم شده باشد! از دورش بد نیست،

اما چیز دیگری هم بلد نیست:

«من همانم که همش میخورم و باز که گفتند بخور خواهم خورد! بله!!»

[...]

- چشمت را ببند و واکن   خوب تماشا کن

شهر شهر دیگریست:

طبلی است کلان! نام این طبل «کوس شهرت» است. هنگامی که باین کوس میکوبند همه با

همهمه از خواب میپرند، چند نفری هم احتیاطاً دق میکنند!

آهای بپّا، بپّا:

«بُمّ! بُمّ!.....»[61]

- Close your eyes and then open them   look thoroughly
The city is another city:
The dust rises, a car passes fast and inside it
a bald, beardless person is swollen with wealth:
'I fulfil wishes!'
'I solve all problems! And cause trouble for the tough guys' pocket.'
'So, shame on you tough guys!'
[...]
- Close your eyes and then open them   look thoroughly
The city is another city:
The statue is standing with two meat grinders in his hands!
Apparently,
he is a warrior; maybe he has also become a hero! He doesn't look
bad from a distance,
But he does not know anything else:
'I am the one who eats everything, and I will eat again when they say
so! Yes!!'
[...]
- Close your eyes and then open them   look thoroughly
The city is another city:
It is a huge drum! The name of it is 'drum of fame'.
When they beat the drum, everyone wakes up in commotion, and a
few people die of jealousy just in case!
Oh, watch out, watch out:
«Bang! Bang!...»

---

[61] Kiā, *Nahib-e Jonbesh-e Adabi-e Shāhin* (1940), pp. 52–3.

In this example, the wealthy man, the warrior, and the drum of fame have their own voices with distinctive tones and even rhythmic systems. The wealthy man, probably a pimp or someone who earns money by fooling or entertaining tough guys, talks in a colloquial manner with a light rhythm approximating *mostafʿelon faʿulon* (–⌣-/⌣–). The warrior has a single prosodic line with a much stronger rhythm: *fāʿelāton, faʿalāton, faʿalāton, faʿalāton, faʿalāton, faʿlon* (-⌣–/⌣⌣–/ ⌣⌣–/ ⌣⌣–/ ⌣⌣–/–). Finally, the drum contributes with a simple non-metrical onomatopoeia. The part of the narrator, on the other hand, is offbeat in order to highlight the rhythm of the other parts' specific characters.

By giving rise to inharmonious voices and sounds in his poetry, Kiā attempts to compose a primary text to be presented as an early form of performance poetry. His poems include many variations of sound, rhythm, tone, and diction in a way that makes them more performative. Indeed, these poems were written to be performed on stage or in cafes rather than being printed on paper. By highlighting their performative and musical nature, Kiā emphasizes that his poems should ideally be delivered as various kinds of performances.[62]

In his performative poems, Kiā seems to reproduce the voices of imaginary simultaneous performers in the text. He calls up the Dada artists of Cabaret Voltaire in his poems through the interaction of noises and rhythms. In the real world, however, Kiā saw himself as an individual avant-garde being constantly pushed out of the literary community. Besides, his refusal to cooperate with other Iranian avant-gardes of the 1930s and 1940s excluded him from any sort of collective activities such as performances, exhibitions, and journal contributions. However, perceiving the collective nature of avant-garde movements, another group of artists organized such activities for the first time under the title of *Anjoman-e Honari-e Khorus Jangi* (the Khorus Jangi Society for the Arts) in the late 1940s.

Hushang Irāni: Slaughterer of the nightingale

Hushang Irāni, born in Hamedan in 1925, pursued his primary and secondary education in Tehran. In 1942, he obtained his high school diploma. Four years later, in 1946, he successfully completed his Bachelor of Mathematics degree at the University of Tehran. Simultaneously, he cultivated his passion for painting and began establishing himself as a painter within the contemporary art community.[63] Irāni enrolled in the navy in 1946 and was

---

[62] Tondar Kiā, *Nahib-e Jonbesh-e Adabi-e Shāhin* (Tehran: [no publisher], 1976), pp. 842–43.
[63] Sirus Tāhbāz, ed., *Khorus Jangi-e Bi-Mānand* (Tehran: Farzān-e Ruz, 2001), p. 7.

transferred to England for further training; however, not finding himself well suited to military life, he soon left England for France, where he lived for a year before returning to Iran. In 1948 he moved to Spain and in October 1950 received his PhD in mathematics, for which he wrote a thesis entitled *Fazā va Zamān dar Tafakkor-e Hendi* (Time and Space in Indian Thought).[64] A couple of years after Irāni's return to Tehran, Mohammad Mosaddeq's nationalist government was overthrown by the American- and British-led coup d'état of 1953. This incident, and the severe suppression of the activities of cultural and political intellectuals, had a devastating impact on all artists of the time. Irāni was one of those who never recovered from the destructive impact of the coup, leading him to end his career as a poet and painter. As Manuchehr Ātashi says, after the coup he retreated into silence, although he was present at a few intellectual gatherings and debates.[65] However, his alcoholism, as well as his propensity for leading a solitary, mystic lifestyle, kept him out of the literary community until his death in 1973. According to most biographical accounts, he passed away in Kuwait, where he was undergoing treatment for throat cancer.

Hushang Irāni's fame as a poet is mostly associated with his involvement in the second series of the *Khorus Jangi* (Fighting Rooster) magazine. *Anjoman-e Honari-e Khorus Jangi* started its activities in Tehran in 1948. The founders of this society, the painter Jalil Ziā'pur, the writer Gholām-Hoseyn Gharib, the playwright Hasan Shirvāni, and the poet Manuchehr Sheybāni, were all pioneer figures in their fields. In 1949 this group initiated the publication of a magazine, also titled *Khorus Jangi*. This controversial journal, however, was suspended after five issues in 1950, and members of the editorial team, particularly Ziā'pur, were questioned by security officials owing to an imagined association between Cubism and communism. Because of the role this journal played in introducing Cubism to Iranian artists, they were condemned as communist sympathizers.[66] The first issue of this groundbreaking journal contains some articles and literary works by the members of the editorial board, reflecting their modernist approach towards Iranian art and literature. Specifically, this issue contains a poem by Nimā Yushij, *Az Shāhr-e Sobh* (From the City of Morning), to show the group's support for *Nimāic* modernism.[67]

---

[64]Tāhbāz, *Khorus Jangi-e Bi-Mānand*, p. 7.
[65]Manuchehr Ātashi, 'Sohāngar-e Sonnt-hā va Mote'āref-hā', in *Az Banafsh-e Tond tā be to Miandisham*, ed. by Shahrām Anāri (Tehran: Nakhostin, 2000), p. 11.
[66]Ayda Forutan, 'Why the Fighting Cock? The Significance of the Imagery of the *Khorus Jangi* and Its Manifesto "The Slaughterer of the Nightingale"', *Iran Namag*, 1 (2016), 28–49 (p. 38).
[67]Tāhbāz, *Khorus Jangi-e Bi-Mānand*, p. 7.

In 1951 Jalil Ziā'pur and Manuchehr Sheybāni left the group.[68] Hushang Irāni joined the team to kick-start the second series of the journal, which was now different both in appearance and in its approach to modern arts. Gharib, Shirvāni, and Irāni expressed their opinion about the new art (*Honar-e Now*) in a manifesto entitled *Sallākh-e Bolbol* (The Slaughterer of the Nightingale).[69] Arta Khakpour interprets this as a reference to the *bolbol*, the bird that is the 'standard metaphor for the singing, reciting lover or the poet in classical Persian poetry'.[70] Also, it may refer to the term '*gol-o-bolbol*' (the flower-and-nightingale pattern), a very popular but overused Persian ornamentation.[71] This manifesto, which advocated a radical, destructive approach towards both traditional and moderate modern art forms in Iran, appeared in the back cover of all four issues of the second series in red ink:

(1) *Khorus Jangi*'s art is the art of the living. This rooster [*khorus*] will silence the voices of all who sing dirges at the grave of the old art.

(2) For the sake of initiating a new era in art, we have mercilessly declared war upon the artistic traditions and conventions [*qavānin*] of old.

(3) Contemporary artists are the children of this age [*farzand-e zamān-and*]; in the arts, the right to life belongs only to the innovators.

(4) The first step of any new movement is the smashing of the idols of the old.

(5) We sentence to annihilation those who worship the old and outdated [*kohneparast*] in all realms of art: theatre, painting, novel writing, poetry, music, sculpture, and we obliterate the idols of the old and the carrion-eating imitators.

---

[68] According to Ayda Forutan, after the termination of the first series of *Khorus Jangi*, Ziā'pur 'started another magazine called *Kavir* (Desert). Soon this, too, was stopped by the government, and Ziā'pur went on to start yet another short-lived magazine entitled *Panjeh-ye Khorus* (The Cock's Claw)'. Forutan, p. 38.

[69] A few months after the end of *Khorus Jangi*'s publication in March 1952, Irani contributed to the founding of a new journal called *Mowj* (Wave). However, *Mowj* was only published for one issue and in a limited number of copies. In July 1956 the same editorial team with a few changes published two issues of another journal called *Apādānā*. The third and last issue of this journal was published in December 1956 under the title *Honar-e Now*. Mohammad Shams Langrudi, *Tārikh-e Tahlili-e She'r-e Now*, 4 vols (Tehran: Markaz, 1998), 1–2, p. 525 and pp. 278–86.

[70] Khakpour, p. 127.

[71] Bavand Behpoor, 'Introduction to "The Nightingale's Butcher Manifesto" and "Volume and Environment ii"', *ARTMargins*, 3 (2014), 118–28 (p. 123).

(6) The new art, which considers introspection [*samimiyat ba darun*, intimacy with the internal] to be the wellspring of artistic creation, contains within it all the turmoil and turbulence of life, and can never be separated from it.

(7) The new art treads upon the grave of idols and their accursed imitators in order to break the chains of tradition and promote the freedom of expressing emotions [*āzādi-ye bayān-e ehsās*].

(8) The new art voids all the conventions of the past, and locates newness as the source of all beauty.

(9) The essence of art is in moving and progressing. The only living artists are those whose intellects are fortified with the knowledge of the new.

(10) The new art rejects all the claims of the proponents of 'art for society', 'art for art's sake' [*honar barāye Ejtemā', honar barāye honar*], etc.

(11) The advancement of art in Iran necessitates the annihilation of all societies that promulgate the art of the old.

(12) Let all creators of artistic works beware that the artists of *Khorus Jangi* will combat with the greatest ferocity the dissemination of archaic and banal works.

(13) Death to idiots [or 'down with fools,' *marg bar ahmaqān*].[72]

One could consider this declaration the manifesto of the first Iranian avant-garde movement which, for two reasons, is comparable to those of other avant-garde movements throughout the world. First of all, unlike other individual attempts preceding the *Khorus Jangi* society, this manifesto is a collective endeavour intended to create an avant-garde movement. Second, the style and phraseology of the manifesto are in line with those of the worlds' leading, historical avant-garde movements. For instance, Khakpour states that the group's manifesto, *Sallākh-e Bolbol*, is structurally similar to the manifestos of Futurism and Vorticism. One may also see a resemblance between phrases in *Sallākh-e Bolbol* and those of a Dutch Neoplasticism manifesto in *De Stijl* (The Style) 1918.[73] In addition, Ayda Forutan spots various combinations of language typical of avant-garde manifestos in *Sallākh-e Bolbol*. She states that the 'predominance of romanticised, poetic idealisation', 'angry, heroic, violent, revolutionary language', 'religion sub-themes', and 'cursing, dehumanising and threatening language typical of

---

[72] Behpoor, p. 127.
[73] Behpoor, p. 128.

revolutionary slogans' are phraseological substitutions that *Sallākh-e Bolbol* shares with other avant-garde manifestos.[74]

In terms of content, one can spot all four of Poggioli's avant-gardes' shared 'moments' in *Sallākh-e Bolbol*. Statements 6 and 9 illustrate the activist moment of avant-garde artists: the moment in which they recreate 'the turmoil and turbulence of life' in their dynamic artistic works and seek 'the essence of art' in 'moving and progressing'. The hostility of this manifesto's contributors towards tradition and traditionalists is visible in most of the statements, particularly statements 1, 4, 7, and 11. This sense of opposition to both the public and the intellectuals reveals this as a potentially antagonistic moment. The writers condemn 'all who sing dirges at the grave of the old art', whether intellectuals or ordinary people. Also, they do not differentiate between moderate modernists, particularly those associated with *Sokhan*, and traditionalists, calling for the destruction of 'all societies that promulgate the art of the old'.

Mashi'at Alā'i compares the destructive antagonism of the *Khorus Jangi* movement, particularly Irāni's poetry, with other post-war avant-garde movements. He states that *Khorus Jangi* artists, like Western avant-gardes, tried to portray an original image of the reality of their surrounding world. In so doing, they intended to destroy 'the literary language, traditional forms, and current rules' to avoid the clichés of mainstream art. Therefore, they dived into their own personal, mental, and intuitive experiences to give the reality an unfiltered expression.[75]

An argument can be made that the artists of *Khorus Jangi* inclined more towards the destruction of existing structures rather than the construction of new ones. This approach, in turn, led them to the nihilistic moment of avant-gardism. The nihilistic perspective of this manifesto becomes apparent when, in statement 10, the writers reject both ideas of art for society and art for art's sake. Also, in statement 12, they introduce themselves as the guardians of the 'new art' and warn other artists that they oppose the 'banal works' of both the traditionalists and the moderate modernists.

In addition, *Khorus Jangi* artists not only wished to abolish all aspects of institutionalized art but also placed their careers in danger of being erased from the history of art by the majority of literary historians belonging to what Harold Bloom terms 'the school of resentment': academic critics who are primarily occupied with social and political activism. These historians prioritize the sociopolitical commitment of the literary work, even at the expense of aesthetic values.[76] In contrast, Irāni condemns

---

[74] Forutan, p. 46.
[75] Mashi'at Alā'i, 'Hushang Irāni va Sureālism-e Irāni', *Goharān*, 7–8 (2005), 94–9 (p. 97).
[76] Bloom, pp. xvi–xvii.

the politically charged works of Nimāic poets as being 'custom-made' (sefāreshi). He believes that sociopolitically committed Nimāic poetry should not be considered avant-garde. He criticizes Nimā's foreword to Esmāʿil Shāhrudi's first collection of poetry, Ākharin Nabard (Last Battle, 1951), for encouraging young poets to deviate from the expression of their thoughts and to try to serve a sociopolitical purpose or to bend innovation to norms.[77] Such an approach to the main trend of high modernist literature at the time marginalized Irāni and his fellow colleagues in Khorus Jangi. Indeed, Khorus Jangi artists, in their agonistic moment, dedicated all of their energy to the destruction of institutionalized art and devoted their careers to the future generation of artists.

Irāni's violet scream

In addition to declaring Khorus Jangi's perspectives on current issues relating to Iranian art, this manifesto also served as Irāni's initial proclamation of a new poetic style. Although he did not receive much attention from his contemporary poets at the time of publication, he insisted on his style and published several groundbreaking poems in the journal. Peyman Vahabzadeh assumes that some of the young literary figures of the time instantly realized the 'poetic novelty' of Irāni's works. However, to protect themselves from the 'authoritarian' onslaughts of the mainstream poetic community, most of these perceptive poets and critics joined the collective silence about Irāni's poetry.[78] Nevertheless, although the poets of Khorus Jangi were pushed to the margin of modern Persian poetry, their works, particularly Irāni's poems, influenced some of the most prominent poets of the time, such as Sohrāb Sepehri (1928–1980), as well as Ahmad-Rezā Ahmadi (1940–2023), and the Sheʿr-e Digar poets (active in the 1960s) of the next generation.[79]

The first collection of Irāni's poetry, Banafsh-e Tond bar Khākestari (Intense Purple on Grey), was published in September 1951 in 200 copies. This collection included thirteen poems and an epilogue illustrated by the poet's drawings. Although most critics and poets attempted to overlook this book, a few poems found their way into the canon of Persian avant-garde

---

[77] Tāhbāz, Khorus Jangi-e Bi-Mānand, pp. 221–3.
[78] Peyman Vahabzadeh, 'The Space between Voices', in Essays on Nimā Yushij: Animating Modernism in Persian Poetry, ed. by Ahmad Karimi-Hakkak, Kamran Talattof (Leiden: Brill, 2004), pp. 193–219 (p. 208).
[79] For a thorough discussion of this, see Abdolali Dastgheyb, Sāyeh Rowshan-e Sheʿr-e Now-e Pārsi (Tehran: Farhang, 1969), pp. 165–243.

poetry. Among these poems, *Kabud* (Indigo) has received both the most attention and the most objection. The poem opens with the following lines:

هیماهورای
گیل ویگولی
...
نیبون .... نیبون
غار کبود می‌دود
دست به گوش و فشرده پلک و خمیده
یکسره جیغی بنفش
می‌کشد⁸⁰

Himahooray!
Gil vigooli
...
Niboon! Niboon!
The indigo cave runs
Hands on ears, pressing its eyelids, hunching
Screams a continuous scream in violet.⁸¹

The poem is composed in a free verse style. Some lines start with the prosodic foot *mofta'elon* (-⌣⌣-) and then turn into a rhythmic prose. The imagery is also unique and somehow unprecedented in Persian poetry. The hallucinatory imagery of the poem is similar to expressionist painter Edvard Munch's work, *The Scream* (1893). The indigo cave is pictured as a human running and radiating a shade of violet light which can be seen as the embodiment of screaming noise.

Sirus Tāhbāz states that the negative reception received by this poem from both the literary community and the general public caused many difficulties in the process of modernizing Persian poetry as a whole. He believes that although parts of this poem can be regarded as some of the best poetic pieces of the time, opponents of Persian avant-garde movements misused it as a means of discouraging the young generation of avant-garde poets. They mocked every controversial change in the form and content of Persian poetry, labelling it as a '*jigh-e banafsh*' (violet scream), a phrase that they had coined from the above poem. Abdol'ali Dastgheyb, too, denounced Irāni's poetry as being merely an excuse for the opponents of poetic modernization to attack all modernist movements.⁸² He believed Irāni's poems to be blind imitations of Buddhist and Islamic mystical poetry, with no added value.

---

[80] Tāhbāz, *Khorus Jangi-e Bi-Mānand*, p. 59.
[81] Translations are from: Behpoor, pp. 118–24.
[82] Dastgheyb, p. 179.

Dastgheyb even refers to the poem *Kabud* as a 'pastime' which can 'never' be defined as a poem.[83]

Another significant poem in *Banafsh-e Tond bar Khākestari* is *Hāh*. Following the dominant readings of this poem, Vahabzadeh describes it as a portrayal of 'an apocalypse or cataclysmic event' being narrated from an 'omniscient' perspective.[84] On the other hand, one may read this as a pseudo-prayer in which the poet seeks shelter with his almighty God, the one who momentarily appears in the poem as 'You':

پنجه ای از – خشم – آبی خرد گردد
در درونش
هستی توفان شود، همچون غباری
زیر چنگ دره‌ها پیچان
برکند نفرت از بند مهره
شکافد
قلعه های سهمگین خیره بر دریا
مرداب آهن های دود
دشنه چشمش گلوی نهرها را یخ زند
تو و این سپید
تو این نقب ابد[85]

Turned blue in fury, a claw shatters
Within it
Tornado's being turns to dust
Twists in the grip of the valleys
Hatred tears the beads off the string
It splits open
The dreadful sea-gazing castles
The swamp of steel rushes
The dagger of its eyes freezes the throats of creeks
You and the white
You and the eternal tunnel[86]

This poem consists of seven stanzas which portray images of an apocalyptic situation; however, each stanza is relatively autonomous. Vahabzadeh states that this poem is made of stanzas which barely address each other, and that its 'distorted' images are built upon 'uncertain relationships among signifiers'.[87] One can observe similar concerns about the notion of the organic unity of

---

[83] Dastgheyb, p. 165.
[84] Vahabzadeh, p. 209.
[85] Tāhbāz, *Khorus Jangi-e Bi-Mānand*, p. 55.
[86] Translation of this poem is from Vahabzadeh, pp. 209–10.
[87] Vahabzadeh, p. 210.

modern poetry among critics contemporary to the poet. For instance, Parviz Nātel Khānlari argues that there is no relevance or unity between the beginning and end of the text in most pioneer Persian poems. He states that the forms in these poems are 'bunches of dispersed fragments' rather than unified and coherent structures.[88] Moreover, Vahabzadeh criticizes the open structure of the sentences, which results in 'contingent' and 'ambiguous' lines. He concludes that since the segments are not composed 'to generate an integrational effect', this poem has failed to create a proper narrative form. He writes:

> One can easily see how, unlike Nimā's poem, the structure of the narrative is disturbed by moments of radical ambiguity. Put in Barthesian terms, the functional units of the narrative ('Turned blue in fury, a claw shatters'; 'tornado's being turns to dust'; and so on) do not quite imply, but rather stand in external relations with one another in an 'unorderly' fashion within passages.[89]

However, one may conclude these statements differently and suggest that *Hāh*, as an avant-garde poem, aims to create an un-coherent, non-organic form. Vahabzadeh's understanding of poetic forms fails to grasp Irāni's approach because Irāni's poetry cannot be constructed based on 'contingent sequences of segments' which are fixed through articulation. *Nimāic* poetry seems to have interrelated and consequential components in which, as Bürger writes, the parts can be understood only through the whole, the whole only through the parts.[90] This rule, however, does not apply to all post-Nimā modern poems. One must bear in mind that the 'unorderly fashion' within the lines and stanzas is in order to harmonize the form with the apocalyptic mood of the poem. The poet envisions cataclysmic moments which, through nature, disturb the logical structure of the language, the sequence of thoughts, and the form of narration.

Tāhbāz, too, asserts that Irāni's deviation from the formal norms of Persian poetry does not indicate his lack of knowledge or his inability to create a standard and coherent form. He argues that stanzas in disarray and the disorganization of components in each line are the result of the poet's 'internal eruption' and are derived from his subconscious.[91] Tāhbāz's emphasis on the active subconscious of the poet probably refers to the idea of automatic writing or psychography. Thus, it can be argued that these poems should not be analysed based on modernist preconditions of organic unity. According to Bürger, in an automatic text 'the parts emancipate themselves

---

[88] Iraj Pārsinezhād, *Khānlari va Naqd-e Adabi* (Tehran: Sokhan, 2008), p. 223.
[89] Vahabzadeh, p. 210.
[90] Bürger, p. 79.
[91] Tāhbāz, *Khorus Jangi-e Bi-Mānand*, p. 17.

from a superordinate whole; they are no longer its essential elements ... In an automatic text that strings images together, some could be missing, yet the text would not be significantly affected'.[92] In Irāni's poetry one can see that new images of the same type could be added to or omitted from the text with no noticeable impact on the composition of the poem as a whole. The order of images is also uncertain. In other words, as Bürger states, 'what is decisive are not the events in their distinctiveness but the construction principle that underlies the sequence of events'.[93]

Moreover, in terms of the smaller units of the poem, such as lines and words, the poet releases his writing from the conventions of the literary language. Towards the end, the poet not only permits his unconscious mind to disturb the logical structure of sentences but also, at the very last stanza, emancipates his language from the standard meaning:

سوز سایه‌ای
سر فراکشد
دخمه بسته‌ها
از هوار او
رشته‌ها درند
سایه برجهد
سایه   بر   جهد
....

هایی   یی   یا   یا
هایی   یی   یا   یا
نی   دا   دا   دا ا ا ا ا ا ا ا ا
هاه[94]

The cold breeze of a shadow
arises
those in tight crypts
break the chains
from its cry
the shadow leaps,

---

[92] Bürger, p. 80.
[93] Bürger, p. 80.
[94] Tāhbāz, *Khorus Jangi-e Bi-Mānand*, p. 56.

```
the     shadow    leaps
................................
Haii  yee  ya  ya
Haii  yee  ya  ya
Ni da da da a a a a a a
Huh
```

The unintelligible sounds at the very end of the poem are excellent examples of unconscious outbursts in Irāni's poetry. Parviz Dāryush, one of the first critics who examined Irāni's poetry, interprets this type of sound as representative of the poet's delusions being transmitted into letters. Although Dāryush does not discuss the notion of oneiric language, which is associated with the automatic writing technique, he notices the connection between Irāni's use of unintelligible sounds and that of surrealists.[95]

Tāhbāz argues that Irāni's surrealism in theory and practice are indigenous. Indeed, he refers to Irāni's non-organic forms as a hybrid: surrealist notions of automatic writing combined with the Eastern mystical heritage, particularly Persian Sufi poetry.[96] Dāryush, in a similar vein, states that Irāni's work is indebted to his experiences in the intellectual and artistic communities of 1940s France and his constant readings of Rumi and Attar.[97]

Irāni's second collection entitled *Khākestari* (Grey, 1952) is a small pamphlet of twenty-two pages, published in just 110 copies. There are eight prose poems in this collection, illustrated with the poets' drawings. Tāhbāz states that Irāni changes his poetic strategy from his second book onwards. He asserts that there are no more controversial poetic forms and melancholic sounds in this book; instead, the mystical overtone of the poems has increased considerably.[98] However, although the style of the collection is generally less subversive in comparison to the first collection, the book still contains a few controversial pieces. Among the few innovative sections of the collection is a visual poem titled *Unio Mystica* (Mystical Union), which has been recognized as one of the earliest instances of Persian concrete poetry.[99]

However, it is possible to categorize this work as a more traditional form of visual poetry known as 'pattern poetry' (also called a figure poem, shaped

---

[95] Parviz Dāryush, 'Dar Resā-ye Veylāni', in *Khorus Jangi-e Bi-Mānand*, ed. by Sirous Tāhbāz (Tehran: Farzān-e Ruz, 2001), pp. 318–29 (p. 320).
[96] Tāhbāz, *Khorus Jangi-e Bi-Mānand*, p. 17.
[97] Dāryush, pp. 324–5.
[98] Tāhbāz, *Khorus Jangi-e Bi-Mānand*, p. 21.
[99] Sayeh Eghtesadinia, 'Irani, Hushang', in *Encyclopaedia Iranica*, http://www.iranicaonline.org/articles/irani-hushang [accessed 18 March 2018].

verse, or *carmen figuratum*), in which the poet supports the coherence of his/her poem through the typographical presentation. According to the *Encyclopedia Britannica*, pattern poetry consists of verses 'in which the typography or lines are arranged in an unusual configuration, usually to convey or extend the emotional content of the words'.[100] Likewise, in this poem, the arrangement of the words on the page represents the notion of union between the mystic's soul and God. In fact the main idea behind the arrangement of these words is to illustrate the concept of *Unio Mystica*. This notion refers to the 'ultimate aim of man for his soul to be absorbed in the transcendent' in both this life and the hereafter during 'rare moments of religious ecstasy'.[101]

آ

آ، یا

«آ» بون نا

«آ»، «یا»، بون نا

آ اوم، آ اومان، تین‌تاها، دیژ داها

میگ تا اودان: ها

هوماهون: ها

یندو: ها

ها[102]

"A, ya

"a", bun na

"a", "ya", bun na

A um, A uman, tintaha, dizh daha

Mig ta udan: ha

Humahun: ha

Indu: ha

Ha

---

[100] 'Pattern Poetry', in *Encyclopedia Britannica* https://www.britannica.com/art/pattern-poetry [accessed 26 February 2020] (para. 10 of 19).
[101] 'Unio Mystica', in *Oxford Reference* https://www.oxfordreference.com/view/10.1093/oi/authority.20110803110707752 [accessed 19 February 2020].
[102] Tāhbāz, *Khorus Jangi-e Bi-Mānand*, p. 109.

It is not just the visual aspect of this poem which is controversial; the words and sounds are also unintelligible for the Persian reader. The poem engages in a dialogue with the sound poetry traditions of historical avant-gardes, including the Futurists and Dadaists. Sound poetry prioritizes the phonetic elements of human speech over the conventional semantic and syntactic values of traditional forms of expression. It is often characterized as verse without words, focusing on the sonic qualities and oral delivery. Designed primarily for live performances, sound poetry allows the audience to experience the immersive power of sound and its artistic potential beyond traditional linguistic structures.[103] However, numerous critics have offered interpretations of the sounds in this poem, associating them with hymns derived from mystical or ancient Iranian and Indian Vedic texts. For instance, Tāhbāz compares the use of unintelligible words in Irāni's poems to the repetitive sounds in the *samaʿ* dance songs of the Molavi (Rumi) Order of Sufism.[104] Alternatively, some scholars, such as Sayeh Eghtesadinia, compare the sounds used in this poem to 'Sanskrit letters and sounds in a particular geometrical arrangement'.[105]

The mystical overtone is maintained in Irāni's third and fourth collections of poems. The third collection, *Sholeh-ʿi Pardeh ra bar Gereft va Eblis be Darun Āmad* (A Flame Embraced the Curtain, and Iblis Entered, 1952), too, is a 24-page pamphlet containing seven prose poems, printed in 110 copies. Even in the prologue to this collection, the mystical tendencies of the poet are explicit. Eghtesadinia believes that this mystical overtone does not stem from Islamic mysticism. In this introduction, it is argued that Irāni delves into the mystical journey as experienced by the modern individual, engaging in a profound dialogue with Buddha.[106] In 1955 Irāni published his final collection of poetry, *Aknun be to Miandisham, be to-hā Miandisham* (I Think of You Now, I Think of All Like You), containing nine poems. The physical features and scope of the collection are similar to the previous one. The only difference is the slightly larger number of copies printed in the first instance. All the poems in this collection are more or less in line with those of the previous one. Shams Langrudi, however, believes that Irāni's prologue to this book is 'the first theoretical text on modern, Persian mystical poetry'.[107]

---

[103] Filippo Tommaso Marinetti's (1876–1944) renowned work *Zang Tumb Tumb* stands out as a prominent example of Futurist sound poetry. As previously mentioned the Dadaists delved deeper into the realm of sound poetry and introduced distinct categories, such as Bruitist, phonetic, and Simultaneous poetry. For a thorough discussion of the history of sound poetry, see Greene Roland et al., *The Princeton Encyclopedia of Poetry and Poetics* (Princeton: Princeton University Press, 2012), pp. 1327–29.
[104] Tāhbāz, *Khorus Jangi-e Bi-Mānand*, p. 17.
[105] Eghtesadinia (para. 10 of 19).
[106] Eghtesadinia (para. 11 of 19).
[107] Shams Langrudi, *Tārikh-e Tahlili-e Sheʿr-e Now*, 1, p. 255.

A different way of sociopolitical engagement

The prevailing consensus among scholars is that due to his mystical inclinations, Irāni tended to overlook the sociopolitical dilemmas of his era. According to Ātashi's recollections, during the 1960s, Irāni would frequent the café at Marmar Hotel, where gatherings of poets and critics convened to engage in discussions on literary and political matters. However, Irāni was known to abstain from actively participating in these debates. Instead, he would often be found playing darts in a corner of the hall, distancing himself from the ongoing conversations. Ātashi interprets this behaviour as Irāni's reaction to the politicized atmosphere of the literary community, implying that he was not interested in political issues.[108] Tāhbāz writes that even the 1953 coup and its tremendous consequences on society did not 'wake our mystic wayfarer'.[109] Furthermore, some leftist critics condemned avant-garde poets like Irāni of 'individualism' and of acting as outsiders who did not speak 'the language of the public' (*zabān-e tudeh-hā*). Notably, a journal called *Kabutar-e Solh* (The Peace Pigeon), which was considered the main rival to *Khorus Jangi*, had a significant impact on the creation of the 'committed' and 'uncommitted' dichotomy among modern poets of the time.[110]

However, one may argue that Irāni's avant-garde antagonism towards the institutionalized literary modernism supported by leftist activists drove him to possess a distinct opinion about the means of sociopolitical engagement in the arts. In other words, Irāni attempted to change the nature of sociopolitical engagement in Persian poetry, the very nature which was considered unalterable by sociopolitically committed poets and critics promoting communist/socialist perspectives towards art and literature. Bürger suggests that the structural principle of an avant-garde work is emancipatory in itself 'because it permits the breakup of an ideology that is increasingly congealing into a system'.[111] Hence the political engagement of an avant-garde work cannot be examined on the basis of its content, but should rather be assessed through an investigation of its resistance to dominant forms. Therefore, one should see Irāni's endeavour to resist the old dichotomy of pure and political art as a political act in itself, manifested in his practice of poetry.

According to Bavand Behpoor, Irāni held a stance against both the Iranian communists, who advocated a social approach to art, and those who, despite their formal modernist inclinations, sought to maintain some connection

---

[108] Ātashi, pp. 11–12.
[109] Tāhbāz, *Khorus Jangi-e Bi-Mānand*, p. 27.
[110] Shams Langrudi, *Tārikh-e Tahlili-e She'r-e Now*, pp. 13–14.
[111] Bürger, p. 91.

with the past.¹¹² From Irāni's point of view, Nimā Yushij, who had by then been established as the father of modern poetry, had become an elderly poet who had compromised with both traditionalists and political activists. In his critical article about Nimā's foreword to Shāhrudi's *Ākharin Nabard (Last Battle, 1951)*, Irāni states that Nimā compromised his innovations in order to still be acknowledged by the institutionalized literature of his time. He finishes his article thus: 'Nimā Yushij will always be remembered with respect as he is the founder of a precious movement. However, the right to artistic life is exclusive to pioneers.'¹¹³

Irāni's perspective is similar to the notion of the 'continual process of standardisation' in Poggioli's theory. According to him, the process of standardization puts 'a rarity or novelty into general and universal use', then passes on 'to another rarity or novelty when the first has ceased to be such'.¹¹⁴ Irāni criticized Nimā for his simultaneous conservative stance and role as a propaganda tool for the leftists:

> Nimā Yushij has understood his time and pushed the boundaries of art in many cases. He breathed in that time and generated great value in the art community. However, today his art suffers from stagnation and obsolescence … He, wrongly, seeks the acceptance of the artist among different strata of society. He foists custom-made art as a way to keep the arts alive while they are eventually subject to death.¹¹⁵

By condemning Nimā, Irāni suggests that public acceptance should not be regarded as a characteristic of avant-garde poetry, as it has the potential to push the poet towards conservativism. He believes that a work of art is created to satisfy the artist's desires and that an artist never commits himself to ethics, society, and traditions.¹¹⁶ Accordingly, he himself experimented recklessly with various aspects of poetry, regardless of resistance from the general public and literati. Unlike Nimā, who wanted to establish his movement as an acceptable tradition, Irāni, as an anti-establishment artist, sacrificed the chance for his work to become a tradition of sorts by refusing to tailor his art according to public acceptance. Vahabzadeh argues that Irāni's poetry is a warning about the institutionalization of young *Nimāic* modernism. So he interprets Irāni's radicalism as a 'cry for a collective

---

¹¹²Behpoor, p. 123.
¹¹³Tāhbāz, *Khorus Jangi-e Bi-Mānand*, pp. 222–3.
¹¹⁴Poggioli, pp. 79–80.
¹¹⁵Tāhbāz, *Khorus Jangi-e Bi-Mānand*, pp. 221–2.
¹¹⁶Shahrām Anāri, *Majmu'eh-ye Ash'ār va Andisheh-ye Hushang Irāni: Az Banafsh-e Tond tā be to Miandisham* (Tehran: Nakhostin, 2000), pp. 49–50.

emancipation from stagnation and establishment' and a call for the revival of the main objectives of the movements leading to modern poetry.[117]

By denying the importance of being acceptable to the public, Irāni risked being seen as a 'one-off', an inappropriate cultural phenomenon. Karimi-Hakkak argues that 'such risks are an inherent part of all efforts at innovation as they arrive on the cultural scene'.[118] This might happen when the readers fail to comprehend the innovative aspect of a work and label it as absurd, nonsensical, and even non-poetry. Karimi-Hakkak articulates that readers' rejection can be a simple reaction to what they see as aesthetically pleasureless works or merely 'cultural noise'.[119]

The repressive social and cultural atmosphere of Iranian society in this era not only marginalized radical poets such as Irāni but also affected the more publicly accepted side of poetry's modernization. Even Nimā himself, at some point, became a victim of the process of marginalization. After the establishment of Nimāic modernism within the literary mainstream, all avant-garde poets whose poetry was not politically engaged were ignored by the public. Indeed, even some of Nimā's poems in which he had experimented with the aesthetic system of Persian poetry were considered as 'unwanted noises'. According to Vahabzadeh, modernist Persian poetry following Nimā has been affected by the standardization process, becoming constrained within a predetermined framework. In an attempt to maintain its discursive continuity, modernist Persian poetry not only emphasizes specific elements, symbols, and interpretations but also seeks to legitimize them through historicization. Vahabzadeh argues that this discourse of modernist Persian poetry suppresses the disruptive ruptures brought forth by Irāni's poetic output, which challenges the established norms and boundaries.[120]

Many critics have tried to justify Irāni's exclusion from the modern literary community by portraying his works as irrelevant to the reality of society and as alien to Iranian culture. For instance, Enāyat Sami'i states that Irāni failed because he never succeeded in creating an alternative to Nimāic political symbolism. Additionally, his intended replacement for Nimāic poetry did not stem from Iranian cultural traditions. As highlighted by Sami'i, this refers to both contextual and formal innovations in Irāni's poetry, such as the novel use of sense analogy/synaesthesia, automatic writing, and sound poetry. Sami'i maintains that although these elements influenced some influential poets, particularly Sohrāb Sepehri, they were

---

[117] Vahabzadeh, p. 215.
[118] Karimi-Hakkak, *Recasting Persian Poetry*, p. 283.
[119] Karimi-Hakkak, *Recasting Persian Poetry*, p. 283.
[120] Vahabzadeh, p. 218.

incompatible with Iranian literary traditions.[121] Likewise, Esmā'il Nuri 'Alā perceives the anti-traditional nature of Irāni's poetry to be the main reason behind his failure and argues that Irāni completely disregarded the parameters of Iranian classical poetry and Iranian social conventions.[122]

Revisiting the hypothesis initially presented in this chapter, it becomes evident that Hushang Irāni and Tondar Kiā should be acknowledged as pivotal figures within the Persian avant-garde movement of the 1940s and 1950s. Their visionary perspectives challenged and sought to dismantle the established literary traditions, advocating for the creation of a wholly new aesthetic framework for Persian poetry. While these poets displayed a strong affinity for the aesthetic and figurative aspects of the avant-garde, their poetics went beyond mere artistic expression and assumed a political dimension through their anti-hierarchical and anarchistic approach. It is important to note that Kiā and Irāni vehemently fought against the exclusive attitudes of institutionalized cultural bodies that accused avant-garde art of undermining society's 'good taste' and jeopardizing its cultural heritage. This selective stance towards the Persian avant-garde, particularly within the historiography of literary modernism in Iran, has obscured significant aspects of the history of modern Persian poetry.

---

[121] Enayat Sami'i, 'Khiyāl Pardāz-e Ofoq-hā-ye Bāz', *Goharān*, 7 & 8 (2005), 91–3 (pp. 92–3).
[122] Esmā'il Nuri 'Alā, *Teori-e She'r; az Mowj-e Now ta She'r-e Eshq* (London: Ghazal, 1994), p. 225.

Conclusion

The primary objective of this book was to explore the connection between aesthetic transformations in poetry and the resistance against established political, cultural, and aesthetic hierarchies within the works of a specific group of pioneering Iranian poets spanning from the 1800s to the 1950s. Dividing this one hundred and fifty year timespan into four periods – the Literary Return Movement (1780–1900), the Constitutional Revolution (1900–1920), the post-constitutional era (1920–40), and the domination of modernism (1940–60) – I analysed the aesthetic, cultural, and political aspects of alternative poetic movements and chosen pioneer individuals. I sought to give prominence to the voices of poets whose careers were overshadowed by traditionalists and by the mainstream trends of poetic modernization. Labelled as 'cultural noise', some of these poets' experiential works have been neglected or pushed out of the picture by literary critics and historians. In some cases, the entire oeuvre of an unconventional poet has been eliminated from the history of modern Persian poetry. One can contend, though, that the significance of these very poets and their groundbreaking advancements in poetics is equally vital in driving the transformation of literature, alongside the reforms introduced by Persian modernists.

The main purpose of Chapters 1 and 2 was to present an argument that the formal changes observed in the poetry of the constitutional and post-constitutional eras should be understood as independent emancipatory actions, rather than mere by-products of the sociopolitical upheavals that occurred during those periods. These chapters determined that the very act of renewing literary forms, even when the content was not sociopolitically engaged, was the space of revelation for the politics of literature. Creating the new was, in many cases, associated with breaking the dominance of the solidified old and resistance against entrenched hierarchies of any sort.

The first chapter touched upon the ways in which early sociopolitically engaged poetry of the nineteenth century contributed to the modernization and reformulation of poetic forms, setting the stage for a poetic revolution in subsequent generations. I briefly examined the political dimensions of Qā'em Maqām Farāhāni and Fathollāh Khān Sheybāni's poetry. My analysis revealed these poets' attempts at politicizing their works to have been mostly limited to advisory and didactic content, while the formal aspects of their poems remained representative of the hierarchical regime of power relations. In contrast, Yaghmā Jandaqi ventured into exploring various innovative poetic forms that drew inspiration from contemporary popular religious performances. These experimental forms became pivotal sources for the literary revolution in the following generation of poets, making a significant impact on the trajectory of poetic expression. I, therefore, continued the first chapter by demonstrating the effect of new trends of literary modernization on the works of the followers of pre-revolutionary classical literature during and after the Constitutional Revolution of 1905–11. I then analysed two contradictory approaches adopted by Malek al-Sho'arā Bahār towards the form and function of the traditional poetic templates and literary language of this era: preservation and reconfiguration. The chapter ended with an analysis of colloquialism in constitutional poetry, its relationship with folk performing arts and its significance as a form of artistic resistance.

This discussion led to the second chapter, which examined the performing aspects of constitutional poetry in the works of interdisciplinary artists such as Āref Qazvini and Mirzādeh Eshqi. Chapter 2 also depicted the emancipatory spirit of performed poetry in the form of collective singing and dramatic poems. The chapter argues that the experimentation and public performance of poetry during this era were not solely motivated by political shifts. Rather, they served as a manifestation of independent resistance against sociopolitical and cultural hegemony, showcasing the poets' self-reliance in driving poetic transformation.

The third chapter opened with a very brief account of Taqi Raf'at's life and career as the leading figure of the *Tajaddod* group, before going on to explore the theoretical dimensions of long-lasting disputes between *Tajaddod* poets and the *Dāneshkadeh* Association on their different understandings of the literary revolution. It then turned to a short overview of the life and oeuvre of Abolqāsem Lāhuti, enabling me to analyse Lāhuti's transition from conventional, mystical subject matters to sociopolitically committed, counter-sublime ones. I also examined the figurative transformations in Lāhuti's poetry following his involvement with Soviet socialist realism and discussed his experiments in poetic forms, particularly his innovative rhythmic systems and unconventional rhyme patterns. This led me to scrutinize the experimentations of *Tajaddod* poets – mainly Shams Kasmā'i, Ja'far Khāmene'i, and Taqi Raf'at – in generating poetic forms, as well as adopting novel rhyme patterns inspired by French and Russian sonnets. I then addressed the role of these experiments in developing a new understanding of stanza in Persian poetry. The new conception of stanza introduced by these poets, in turn, led to the introduction of a new poetic form called *chārpāreh* (four-liner). Due to its hybrid nature, this poetic form quickly gained popularity and appealed to both gradualists and radical modernists. The former readily accepted *chārpāreh* since it stemmed from traditional Persian literary forms, while the latter, who were inclined to follow the process of poetic change in Europe, found it a relatively freer form that enabled them to reconfigure their immediate literary tradition. I concluded the chapter by demonstrating the significant role played by *chārpāreh* in changing the classical, generic classification system.

My aim in Chapters 4, 5, and 6 was to determine the various forms of poetic change as methods of resistance against sociopolitical and cultural domination in the works of the literary groups and individuals who undertook the process of reconstructing literary traditions during the first half of the twentieth century. The first of these groups were the modernists, whose followers can be divided into two subgroups: modern poets, who supported a gradual trend of literary modernization, and high-modernists, known as *Nimāic* poets, who favoured radical amendments to classical poetics. The second major group were the experimental artists who, while not directly challenging the literary mainstream, embarked on diverse approaches to experiment with the foundations of Persian poetry. Their aim was to attain a new understanding of poetic form and propose novel styles. The third group were the avant-garde poets who called for the destruction of all dominant, institutionalized literary traditions and the introduction of radical changes in poetic structures and aesthetics to achieve new forms of creativity.

In the fourth chapter, I therefore set out to determine a new classification for Persian pioneer poets in the 1930s and 1940s, including modernists, high modernists, avant-gardes, and experimentalists. I started by redefining all the pioneer movements of modern Persian poetry, assessing the role each played in the process of poetic change. I then focused on the self-revisionary, reformist movement of Nimā Yushij, which enabled him to transcend his own neo-romantic phase and develop his later social symbolism. I drew particular attention to Nimā's *Khāneh-ye Sarivoyli* and established that the poetic change which occurred in this poem resulted in a division between the gradualist modernists and the high-modernists of Persian poetry. Nimā's shift from explicit political subject matter to his aesthetic movement towards more democratic forms of poetry led the discussion to some of the deconstructive and emancipatory works of his contemporary experimentalists.

Chapter 5 demonstrated how Persian experimentalism shattered the established regime of aesthetics and deconstructed the prevailing literary tradition as a means of political engagement. Focusing on Mohammad Moqaddam's, Zabih Behruz's, and Shin Partow's experimentation with traditional poetic forms, I studied specific aspects of their works through analysing the dialogue between Persian experimental poetry and the fictional and non-fictional prose of the time. I also examined the conscious misreading of traditional rhetoric as a corrective approach adopted to reconfigure it and the introduction of free verse as an alternative rhythmic system by experimentalists. My analysis lent further support to the idea that Persian experimentalism facilitated the process of development for high-modernist and, particularly, avant-garde poets.

The sixth chapter began with a brief account of Tondar Kiā's life and oeuvre, before employing Renato Poggioli's idea of avant-garde 'moments', termed as activism, antagonism, nihilism, and agonism, to analyse the avant-garde features of Kiā's creative and theoretical works. I then used Benjamin's concept of the 'ragpicker' to examine Kiā's approach to creation, illustrating that by producing miscellanies from the refuse of art history, Kiā recycled cultural waste such as street songs in order to resist the hierarchical, archival regime of cultural values. Kiā's destructive approach was also associated with the non-organic nature of both poetic forms and the arrangement of parts in his books. The study also examined the similarities and differences between Kiā's visual, phonetic, and performance poems and the parallel practices of historical avant-gardes, subjecting them to careful scrutiny.

In the latter part of Chapter 6, I explored the avant-garde moments in the manifesto of the *Khorus Jangi* association, *Sallākh-e Bolbol* (The Slaughterer of the Nightingale), and analysed some of Hushang Irāni's most controversial poems. This analysis demonstrated that Irāni's controversial poetry resisted the institutionalized art supported by the dominant culture and political groups of the time through its non-organic forms and techniques associated with automatic writing, as well as through experimentation with unintelligible sounds and pattern poetry.

My research contributes to existing scholarship on Persian literary history by challenging the canonical narratives of modern Persian poetry. Selected radical pioneer poets, who can be loosely referred to as alternative poets or avant-gardes, have been given a platform to be heard, and the role they played in the process of literary modernization in Iran acknowledged and appreciated. It is noteworthy that the analysis of the life and works of certain alternative poets in this book marks the first instance of their inclusion in academic research. Despite the dominant approach that marginalizes the radical frontier of literary modernization, this study, rejecting the centre/margin model of literary historiography, suggests that the unconventional formal experiments of these poets were as significant to the fundamentals of Persian poetry as the enduring changes of gradualist modernists and high modernists. Had it not been for the radicals pushing the genre's boundaries, none of the moderate changes would have been welcomed by the readers of Persian. Moreover, the analysis conducted in this work, which explores the relationship between aesthetic innovation and the politics of literature, seeks to broaden our comprehension of political literature in modern Iran. Finally, this work utilizes theoretical sources that have not previously been employed in the study of modern Persian poetry, thus expanding the scope of critiques on Persian poetry and enhancing our understanding of experimental and avant-garde poetic practices.

In terms of limitations facing this research, my highest hurdle lay in the fact that there have been very few academic studies on the marginalized poets of modern Persian poetry. Most of the current literature focuses on the publicly accepted practices of the main trends of modernization in Persian poetry. Even in the cases of constitutional and *Nimāic* poetry, two of the most frequently studied subjects in this field, scholars have been inclined to develop their ideas by examining the famous, mainstream works of the renowned poets. Moreover, much of the existing literature on nineteenth- and twentieth-century Persian poetry primarily focuses on the political subject matter and historical significance, resulting in limited analysis of the aesthetic aspects of Persian poetry during this era.

Prospects for further research

My work lays the ground for further research into the alternative, avant-garde movements of the 1960s–1970s, such as *Mowj-e Now* (New Wave), *She'r-e Digar* (Other Poetry), and those which emerged between the 1979 Iranian Revolution and the end of the 2000s, namely *Mowj-e Nāb* (Pure Wave) and *She'r-e Zabān* (Language Poetry).

Shams Langrudi divides the poetry of the second half of the 1960s into two major groups: guerrilla poetry and *Mowj-e Now*.[1] Although the publication of *Tarh* (Sketch, 1962) by Ahmad-Rezā Ahmadi has been considered as the starting point for *Mowj-e Now*, the notion of *Mowj-e Now* as an avant-garde and un-*Nimāic* poetic movement was developed by two literary journals: *Jong-e Torfeh* (Novel Collection, 1964) and *Jozveh-ye She'r* (Poetry Booklet, 1966–7).

Esmā'il Nuri 'Alā states that *Mowj-e Now* was advanced during the 1960s and 1970s in the works of two different branches: *She'r-e Digar* and *She'r-e Hajm* (Espacementalisme).[2] The former group was inclined towards the experimental and avant-garde poets of the previous generation, particularly Tondar Kiā and Hushang Irāni. Poets of *She'r-e Digar* published a journal under the same name during 1968. In this journal's first issue, the editors unconventionally published two poems by Kiā and Irāni alongside a poem by Nimā in a separate section. In doing so, they demonstrated their recognition of Kiā and Irāni as the co-founders of modern Persian poetry. In

---

[1] Mohammad Shams Langrudi, *Tārikh-e Tahlili-e She'r-e Now*, 4 vols (Tehran: Markaz, 1998), 3, p. 2.
[2] Esmā'il Nuri 'Ala, *Sovar va Asbāb dar She'r-e Emruz-e Irān* (Tehran: Bamdad, 1969), p. 319.

terms of aesthetics, too, the poems of the leading poets of this group, such as Bizhan Elāhi (1945–2010), Bahrām Ardebili (1942–2005), and Parviz Eslāmpur (1944–2012), stem from the alternative movements of modern Persian poetry rather than the mainstream *Nimāic* style.

The central ideas of *She'r-e Digar* as the main branch of Persian avant-garde poetry persisted in *Mowj-e Nāb* poetry from a few years before the Iranian revolution of 1979 until the end of the Iran–Iraq War in 1988. Due to the upheavals of the time – from the Revolution to the War and the violent suppression of political activists by the state during the 1980s – many readers did not welcome the less-politically charged *Mowj-e Nāb* poetry. However, in contrast with their poetic fathers, the leading poets of this movement, such as Manuchihr Ātashi (1931–2005), Sayyed Ali Sālehi (1955–), Hormoz Alipur (1946–), and Hushang Chālangi (1940–2021), were held in high regard by the literary community of that era.

Later in the 1990s, avant-garde movements found the chance to express their ideas more openly and revolt against modern poetry monuments. These movements were mainly influenced by Rezā Barāhani's (1935–2022) poetic practices, and theoretical works centred on the idea of Persian language poetry. These ideas were first presented in Barāhani's well-received book *Khatāb be Parvāneh-hā va Cherā man Digar Shā'er-e Nimā'i Nistam* (Addressing Butterflies and Why Am I No Longer a Nimāic Poet, 1995). Subsequently, critics of *She'r-e Zabān* argued that Barāhani and his followers' deliberate avoidance of being associated with the label of Nimāic poets indicated that they should be categorized as 'Kiāic poets', aligning themselves with the style and approach advocated by Tondar Kiā.[3]

The subjects related to the post-1960s experimental and avant-garde poetic movements, especially those pertaining to early post-revolutionary poetic trends, have received relatively less scholarly attention. This neglect can be attributed to a combination of limited documented information on the poetic practices of marginalized artists and the predominance of mainstream narratives in primary research conducted in this field. Consequently, a natural progression of this work would involve analysing post-1960s pioneer poetry as a continuation of the historical trajectory established by the present study.

---

[3] Yadollāh Royā'i, *Ebārat az Chist?* (Tehran: Āhang-e Digar, 2007), pp. 49–51.

BIBLIOGRAPHY

Abbāsi, Mohammad, ed., *Divān-e Ash'ār-e Abolqāsem Lāhuti* (Tabriz: Helal-e Nāseri, 1941).
Ābedi, Kamyār, *Be Raghm-e Panjereh-hā-ye Basteh: She'r-e Mo'āser-e Zanān* (Tehran: Nāder, 2001).
Abrams, M. H., and Geoffrey G. Harpham, *A Glossary of Literary Terms* (Boston & Mass: Thomson Wadsworth, 1999).
Ahmad, Āmer Tāher, 'Peydāyesh-e Chāhārpāreh va Jāygāh-e Ān dar Tajaddod-e She'r-e Fārsi', *Adabiyāt-e Tatbiqi*, 2 (2010), 7–31.
Ājudāni, Lotfollāh, *Rowshanfekrān-e Irān dar Asr-e Mashruteh* (Tehran: Akhtaran, 2008).
Ājudāni, Mashāllāh, *Yā Marg yā Tajaddod; Daftari dar She'r va Adab-e Mashruteh* (London: Fasl-e Ketab, 2002).
Akhavān Sāles, Mehdi, *Bed'at-hā va Badāye'-e Nimā* (Tehran: Zemestān, 1997).
Alā'i, Mashi'at, 'Hushang Irāni va Sureālism-e Irāni', *Goharān*, 7–8 (2005), 94–9.
Alavi, Bozorg, *Tārikh-e Tahavvol-e Adabiyāt-e Jadid-e Irān* (Tehran: Negāh, 2007).
Āl-e Dāvud, Sayyed Ali, ed., *Majmu'eh-ye Āsār-e Yaghmā-ye Jandaqi*, 2 vols (Tehran: Tus, 1988).
Ali Akbari, Nasrin, and Ali Nazar Nazari, 'Barresi-e Janbe-hā-ye Nowgarā'i dar Vazn-e She'r-e Abolghāsem Lāhuti va Mansha'-e Ān', *Fonun-e Adabi*, 4 (2016), 143–56.
Anāri, Shāhram, ed., *Majmu'eh-ye Ash'ār va Andisheh-ye Hushang Irāni: Az Banafsh-e Tond tā be to Miandisham* (Tehran: Nakhostin, 2000).
Anushiravani, Ali-Rezā, and Kavoos Hasanli, 'Trends in Contemporary Persian Poetry', in *Media, Culture and Society in Iran: Living with Globalization and the Islamic State*, ed. by Mehdi Semati (London: Bürger Routledge Taylor & Francis Group, 2010).
Aqā Hoseyni, Hoseyn, 'Fereshteh-ye She'r', *Nashriyeh-ye Dāneshkadeh Adabiyāt va Olum Ensani Tabriz*, 185 (2002), 73–93.
Āriānpur, Yahyā, *Az Sabā tā Nimā*, 2 vols (Tehran: Franklin, 1976).
Ashbery, John, 'The Invisible Avant-Garde', in *Poetry in Theory: An Anthology 1900–2000*, ed. by Jon Cook (Oxford: Blackwell, 2004).
Āshurpur, Sādeq, *Namāyesh-hā-ye Irāni*, 7 vols (Tehran: Sureh Mehr, 2010).
Ātashi, Manuchehr, 'Sohāngar-e Sonnat-hā va Mote'āref-hā', in *Az Banafsh-e Tond tā be to Miandisham*, ed. by Shāhram Anāri (Tehran: Nakhostin, 2000).
Ātashi, Manuchehr, *Nimā rā Bāz ham Bekhānim; Khiyāl-e Ruz-hā-ye Rowshan* (Tehran: Āmitis, 2002).
Attridge, Derek, *Poetic Rhythm: An Introduction* (Cambridge: Cambridge University Press, 1995).

Ayubi, Vahid, *Zabih Behruz: Zendegi va Gozideh-ye Āsār* (Tehran: Nik, 2007).
Āzhand, Ya'qub, *Tajaddod-e adabi dar dowreh-ye mashruteh* (Tehran: Mo'asseseh-ye Tahqiqāt va Towse'eh-ye 'Olum-e Ensāni, 2006).
Bahār, Mohammad Taqi, *Divān-e Malek al-Sho'arā Bahār* (Tehran: Negāh, 2008).
Bakhshi, Hoseyn, 'Barresi-e Se Now'-e Jadid-e Qāfiyeh dar She'r-e Mashruteh', *Adabiyāt Pārsi Mo'āser*, 3 (2014), 1–14.
Baldick, Chris, *The Concise Oxford Dictionary of Literary Terms* (Oxford – New York: Clarendon Press – Oxford University Press, 1990).
Balim, Çiğdem, 'Therwet-i Fünūn', in *Encyclopaedia of Islam* http://dx.doi.org/10.1163/1573-3912_islam_SIM_7529 [accessed 18 June 2020].
Bāmdād, Mehdi, *Sharh-e Hāl-e Rejāl-e Irān dar Qarn-e 12 va 13 va 14 Hejri*, 6 vols (Tehran: Zavār, 1969).
Barāhani, Rezā, *Kimiyā va Khāk; Moqadameh-i bar Falsafeh-ye Adabiyāt* (Tehran: Morgh-e Āmin, 1985).
Barāhani, Rezā, *Khatāb be Parvāneh-hā va Cherā man Digar Shā'er-e Nimā'i Nistam* (Tehran: Markaz, 1995).
Bashiri, Ahmad, ed., *Divān-e Lāhuti* (Tehran: Amir Kabir, 1979).
Bayāt, Kāveh, *Kudetā-ye Lāhuti* (Tehran: Shirazeh, 1997).
Becka, Jiri, 'Two Iranians in Modern Tajik Poetry', *Oriente Moderno*, 1 (2003), 29–35.
Behpoor, Bavand, 'Introduction to "The Nightingale's Butcher Manifesto" and "Volume and Environment ii"', *ARTMargins*, 3 (2014), 118–28.
Behruz, Zabih, *Shāh-e Irān va Bānu-ye Arman* (Tehran: Farus, 1928).
Behruz, Zabih, *Dar Rāh-e Mehr* (Tehran: Irānkudeh, 1944).
Behruz, Zabih, *Shab-e Ferdowsi* (Tehran: Sazmān-e Namāyesh-e Irān, 1967).
Benjamin, Walter, *The Arcades Project*, trans. by Howard Eiland (Cambridge, MA: Harvard University Press, 2002).
Beyzā'i, Bahrām, *Namāyesh dar Irān* (Tehran: Rowshangarān va Motāle'āt-e Zanān, 2001).
Bloom, Harold, *The Anxiety of Influence: A Theory of Poetry* (New York: Oxford University Press, 1997).
Browne, Edward G., *The Press and Poetry of Modern Persia* (Cambridge: Cambridge University Press, 1914).
Browne, Edward G., *A Literary History of Persia*, 5 vols (Cambridge: The University Press, 1959).
Bürger, Peter, *Theory of the Avant-Garde* (Minneapolis: University of Minnesota Press, 1984).
Carleton, Greg, 'Genre in Socialist Realism', *Slavic Review*, 4 (1994), 992–1009.
Caton, Margaret, 'Tasnif', in *Encyclopaedia Iranica* http://www.Iranicaonline.org/articles/tasnif-music-term [accessed 9 March 2016].
Chelkowski, Peter J., *Ta'zieh: Ritual and Drama in Iran* (New York: New York University Press & Soroush Press, 1979).
Clark, Katerina, 'Socialist Realism in Soviet Literature', in *From Symbolism to Socialist Realism: A Reader* (Boston: Academic Studies Press, 2012).
Cook, Jon, *Poetry in Theory: An Anthology 1900–2000* (Oxford: Blackwell, 2004).
Cronin, Stephanie, *Soldiers, Shahs and Subalterns in Iran: Opposition, Protest and Revolt, 1921–1941* (New York: Palgrave Macmillan, 2010).

Dabashi, Hamid, 'The Poetics of Politics: Commitment in Modern Persian Literature', *Iranian Studies*, 2/4 (1985), 147–88.

Dabirsiyāqi, Mohammad, 'Bahr-e Tawil', in *Encyclopaedia Iranica* https://Iranicaonline.org/articles/bahr-e-tawil-type-of-persian-verse [accessed 11 May 2019].

Dāryush, Parviz, 'Dar Resā-ye Veylāni', in *Khorus Jangi-e Bi-Mānand*, ed. by Sirus Tāhbāz (Tehran: Farzān-e Ruz, 2001).

Dastgheyb, Abdol'ali, *Sāyeh Rowshan-e She'r-e Now-e Pārsi* (Tehran: Farhang, 1969).

E'tezād Al-saltaneh, Ali-Qoli Mirzā, ed., *Kolliyāt-e Yaghmā-ye Jandaqi* (Tehran: [n. pub.], 1921).

Eagleton, Terry, *The Ideology of the Aesthetic* (Oxford: Blackwell, 1990).

Eghtesadinia, Sayeh, 'Irāni, Hushang', in *Encyclopaedia Iranica* http://www.Iranicaonline.org/articles/Irani-hushang [accessed 18 March 2018].

Eliot, T. S., 'Tradition and the Individual Talent', *Perspecta*, 19 (1982), 36–42.

Fātemi, Sāsān, *Peydāyesh-e Musiqi-e Mardom Pasand dar Irān* (Tehran: Māhur, 2013).

Floor, Willem M., *The History of Theatre in Iran* (Maryland: Mage Publishers, 2005).

Fomeshi, Behnam M., *The Persian Whitman: Beyond a Literary Reception* (Leiden: Leiden University Press, 2019).

Forutan, Ayda, 'Why the Fighting Cock? The Significance of the Imagery of the Khorus Jangi and Its Manifesto "The Slaughterer of the Nightingale"', *Iran Namag*, 1 (2016), 28–49.

Gary, Martin, *A Dictionary of Literary Terms* (Essex: York Press, 1999).

Ghanoonparvar, Mohammad-Reza, *Prophets of Doom: Literature as a Sociopolitical Phenomenon in Modern Iran* (Maryland: University Press of America, 1984).

Gheissari, Ali, *Iranian Intellectuals in the Twentieth Century* (Austin: University of Texas Press, 1998).

Granger, David, 'Expression, Imagination, and Organic Unity: John Dewey's Aesthetics and Romanticism', *The Journal of Aesthetic Education*, 2 (2003), 46–60.

Hā'eri, Hādi, *Āref-e Qazvini Shā'er-e Melli-e Irān* (Tehran: Javidān, 1985).

Hallward, Peter, 'Staging Equality', *New Left Review*, 37 (2006), 109–29.

Hamidi Shirāzi, Mehdi, *Sher dar Asr-e Qājār* (Tehran: Ganj-e Ketāb, 1985).

Hamidiyān, Sa'id, *Dastān-e Degardisi; Ravand-e Degarguni-ha-ye She'r-e Nimā Yushij* (Tehran: Nilufar, 2004).

Harding, James M., 'From Cutting Edge to Rough Edges: On the Transnational Foundations of Avant-Garde Performance', in *Not the Other Avant-Garde: The Transnational Foundations of Avant-Garde Performance*, ed. by James M. Harding and John Rouse (Ann Arbor, Michigan: University of Michigan Press, 2006), pp. 18–40.

Hedāyat, Jahāngir, *Farhang-e Āmiyāneh-ye Mardom-e Irān* (Tehran: Cheshmeh, 1999).

Hedāyat, Rezā-Qoli Khān, *Majma' al-Fosahā*, ed. by Mazāher Mosaffā, 6 vols (Tehran: Amir Kabir, 2006).

Homā'i, Jalāl al-Din, *Fonun-e Belāghat va Senā'āt-e Adabi* (Tehran: Tus, 1985).

Homā'i, Jalāl al-Din, *Maqālāt-e Adabi* (Tehran: Homā, 1990).
Homā'i, Jalāl al-Din, *Havāshi bar Majma' al-Fosahā* (Tehran: Homā Publication, 2006).
Hopkins, David, *Dada and Surrealism* (New York: Oxford University Press, 2004).
Ja'fari, Mas'ud, *Seyr-e Romāntism dar Irān; as Mashruteh ta Nimā* (Tehran: Markaz, 2007).
Jamālzādeh, Mohammad-Ali, *Yeki Bud Yeki Nabud* (Tehran: Parvin, 1941).
Jāmi, Mehdi, and Esmā'il Kho'i, 'Esmā'il Kho'i az She'r Miguyad', *Radio Zamaneh*, http://zamaaneh.com/idea/2008/07/post_350.html [accessed 17 February 2020].
Jandaqi, Yaghmā, 'Sayyed Abud', *Yaghmā*, 2 (1954), 76–7.
Jannati Atā'i, Abolqāsem, *Nimā; Zendegi va Āsār-e Ou* (Tehran: Safi-Ali Shāh, 1955).
Jorkesh, Shāpur, *Butiqā-ye She'r-e Now* (Tehran: Qoqnus, 2004).
Karami, Ahmad, ed., *Divān-e Ash'ār Mirzā Fathollāh Khān Sheybāni* (Tehran: Mā Publication, 1992).
Karimi-Hakkak, Ahmad, 'Nimā Yushij; A life', in *Essays on Nimā Yushij; Animating Modernism in Persian Poetry*, ed. by Ahmad Karimi-Hakkak and Kamran Talattof (Leiden & Boston: Brill, 2004).
Karimi-Hakkak, Ahmad, 'Eshqi, Mirzadah', in *Encyclopaedia Iranica* http://www.Iranicaonline.org/articles/esqi-mohammad-Rezā-Mirzāda# [accessed 19 January 2012].
Karimi-Hakkak, Ahmad, *Recasting Persian Poetry: Scenarios of Poetic Modernity in Iran* (London: Oneworld, 2012).
Karimi-Hakkak, Ahmad, 'Free verse', in *Encyclopaedia Iranica* https://Iranicaonline.org/articles/freeverse- [accessed 5 February 2019].
Karimi-Hakkak, Ahmad, and Kamran Talattof, ed., *Essays on Nimā Yushij; Animating Modernism in Persian Poetry* (Leiden & Boston: Brill, 2004).
Khakpour, Arta, 'A Divorce of Avant-Gardes: Surrealism and Socialism in Post-Rezā Shāh Iran', *Middle Eastern Literatures*, 2 (2016), 119–34.
Khānlari, Parviz Nātel, 'Dar Vazn-e She'r-e Fārsi', in *Dowreh-ye Majaleh Sokhan* (Tehran: Sokhan, 1954).
Khānlari, Parviz Nātel, *Haftād Sokhan*, 4 vols (Tehran: Tus, 1998).
Khān Malek Sāsāni, Ahmad, 'Mirzā Abolhasan Yaghmā-ye Jandaqi', *Yaghmā*, 213 (1966), 24–27.
Khoshnām, Mahmud, *Az Najvā-ye Sonnat ta Ghoghā-ye Pāp* (Tehran: Farhang-e Javid, 2018).
Kiā, Tondar, 'Che Avāmeli dar Tahavvol Suri-e She'r-e Fārsi Ta'sir Dāshteh ast?', *Andishe va Honar*, Special issue (1961).
Kiā, Tondar, 'Che Avāmeli dar Tahavvol Mohtavā-ye She'r-e Fārsi Ta'sir Dāshteh ast?', *Andishe va Honar*, Special issue (1962).
Kiā, Tondar, Tehran, The Parliamentary Library of Iran, *Nahib-e Jonbesh-e Adabi-e Shāhin*, MS 9548.
Kiā, Tondar, *Nahib-e Jonbesh-e Adabi-e Shāhin* (Tehran: [n. pub.], 1940).
Kiā, Tondar, *Nahib-e Jonbesh-e Adabi-e Shāhin* (Tehran: [n. pub.], 1943).
Kiā, Tondar, *Nahib-e Jonbesh-e Adabi-e Shāhin* (Tehran: [n. pub.], 1975).
Kiā, Tondar, *Nahib-e Jonbesh-e Adabi-e Shāhin* (Tehran: [n. pub.], 1976).

Kiāni Haftlang, Kiānush, 'Nimā va Mardreseh-ye Sant Lu'is', in *Asnādi Darbareh-ye Nimā Yushij*, ed. by Ali Mir Ansāri (Tehran: Sazmān-e Asnād-e Melli-e Irān, 1995).
Kianush, Mahmud, *Modern Persian Poetry* (London: Rockingham Press, 2004).
Lāhuti, Abolqāsem, *Hezār Mesra'* (Moscow: Nashriyāt-e Kargarān Khāreji dar Ettehād-e Showravi, 1935).
Langrudi, Mohammad Shams, *Az Nimā tā Ba'd*, 2 vols (Tehran: Markaz, 1991).
Langrudi, Mohammad Shams, *Maktab-e Bāzgasht* (Tehran: Markaz, 1993).
Langrudi, Mohammad Shams, *Tārikh-e Tahlili-e She'r-e Now*, 4 vols (Tehran: Markaz, 1998).
Le Roy, Frederik, 'Ragpickers and Leftover Performances', *Performance Research*, 8 (2017), 127–33.
Loraine, M. B., and Jalal Matini, 'Bahar, Mohammad-Taqi', in *Encyclopaedia Iranica* http://www.Iranicaonline.org/articles/Bahār-mohammad-taqi [accessed 17 August 2016].
Malekpur, Jamshid, *Adabiyāt-e Namāyeshi dar Irān* (Tehran: Tus, 2006).
Mann, Paul, *The Theory-Death of the Avant-Garde* (Bloomington: Indiana University Press, 1991).
Maqsudi, Nur al-Din, 'Dobeyti-hā-ye Peyvasteh', *Jostarhā-ye Adabi*, 48 (1978), 684–715.
Meier, Prita, 'Authenticity and Its Modernist Discontents: The Colonial Encounter and African and Middle Eastern Art History', *Arab Studies Journal*, 1 (2010), 12–45.
Meisami, Julie S., and Ali-Reza Korangy Esfahani, 'Masnavi', in *The Princeton Encyclopaedia of Poetry and Poetics*, ed. by Roland Green, Stephen Cushman, and Clare Cavanagh (Princeton: Princeton University Press, 2012) https://search-credoreference-com/content/entry/prpoetry/masnavi/0?institutionId=2454 [accessed 20 January 2020].
Meskub, Shāhrokh, *Dāstān-e Adabiyāt va Sargozasht-e Ejtemā'* (Tehran: Farzān-e Ruz, 2007).
Mir Khānd, Mohammad ebn KhāvandShāh, *Rowzat al-Safā-ye Nāseri*, ed. by Jamshid Kiānfar, 15 vols (Tehran: Asatir, 2001).
Mir-Ābedini, Hasan, *Sad Sāl Dāstānneveisi-e Irān* (Tehran: Cheshmeh, 2001).
Mitchell, Roger, 'A Prosody for Whitman', *PMLA*, 6 (1969), 1606–12.
Mitter, Partha, 'Decentering Modernism: Art History and Avant-Garde Art from the Periphery', *The Art Bulletin*, 4 (2008), 531–48.
Mohammadi, Hasan-Ali, *Az Bahār tā Shahriyār* (Arak: [n. pub.], 1993).
Mohammad-Rezā Lāhuti, ed., *Majmu'eh-ye Āsār-e Nimā Yushij* (Tehran: Nashr-e Nāsher, 1985).
Mohammad-Rezā Lāhuti, ed., *Khorus Jangi-e Bi-Mānand* (Tehran: Farzān-e Ruz, 2001).
Mokhtāri, Mohammad, *Cheshm-e Morakkab* (Tehran: Tus, 2009).
Moqaddam, Mohammad, *Rāz-e Nimshab; Rāhi Chand Birun az Pardeh* (Tehran: [n. pub.], 1934).
Moqaddam, Mohammad, *Bāng-e Khorus* (Tehran: [n. pub.], 1935).
Moqaddam, Mohammad, *Bāzgasht be Alamut* (Tehran: [n. pub.], 1935).
Moshir Salimi, Ali Akbar, ed., *Kolliyāt-e Mosavvar-e Eshqi* (Tehran: Amir Kabir, 1971).

Naficy, Majid, *Modernism and Ideology in Persian Literature; a Return to Nature in the Poetry of Nimā Yushij* (Maryland: University Press of America, 1997).
Najmābādi, Seyf al-Din, 'Ostād Doktor Mohammad Moqaddam', *Journal of the School of Humanities and Literature, University of Tehran; Special Issue: Jashn-Nāmeh-ye Doktor Mohammad Moqaddam*, 4 (1977), 1–11.
Niku-Hemmat, Ahmad, 'Sheybāni', in *Divān-e Ash'ār-e Mirzā Fathollāh Khān Sheybāni*, ed. by Ahmad Karami (Tehran: Mā, 1992).
Niku-Hemmat, Ahmad, *Zendegāni va Āsār-e Bahār* (Tehran: Abad, 1982).
Nuri 'Alā, Esmā'il, *Sovar va Asbāb dar She'r-e Emruz-e Irān* (Tehran: Bāmdād, 1969).
Nuri 'Alā, Esmā'il, *Teori-e She'r; az Mowj-e Now ta She'r-e Eshq* (London: Ghazal, 1994).
'Pattern Poetry', in *Encyclopedia Britannica* https://www.britannica.com/art/pattern-poetry [accessed 26 February 2020].
Pārsinezhād, Iraj, *Khānlari va Naqd-e Adabi* (Tehran: Sokhan, 2008).
Parvin, Nasereddin, 'Tajaddod', in *Encyclopaedia Iranica* http://www.Iranicaonline.org/articles/tajaddod [accessed 31 March 2018].
Poggioli, Renato, *The Theory of the Avant-Garde* (Cambridge, MA: Belknap Press of Harvard University Press, 1968).
Qā'ed, Mohammad, *Eshqi; Simā-ye Najib-e Yek Ānārshist* (Tehran: Māhi, 2015).
Ra'isniyā, Rahim, 'Shams Kasmā'i', *Chistā*, 246–7 (2008), 450–8.
Rancière, Jacques, *Politics of Literature*, trans. by Julie Rose (Cambridge: Polity Press, 2011).
Rashid Yāsemi, Gholām-Rezā, *Maqāleh-hā va Resāleh-hā*, ed. by Iraj Afshār (Tehran: Barresi va Gozinesh-e Ketāb, 1994).
Rastgār Fasā'i, Mansur, *Parviz Nātel Khānlari* (Tehran: Tarh-e Now, 1999).
Rockhill, Gabriel, and Philip Watts, 'Jacques Rancière: Thinker of Dissensus', in *History, Politics, Aesthetics: Jacques Rancière* (London: Duke University Press, 2009).
Royā'i, Yadollāh, *Ebārat az Chist?* (Tehran: Āhang-e Digar, 2007).
Rypka, Jan, *The History of Iranian Literature* (Dordrecht: D. Reydel, 1968).
Sadriniyā, Bāqer, 'Peydāyesh va Tahavvol-e Chārpāreh Sorā'i dar Irān', *Fonun-e Adabi*. 12 (2015), 23–32.
Sami'i, Enāyat, 'Khiyāl Pardāz-e Ofoq-hā-ye Bāz', *Goharān*, 7–8 (2005), 91–3.
Schechner, Richard, *The Future of Ritual: Writings on Culture and Performance* (Abingdon Oxfordshire: Routledge, 1993).
Scott, James C., *Domination and the Arts of Resistance* (New Haven: Yale University Press, 1990).
Sepānlu, Mohammad-Ali, *Chahār Shā'er Āzādi* (Stockholm: Baran, 1993).
Sepānlu, Mohammad-Ali, *Bahār Mohammad Taqi Malek al-Sho'arā* (Tehran: Tarh-e Now, 2003).
Sepehrān, Kamrān, *Te'ātrokerāsi dar 'asr-e Mashruteh, 1285–1304* (Tehran: Nilufar, 2008).
Shafi'i Kadkani, Mohammad-Rezā, ed., *Gozideh Ghazaliyāt-e Shams* (Tehran: Sherkat-e Sahāmi-e Ketāb-hā-ye Jibi, 1981).
Shafi'i Kadkani, Mohammad-Rezā, *Advār-e She'r-e Fārsi* (Tehran: Tus, 2000).
Shafi'i Kadkani, Mohammad-Rezā, *Musiqi-e She'r* (Tehran: Āgāh, 2010).

Shafi'i Kadkani, Mohammad-Rezā, *Bā Cherāgh va Āyeneh: dar Jostoju-ye Risheh-ye Tahavvolāt-e She'r-e Mo'āser-e Fārsi* (Tehran: Sokhan, 2011).
Shafi'i Kadkani, Mohammad-Rezā, 'Adib-e Neyshāburi dar Hāshiyeh-ye She'r-e Mashrutiyat', in *The Great Islamic Encyclopaedia* http://cgie.org.ir/fa/news/130399 [accessed 2 August 2016].
Shamisā, Sirus, *Aruz va Qāfiyeh* (Tehran: Payām-e Nur University, 2004).
Shamisā, Sirus, ed., *Al-Mo'jam fi Ma'āyir Ash'ār al-A'jam* (Tehran: Ferdows, 1994).
Shāteri, Ali-Rezā, *Āsār-e Fathollāh Khān-e Sheybāni* (Tehran: Mirās-e Maktub, 2014).
Sheppard, Richard, *Modernism – Dada – Postmodernism* (Illinois: Northwestern University Press, 2000).
Shirāzpur Partow, Ali, *Dokhtar-e Daryā* (Tehran: [n. pub.], 1946).
Shirāzpur Partow, Ali, *Samandar* (Tehran: [n. pub.], 1946).
Shirāzpur Partow, Ali, *Zhinus* (Tehran: [n. pub.], 1946).
Shirāzpur Partow, Ali, *Do Nāmeh* (Tehran: Chāp-e Zarrin, 1950).
Shirāzpur Partow, Ali, Bozorg Alavi, and Sādeq Hedāyat, *Anirān* (Tehran: [n. pub.], 1930).
Sonboldel, Farshād, *Tondar Kiā; Gozaresh-e Nahib-e Jonbesh-e Adabi-e Shāhin* (Tehran: Gusheh, 2015).
Soroudi, Sorour, 'Poet and Revolution: The Impact of Iran's Constitutional Revolution on the Social and Literary Outlook of the Poets of the Time: Part I', *Iranian Studies*, 1/2 (1979), 3–41.
Sprachman, Paul, 'Behruz, Dabih', in *Encyclopaedia Iranica* https://Iranicaonline.org/articles/behruz-dabih-1889-1971-persian-satirist-son-of-the-physician-and-calligrapher-abul-fazl-savaji [accessed 28 March 2019].
Tāhbāz, Sirus, ed., *Daftar-e Yāddāsht-hā-ye Ruzāneh-ye Nimā Yushij* (Tehran: Bozorgmehr, 1990).
Tāhbāz, Sirus, 'Kamāndār-e Bozorg-e Kuhestān', in *Yādmān-e Nimā Yushij*, ed. by Mohammad-Rezā Lāhuti (Tehran: Gostaresh Honar, 1989).
Tartakovsky, Roi, 'Free, Verse, Rhythm: An introduction', *Style*, 1 (2015), 1–7.
Tasnif-e Jadid (Doktor) va Majmu'eh-ye Tasanif (Tehran: Matba'eh Eqbal, 1952) https://golistan.org/pamphlet-1-new-songs-dokhtar-others/ [accessed 20 August 2020].
Tavallali, Fereydun, *Nāfeh* (Shiraz: [n. pub.], 1962).
Torābi, Zia' al-Din, 'Az Dobeyti-hā-ye Peyvasteh ta Chahārpāreh', *Keyhān Farhangi*, 202 (2003) http://ensani.ir/fa/article/240242 [accessed 11 November 2019].
'Unio Mystica', in *Oxford Reference* https://www.oxfordreference.com/view/10.1093/oi/authority.20110803110707752 [accessed 19 February 2020].
Vahabzadeh, Peyman, 'The Space between Voices', in *Essays on Nimā Yushij: Animating Modernism in Persian Poetry*, ed. by Ahmad Karimi-Hakkak, and Kamran Talattof (Leiden: Brill, 2004), pp. 193–219.
Vahid Dastgerdi, Hasan, *Enqelāb-e Adabi* (Tehran: Vahidniyā, 1956).
Yaghmā'i, Habib, 'Sharh-e Hāl-e Yaghmā va Jughrāfiyā-ye Jandaq', *Armaghān*, 7–8 (1918), 404–18.
Yaghmā'i, Sayyed Badr al-Din, ed., *Divān-e Ash'ār-e Qā'em Maqām Farāhāni* (Tehran: Sharq, 1988).

Yushij, Nimā, 'Arzesh-e Ehsāsāt dar Zendgi-e Honarpishegān', in *Darbāreh-ye She'r va Shā'eri*, ed. by Sirus Tāhbāz (Tehran: Negāh, 2006).
Yushij, Nimā, 'Harf-hā-ye Hamsāyeh', in *Darbāreh-ye She'r va Shā'eri*, ed. by Sirus Tāhbāz (Tehran: Negāh, 2006).
Zarrinkub, Abdolhoseyn, *Naqd-e Adabi*, 2 vols (Tehran: Amir Kabir, 1983).

INDEX

Abrams, Meyer Howard 96 n. 84, 124
Adib Neyshāburi, Abdoljavād 27, 30
aesthetic regime 5, 7, 34, 54, 57, 65, 68, 71, 73–4, 91, 103, 106, 109, 118, 122, 131, 144, 152, 160–1
aesthetic revolution 2, 11, 29, 33, 62, 74, 84, 107
Ahl-e Haq (Yarsanism) 85 n.65
Ahmadi, Ahmad-Rezā 189, 205
  Tarh (Sketch, 1962) 205
Akhavān Sāles, Mehdi 84, 124, 152, 161
Akhundzādeh, Fath-Ali 64
Alavi, Bozorg 130, 131 n. 8, 153
Alipur, Hormoz 206
Al-Jamāl (journal) 20 n. 2
Andisheh va Honar (journal) 163–4, 173–4
Anjoman-e Adabi-e Irān (Iran Literary Association) 68
Anjoman-e Dāneshkadeh (the *Dāneshkadeh* Literary Association) 9, 30, 66, 68, 70–2, 98, 103–4, 123, 202
Anjoman-e Honari-e Khorus Jangi (the Khorus Jangi Society for the Arts) 184–5
  Khorus Jangi (journal) 11, 162, 185–9, 197
  Sallakh–e Bolbol (The Slaughterer of the Nightingale) 186–8, 204
Ansāri, Khājeh Abdollāh 148
Apādānā (journal) 186 n. 69
Apollinaire, Guillaume 14, 178
Aragon, Louis 154
Ardebili, Bahrām 206

Āref Qazvini, Abolhasan 8, 23 n. 8, 35, 39, 44–51, 52 n. 36, 62–3, 74, 202
  Az Khun-e Javānān-e Vatan Lāleh Damideh (The Tulip Has Sprouted from the Blood of the Homeland's Youth) 47
  Komite Defā'-e Melli (the National Defence Committee) 45
  Mārsh-e Jomhuri (March of the Republic) 46
  Nāle-ye Morgh (The Birds' Lament) 45
  Rahm Ey Khodā-ye Dādgar (O Merciful God) 45
Ārianpur, Yahya 4, 19, 20 n. 2, 23 n. 8, 27, 31–3, 39, 46, 83, 94 n. 81
Ārmān (journal) 146 n. 38
Ātashi, Manuchehr 114, 185, 197, 206
automatic writing 11, 162, 192, 194
Āzādistān (journal) 67

Bahār, Malek al-Sho'arā 8–9, 22, 28–37, 42, 47, 62–3, 66, 71–2, 74, 92, 104, 113–4, 129, 153, 202
  Anjoman-e Sa'adat (the Society for Prosperity) 30
  direct imagery 36–7, 48, 59, 84
  Habl al-Matin (journal) 30, 76
  Khorāsān (journal) 30, 33
  Morgh-e Sahar (The Morning Bird) 47
  Pand-e Sa'di (Sa'di's Advice) 33
bahr-e tavil 150 n. 48, 151–2
Bakhtin, Mikhail 176
Ball, Hugo 179, 181
band (stanza) 43

bara'at-e estehlāl (poetic introduction) 58
Barāhani, Rezā 4, 70, 206
  Khatāb be Parvāneh-hā va Cherā man Digar Shā'er-e Nimā'i Nistam (Addressing Butterflies and Why am I no Longer a Nimāic Poet 1995) 206
Baudelaire, Charles 110
Bāzgasht-e Adabi (the Literary Return Movement) 8, 22–3, 27, 31, 59
Behruz, Zabih 10, 13, 108, 125, 127, 130, 144–58
  Dar Rāh-e Mehr (In the Path of Love, 1934) 148–149
  Gandestān (Stenchland) 146
  Gand-nāmeh (Stenchbook) 146
  Me'rāj-Nāmeh-ye Ebn-e Deylāq or Gand-e Bādāvard (Ebn-e Deylāq's Book of Ascension or Wind-blown Stench) 145
  Mer'āt al-Sarā'er (Mirror of Secrets) 171
  Shab-e Ferdowsi (Ferdowsi's Night) 146–9
Benjamin, Walter 3, 167, 173
  Arcades Project 6
  ragpicker 6–7, 11, 162, 167–168, 173–4, 204
Bloom, Harold 3, 5, 21, 28, 36–38, 53, 64–5, 68, 71, 91, 104–5, 122, 174, 188
  The Anxiety of Influence: A Theory of Poetry 5, 21, 174
  apophrades 28
  clinamen 122
  daemonization 65
  kenosis 65, 71
  school of resentment 36, 37, 47, 64
  tessera 36, 53, 91, 104
Browne, Edward 33, 85 n. 62, 145
Bürger, Peter 3, 5–6, 109, 111–12, 159–60, 174–5, 192–3
  Theory of the Avant-Garde 5–6

caesura 136, 147, 151
canon 14, 125, 160, 189
carmen figuratum 195

Caton, Margaret 47–48, 50
chained octave 92
Chālangi, Hushang 206
chārpāreh (four-liner) 9, 31, 66, 97–105, 108, 121–122, 203
clinamen (or poetic misprision) 122, 174
Coleridge, Samuel Taylor 175–6
colloquialism 3, 8, 22, 26, 33, 38, 63, 174
  colloquial poetry 36–9, 79
concrete poetry 178, 194
constitutional poetry 2, 4, 8, 19–22, 33, 36–7, 39–41, 44, 51, 57–58, 63, 69, 77–8, 174, 202

Dabashi, Hamid 63–4, 72, 79
Dadaism 15, 124, 162, 169, 177–178, 181, 184, 196
  Cabaret Voltaire 181, 184
Dāneshsarā-ye Āli (Supreme College) 121
Dargazi, Seyd-Ali Khān 30
Dāryush, Parviz 122, 194
  Nemuneh-hā-ye She'r-e Now (Examples of New Poetry) 122
dead metaphor 10, 31, 99, 127, 139–40, 143
Dehkhodā, Ali Akbar Khān 28–9, 31, 74, 92, 98
  Yād Ār (Remember) 29, 92, 98
dobeyti (poem of four hemistichs) 68, 119, 120, 144, 145
dobeyti-hā-ye peyvasteh (connected doublet) 100, 121–2
Dowlatābādi, Yahyā, 85 n. 62
dramatic poetry 8, 57
  dramatizing poetry 40
  poetic dramas 10, 40, 57, 127
Dutch Neoplasticism 187

E'tesāmi, Parvin 92, 123
ekfā (homology) 55
ekhtiyārāt-e vazni (poetic licence) 115
Elahāmi, Mirzā Ahmad 76
Elāhi, Bizhan 164, 206
Eliot, T. S., 96 n. 84, 104–5, 125
enjambment 135, 156

INDEX

Eqbāl Āshtiāni, Abbās 153
Eslāmpur, Parviz 206
experimental poetry 101, 111, 139, 143, 149, 203
  experimentalism 9, 108–10, 143–4, 153, 203–4

Farāhāni, Abolqasem Qā'em Maqām 8, 23–4, 26, 35
  Jalāyer-Nāmeh (Letter of Jalāyer) 23
Farāhāni, Adib al-Mamālek 20 n. 2
Farrokhzād, Forugh 124
Farzād, Mas'ud 131
Ferdowsi, Abolqāsem 29, 131, 146–9
  Shāhnāmeh (The Book of Kings) 29, 146–8
  Ferdowsi's Millennium 131
Fikret, Tewfik 102
Flaubert, Gustave 37
folk comic play 40, 42
  comedic drama 41
  tamāshā, 40–1
  taqlid (mime) 40
folk performances 40, 42, 62
folk poetry 51, 131
folklore 3, 33, 38, 131
Foruzānfar, Badi' al-Zamān 153
free verse 10, 15, 115, 127–8, 130, 132, 134, 146, 149, 150, 154, 156–8, 190, 204
Futurism 177, 187

Ghanoonparvar, Mohammad-Reza 65, 73–4, 101
Gharib, Gholām Hoseyn 185–6
ghazal 77–8, 94, 102, 105, 148, 153
Gilāni, Sayyed Ashraf (Nasim-e Shomāl) 28–9, 33, 83

Hā'eri, Hādi 44–5
Hāfez, Khājeh Shams al-Din Mohammad 148
Hallward, Peter 44, 47, 55, 57, 61, 173
Hamedāni, Moshfeq 163 n. 16
Hamidi Shirāzi, Mehdi 27, 115, 117, 123
Hamidiyān, Sa'id 115, 117
Haydar Khān Amo-oghli 88 n. 69

Hedāyat, Rezā-Qoli Khān 64 n. 3
Hedāyat, Sādeq 130–1, 146, 153
Hekmat, Ali-Asghar 114, 123
Hezb-e Demokrāt-e Āzarbāyjān (the Democratic Party of Azarbaijan) 67
Hezb-e Tudeh-ye Irān (Tudeh Party of Iran) 111 n. 8
high modernism 5, 9, 108–12, 124–5, 144, 158, 159, 189, 204
Homā'i, Jalāl al-Din 27, 96, 145 n. 36
Homā-ye Shirāzi, Tarab ebn–e 27
Hugo, Victor 70, 84, 102–3, 113

Iraj Mirzā, 23, 29, 168
  Āref-Nāmeh (Letter of Āref) 23
irāni, Hushang 2, 11, 15, 108, 159, 161–2, 184–6, 188–94, 196–200, 204–5
  Aknun be to Miandisham, be to-hā Miandisham (I Think of You Now, I Think of All Like You) 196
  Banafsh-e Tond bar Khākestari (Intense Purple on Grey) 191
  Hah 191–2
  Kabud (Violet) 190–1
  Khākestari (Grey, 1952) 189, 194
  Sholeh-'i Pardeh ra bar Gereft va Eblis be Darun Āmad (A Flame Embraced the Curtain, and Iblis Entered, 1952) 196
  Unio Mystica 194–5

Jamālzādeh, Sayyed Mohammad Ali 141, 146
Jariyān-e estehāleh (stream of metamorphosis) 171
Jong-e Torfeh (journal) 205
Jozveh-ye She'r (journal) 205

Kabutar-e Solh (journal) 197
Karimi-Hakkak, Ahmad 1–2, 4, 20, 47, 51, 52 n. 36, 53, 55, 57, 61, 68, 69, 72, 74, 78, 91, 94, 103, 105, 111 n. 8, 113–14, 156, 161, 199

Kasmā'i, Shams 9, 13, 64, 66–7, 88, 90–1, 95, 202
  Medāl-e Eftekhār (The Medallion of Honour) 89
  Mā dar in Panj Ruz Nobat-e Khish (In the Five Days of Our Turn) 88–9, 95, 105
  Omr-e Gol (Life of the Rose) 88 n. 69
  Parvaresh-e Tabi'at (The Nurture of Nature) 90–1
Kasrā'i, Siyāvash 161
Kāveh (journal) 68, 69 n. 14
Kermāni, Aqā Khān 64, 65 n. 3
Khājeh Nuri, A., 163 n. 16
Khāmene'i, Ja'far 64, 67, 91, 94, 98, 202
  Be Qarn-e Bistom (To the Twentieth Century) 94
Khānlari, Parviz Nātel 14, 85, 121–2, 123–4, 135, 192
Khiyābāni, Sheykh Mohammad 67, 75, 88 n. 69
Kho'i, Esmā'il 15
Kiā, Tondar 2, 11, 13, 15, 108, 110, 134, 150, 152, 159, 161–82, 184, 200, 204–6
  Chizak (a small thing) 178–80
  Dans (Dance) 170
  Khāb Didam Mast Kardam! (I Dreamt that I am Drunk!, 1943) 171
  Shāhin-e Guyā (Talking Falcon) 180–1
  Tisfun (Ctesiphon) 163–4
Kurdish poetry 85

Lāhuti, Abolqāsem 9, 15, 64, 66, 74–85, 87–8, 90–1, 94–6, 98, 202
  Vafā-ye be Ahd (Remaining Loyal to One's Oath) 98–9
  Sangar-e Khunin (The Blood-Covered Trench) 84, 90–1, 94, 105
Lālehzār 168–9, 171
Lamartine, Alphonse de 113
Loy, Mina 169–70, 178

Mahmud Khān-e Malek al-Sho'arā, 27
Mallarmé, Stéphane 102, 113
Manuchehri Dāmqāni 33
masnavi 23, 77, 85, 100, 146, 152
mostazād-masnavi (increment couplets) 100
Mayakovsky, Vladimir 154
metrical analyses 10, 127, 132, 134, 151, 158
Mirzādeh Eshqi, Mohammad-Rezā 8, 35, 39–40, 42, 51–63, 74, 92, 113, 122, 168, 202
  Barg-e Bād Bordeh (The Windblown Leaf) 54
  Kafan-e Siyāh (Black Shroud) 52, 57
  Kolāh-namadi-hā (Felt Hats) 56
  Qarn-e Bistom (journal) 52, 94, 113
  Rastākhiz-e Shahriyārān-e Irān (The Resurrection of the Persian kings) 52, 57
  Sargozasht-e Ta'asor Āvar-e Shā'er (The Poet's Pitiful Destiny) 92
  'id-e Khun (The Blood Feast) 52, 61–2
  Tasnif-e Jomhuri (Song of the Republic) 42
monāzereh (poetic debate) 25, 59, 60
monotony 24, 49, 51, 131, 176
Moqaddam, Mohammad 10, 13, 15, 75, 108–9, 125, 127–37, 139, 141–5, 150, 154–5, 158, 203
  Bāng-e Khorus (The Voice of the Rooster) 128, 140–1
  Bāzgasht be Alamut; Pish-darāmad va Nāmeh-ye Yekom (Returning to Alamut; the Introduction, and the First Letter) 128
  Irānkudeh (journal) 131, 145
  Irānvich Forum 131, 145
  Rāz-e Nimshab; Rāhi Chand Birun Az Pardeh (The Mystery of Midnight; A Few Pieces Out of Tune with the Main Melody) 128, 139
mosammat 29, 33, 53–4, 58, 92, 94, 96, 121

Mosāvāt (journal) 20 n. 2
mostazād (increment poem) 33, 100, 102–3, 121, 152
Mowj-e Nāb (Pure Wave) 205–6
Mowj-e Now (New Wave) 144, 205
Munch, Edvard 190

Naficy, Majid 115, 117, 120
Nafisi, Sa'id 154, 163 n. 16
Nedā-ye Vatan (journal) 20 n. 2
Nezāmi, Jamal al-Din Abu Mohammad Elyās 77, 149
Niku-Hemmat, Ahmad 30–1
Nimāic poetry 55, 84, 106, 108, 110–11, 114–15, 118, 120–5, 152–3, 158, 161, 165, 185, 189, 192, 198–9, 203, 205–6
non-organic 5–7, 11, 110–11, 160, 162, 175–6, 192, 194, 204
nowheh (lament) 24, 25 n. 9, 33–4, 41
Nuri 'Alā, Esmā'il 200, 205
Nuri, Sheykh Fazlollāh 162, 164
Nushin, Abdolhoseyn 131 n. 8

octet 92, 94, 99
oneiric language 194
organic unity 97, 101, 110, 175–6, 191–2
organic form 5–7, 11, 99, 110, 152, 160, 162
organicity 6, 160, 177

pattern poetry 194–5, 204
performance 8, 19, 39–42, 44–7, 57, 62, 167, 176–7, 180–1, 184, 196, 202, 204
  performative arts 3, 22, 25, 38, 39–40, 182
  performative poems 55, 57, 62, 181, 184
  performative poetic form 41, 44, 178
Pesyān, Mohammad Taqi Khān 23 n. 8, 45
Petrarchan sonnet 91, 94, 99
Pezhmān, Hoseyn 123
Phonetic poetry 179–80
phrasing (phrasal) analyses 10, 127, 132, 147–8, 151, 156–8

pishpardeh (curtain-raisers) 169
Poggioli, Renato 3, 6–7, 11, 110–11, 160–2, 164–7, 188, 198, 204
  activism 7, 164–5
  agonism 7, 164, 204
  antagonism 7, 164–6, 176, 188, 197
  nihilism 7, 164, 166, 204
polyphony 49, 176
private symbols 10, 127, 139–40

qāfiyeh-ye ma'muleh (feigned rhyme) 55
qasideh 27, 37, 105

Ra'di Āzarakhshi, Gholām-Ali 123
Rab'eh (literary group) 131 n.8
Raf'at, Taqi 8–9, 13, 64, 66, 71–2, 88 n. 69, 91, 93, 102, 105, 202
  Nowruz va Dehqān (Nowruz and the Farmer) 93
Rancière, Jacques 3–5, 20, 32, 37, 44, 56, 173
  disruptive equality 6, 44, 173
Rashid Yāsemi, Gholam-Rezā 40, 57, 71 n. 20, 98, 102–4
rhythmic analysis 10, 127, 132, 158
robā'i 77, 79, 102
Romanticism 64, 70, 120, 177
rowzeh-khāni (martyrdom-recitation) 44
ru-howzi 41, 169

Sab'eh (literary group) 131 n. 8
Safā, Zabihollāh 163 n. 16
Safā'i Esfahāni, Mohammad Hoseyn 27
saj' (prose rhymes) 148–9
Sālehi, Sayyed Ali 206
Sartre, Jean-Paul 37
Sepehri, Sohrāb 189, 199
serate futuriste (futurist evenings) 62
Sereh-Nevisi (Language purification) 145
Servat-e Fonun (Journal) 102
Shafaq-e Sorkh (Journal) 52, 61
Shafi'i Kadkani, Mohammad-Rezā 27–8, 46–7, 76, 85, 98, 100, 123 n. 47, 129, 139, 143–4

Shāhrudi, Esmāʿil 189, 198
  Ākharin Nabard (Last Battle, 1951) 189, 198
Shakespearean sonnet 91
Shāmlu, Ahmad 124, 144
Shams Qeys Rāzi 97
Sheʿr-e Digar (Other Poetry) 144, 189, 205–6
Sheʿr-e Hajm (Espacementalisme) 205
Sheʿr-e Sepid (White Poetry) 144
Sheʿr-e Zabān (Language Poetry) 205–6
Sheybāni Kāshāni, Fathollāh Khān 8, 13, 23–4, 26–7, 202
Sheybāni, Manuchehr 185–6
Sheydā, Ali Akbar 47
  Dokhtar-e Daryā (Girl from the Sea, 1946) 153–4
  Ghazāleh-ye Khorshid (Gazelle of the Sun, 1974) 153
  Ghozhmeh (Grape, 1950) 153
  Khusheh Parvin (The Pleiades, 1946) 153
  Samandar (Salamander, 1946) 153
  Shin Partow (Ali Shirāzpur) 10, 13, 108, 125, 127, 130, 131 n. 8, 153–8, 203
  Zhinus (1946) 153, 156
Shirvāni, Hasan 185–6
Shurideh, Mohammad Taqi 27
Shuster, William Morgan 48–9
Siyāsat (Journal) 52
socialist realism 9, 15, 66, 81–4, 202
Sokhan (Journal) 121–4, 188
sound poetry 177, 196, 199
street songs 168–72, 204
Suratgar, Lotf-Ali 163 n. 16
Sur-e Esrāfil (Journal) 20 n. 2
surrealism 15, 124, 177, 194

taʿzieh (passion play) 25, 41
Tabari, Ehsān 111 n. 8, 123, 161
Tāhbāz, Sirus 123, 190, 192, 194, 196–7
Tajaddod 8–9, 65–74, 88, 91, 93, 95, 96 n. 84, 97–8, 101, 103–7, 110, 123, 202
Tamaddon (Journal) 20 n. 2

Tarāneh-ye degardisi (lyrics of transformation) 171
tarjiʿ-band 92–3, 96
tarkib-band 81, 96
tasnif (light song) 42, 44, 46–51, 63, 169 n. 31
Tavallali, Fereydun 122
  Nāfeh (Musk, 1962) 122
Teʾatr (Journal) 20 n. 2
tekrār-e qavāfi 55
terza rima 95
the First Congress of Iranian Writers 114, 123
theatrocracy 58, 60
typography 178, 195

uneven verses 26, 102, 133, 150, 152

Verhaeren, Émile 113
Vosughi, Nāser 164

Whitman, Walt 129–30, 136

Yaghmā Jandaqi, Abolhasan 2, 8, 13, 23–6, 202
  Āsār-e Morādieh (Moradi's Works) 25
  Kholāsat al-Eftezāh (The Abridged Account of the Scandal) 24
  Sayyed Abud 25–6
Yushij, Nimā 2, 10, 51, 54, 84, 91, 93, 95, 108–9, 111 n. 8, 112–25, 127, 134, 142, 150, 152–3, 155, 157–8, 161, 165–6, 185, 189, 192, 198–9, 203, 205
  Afsāneh (Legend) 121–2
  Harf-hā-ye Hamsāyeh (The Neighbour's Words) 115
  Khāneh-ye Sarivoyli (Sarivoyli's House, 1940) 10, 108, 115, 117, 120–1, 203

Zakāni, Obeyd 25
Ziāʾpur, Jalil 186
  Kavir (journal) 186 n. 68
zu-qāfiatain
  (double rhymed poem) 100

www.ingramcontent.com/pod-product-compliance
Lightning Source LLC
Chambersburg PA
CBHW052039300426
44117CB00012B/1887